Berlitz® Audio

Just listen and repeat

60 minute cassettes t...
accent before you depa...
ation and complete tex...

C000174380

	Cassettes			
Arabic				
Danish				
Dutch	212		237	
Finnish	201		226	
French	202		227		802
German	203		228		803
Greek	204		229		
Hebrew	205		230		805
Italian	206		231		806
Japanese	207		232		
Norwegian	208		233		
Portuguese	214		239		
Russian	209		234		809
Serbo-Croatian	215				
Spanish (Castil)	210		235		810
Spanish (Lat Am)	213		238		813
Swedish	211		236		

English for Visitors	Cassettes	LP BRIT	LP USA
For French	250	830	246
For German	260	835	247
For Italian	280		248
For Spanish*	290		249
For Danish	300	850	
For Dutch	270	855	
For Finnish	310	860	
For Norwegian	320	870	**Total Units**
For Swedish	330		
For Japanese	Cas. BRIT 340	Cas. USA 345	
* also available as 8-Track	890		

Please count the total number of units requested and complete the reverse side of this order form.

11403

<table>
<tr><td>

$
From New Jersey
Total units _____
at $ 7.95 each
Total amount enclosed
$ _____
(N. J. residents add
sales tax)

</td><td>

£
From London
Total units _____
at £ 4.95
Total amount enclosed
£ _____
(VAT is included)

</td></tr>
</table>

Name _____

_____

Address _____

_____

_____

Please complete and return this order form to:

Traveller's
Shopping Service   or
600 Grand Avenue
Ridgefield, NJ 07657
USA

Traveller's
Shopping Service
8, Trident Way
Brent Road
Southall
Middlesex UB2 5LS
England

Please order Berlitz books through your bookseller. Should you encounter any difficulties, write directly to any of the distributors listed on the back cover.

11403

BERLITZ®

EUROPEAN
PHRASE BOOK

By the staff of Editions Berlitz

Library of Congress Catalog Card Number: 73-20997

7th printing 1981

Printed in Switzerland

Editions Berlitz
1, avenue des Jordils
1000 Lausanne 6, Switzerland

Contents

Preface

You're about to visit several countries in Europe and we've attempted to provide you with a useful phrase book featuring key phrases in 14 different European languages.

Our book is simple to use, since the language sections are divided into topics, from arrival to eating out, from shopping to emergencies. Each expression appears with a code to pronunciation next to it. Simply read this imitated pronunciation as if it were English, stressing the syllables that are printed in bold type.

This European Phrase Book is made up of key extracts from 14 complete phrase books published by Berlitz. If you plan to spend a longer period of time in one country or language area, you'd be well advised to obtain a complete 192-page single language phrase book. It contains detailed travel information and tips, as well as useful phrases.

The phrases featured in each language of this book are also available in cassette form to help you prepare for your trip. The cassette is also available with a full-length phrase book at booksellers and record shops as a "Cassettepak" or "8-track Cartridgepak".

Bon Voyage!

DANISH

Guide to Pronunciation

Letter	Approximate pronunciation	Symbol	Example	
Consonants				
b, c, f, h, l, m, n, v	as in English			
d	1) when at the end of the word, or between two vowels, like **th** in **this**	dh	**med**	mehdh
	2) otherwise, as in English	d	**dale**	darler
g	1) at the beginning of a word or syllable, as in **go**	g	**glas**	glahss
	2) when at the end of a word after a long vowel or before unstressed **e**, like **ch**s in Scottish lo**ch**, but weaker and voiced	ǧ	**kage**	karǧer
	3) usually mute after **i**, **y**, and sometimes mute after **a**, **e**, **o**		**sige**	seeer
j, hj	like **y** in yet	y	**ja**	yah

k, p, t	1) when at the beginning of a word, as in kite, pill and to	k p t	**kaffe** **pude** **tale**	kahfer poodher tarler
	2) otherwise like **g**, **b**, **d** in go, bit and **do**	g b d	**lække** **stoppe** **sætte**	lehger sdober sehder
l	always as in leaf, never as in bell	l	**vel**	vehl
r	pronounced in the back of the throat, as in French	r	**rose**	roaser
s	always as in see	s/ss	**skål** **haster**	sgawl hahssderr
sj	like **sh** in sheet	sh	**sjælden**	shehlern
w	for Danes this is the same as **v**			
z	like **s** in so	s	**zone**	soaner

Vowels

Vowels are generally long in stressed syllables when followed by *at most* one consonant. If followed by two consonants (or more), or in unstressed syllables, they are generally short.

a	1) when long, like **a** in car; it can also be pronounced like **a** in bad, but longer	ar	**bade**	bardher
	2) when short, like long **a**, or more like **a** in cart	ah	**hat**	hahd
	3) you will also hear, as alternatives to the above, a more or less "flat" pronunciation of **a**, which can be like **a** in hat, or tend towards **e** in let; it can be long or short	ai æ	**tale** **tak**	tailer tæg
e	1) when long, the same quality as **a** in plate, but longer, and a pure vowel, not a diphthong	ay	**mere**	mayrer
	2) when short, somewhere between the **a** in plate and the **i** in hit	ay	**fedt**	fayd
	3) when short, also like **e** in met	eh	**let**	lehd
	4) when unstressed, like **a** in about	er	**gammel**	gahmerl
i	1) when long, like **ee** in bee	ee	**bide**	beedher
	2) when short, like **ee** in meet	ee	**liter**	leederr

o				
o	1) when long, like **aw** in **saw**, but with the tongue higher in the mouth; quite like **u** in **put**	oa	**skole**	sgoaler
	2) when short, more or less the same quality of sound	oa	**bonde**	boaner
	3) when short, also like **o** in **lot**	o	**godt**	god
u	1) when long, like **oo** in **pool**	oo	**pude**	poodher
	2) when short, like **oo** in **loot**	oo	**nu**	noo
y	put your tongue in the position for the **ee** of **bee**, but round your lips as for the **oo** of **pool**; the vowel you pronounce like this should be more or less correct	ew	**byde** **lytte**	bewdher lewder
æ	1) when long, like the first part of the word **air**	ai	**bære**	bairer
	2) when short, like **e** in **get**, but next to **r** it sounds more like the **a** of **hat**	eh æ	**ægte** **værre**	ehgder værer
å	1) when long, like **aw** in **saw**	aw	**åben**	awbern
	2) when short, like **o** in **on**	o	**ånd**	on
ø	like **ur** in **fur**, but with the lips rounded; can be long or short	ur	**frøken** **øl**	frurgern url

DANISH

Diphthongs

av	like **ow** in **now**	ow	**hav**	how
ej	like **igh** in **sigh**	igh	**nej**	nigh
ev	like **e** in **get** followed by a short **u** as in **put**	ehoo	**evne**	ehooner
ou	like **o** in **got** followed by a short **u** as in **put**	ooo	**lov**	looo
øi	like **oi** in **oil**	oi	**øje**	oier
øv	like **ur** in **hurt** followed by a short **u** as in **put**	uroo	**søvnig**	suroonee

N.B. 1) Many Danish speakers put a glottal stop in or after long vowels (like the Cockney pronunciation of **t** in **wa'er**). Although it has a certain distinctive role, you will be understood perfectly well if you do not use it, so we have not shown it in our transcriptions;

2) **dd** and **gg** between vowels are pronounced like **d** in **do** and **g** in **go**;

3) the letter **d** is not pronounced in **nd** and **ld** at the end of a word or syllable (*mand* = **mahn**, *guld* = **gool**) or before unstressed **e** or before **t** or **s** in the same syllable (*plads* = **plahs**).

Some basic expressions

Yes.	**Ja.**	yar
No.	**Nej.**	nay
Please.	**Vær så venlig.**	vair saw **vehn**lee
Thank you.	**Tak.**	tahk
Thank you very much.	**Mange tak.**	**mahng**er tahk
That's all right.	**Å, jeg be'r.**	aw yay bayr

Greetings

Good morning.	**Godmorgen.**	goadh**mor**ern
Good afternoon.	**Goddag.**	goadh**dai**
Good evening.	**Godaften.**	goadh**ahf**dern
Good night.	**Godnat.**	goadh**nahd**
Good-bye.	**Farvel.**	fahr**vehl**
See you later.	**På gensyn.**	paw **gehn**sewn
This is Mr....	**Det er hr....**	day air hehr
This is Mrs....	**Det er fru....**	day air froo
This is Miss...	**Det er frøken...**	day air **frur**gern
I'm very pleased to meet you.	**Det glæder mig at træffe Dem.**	day **glaid**herr migh aht **treh**fer dehm
How are you?	**Hvordan har De det?**	**vor**dahn harr dee day
Very well, thank you. And you?	**Fint, tak. Og De?**	fint tahk. o dee
Fine.	**Fint.**	fint
Excuse me.	**Undskyld.**	**oons**gewl

Questions

Where?	**Hvor?**	vor
Where is...?	**Hvor er...?**	vor air
Where are...?	**Hvor er...?**	vor air
When?	**Hvornår?**	vor**nawr**
What?	**Hvad?**	vah(dh)
How?	**Hvordan?**	vor**dahn**
How much?	**Hvor meget?**	vor **migh**erd

How many?	**Hvor mange?**	vor **mahng**er
Who?	**Hvem?**	vehm
Why?	**Hvorfor?**	vor**for**
Which?	**Hvilken/Hvilket?**	**vil**gern/**vil**gerd
What do you call this?	**Hvad hedder dette?**	vahdh **hehd**err **dehd**er
What do you call that?	**Hvad hedder det?**	vahdh **hehd**err day
What does this mean?	**Hvad betyder dette?**	vahdh ber**tewd**err **dehd**er
What does that mean?	**Hvad betyder det?**	vahdh ber**tewd**err day

Do you speak...?

Do you speak English?	**Taler De engelsk?**	**tai**lerr dee **ehng**erlsg
Do you speak German?	**Taler De tysk?**	**tai**lerr dee tewsg
Do you speak French?	**Taler De fransk?**	**tai**lerr dee frahnsg
Do you speak Spanish?	**Taler De spansk?**	**tai**lerr dee spahnsg
Do you speak Italian?	**Taler De italiensk?**	**tai**lerr dee eetahlee**aynsg**
Could you speak more slowly, please?	**Vil De tale lang-sommere?**	vil dee **tai**ler **lahng**somerrer
Please point to the phrase in the book.	**Vær så venlig at pege på sætningen i bogen.**	vair saw **vehn**lee ahd **pigh**er paw **sehd**ningern ee **baw**(g)ern
Just a minute. I'll see if I can find it in this book.	**Et øjeblik. Jeg vil se, om jeg kan finde det i denne bog.**	ehd **oier**blig. yay vil say om yay kahn **finn**er day ee **dehn**er baw(g)
I understand.	**Jeg forstår.**	yay for**sdawr**
I don't understand.	**Jeg forstår ikke.**	yay for**sdawr** **igg**er

Can...?

| Can I have...? | **Kan jeg få...?** | kahn yay faw |
| Can we have...? | **Kan vi få...?** | kahn vee faw |

DANISH

DANISH

Can you show me...?	Kan De vise mig...?	kahn dee **vee**sser migh
Can you tell me...?	Kan De sige mig...?	kahn dee **see**yer migh
Can you help me, please?	Vil De være så venlig at hjælpe mig?	vil dee **vai**rer saw **vehn**lee ahd **yehl**per migh

Wanting

I'd like...	Jeg vil gerne have...	yay vil **gehr**ner **hai**(wer)
We'd like...	Vi vil gerne have...	vee vil **gehr**ner **hai**(wer)
Please give me...	Vær så venlig at give mig...	vair saw **vehn**lee ahd **gee** migh
Give it to me please.	Vær så venlig at give mig det.	vair saw **vehn**lee ahd **gee** migh day
Please bring me...	Vær så venlig at hente...til mig.	vair saw **vehn**lee ahd **hehn**der...til migh
Bring it to me, please.	Vær så venlig at hente det til mig.	vair saw **vehn**lee ahd **hehn**der day til migh
I'm hungry.	Jeg er sulten.	yay air **sool**tern
I'm thirsty.	Jeg er tørstig.	yay air **turrs**stee
I'm tired.	Jeg er træt.	yay air trehd
I'm lost.	Jeg er faret vild.	yay air **far**rerd veel
It's important.	Det er vigtigt.	day air **vig**dee(t)
It's urgent.	Det haster.	day **hahss**derr
Hurry up!	Skynd Dem!	sgurn dehm

It is/There is...

It is/It's...	Det er...	day air
Is it...?	Er det...?	air day
It isn't...	Det er ikke...	day air **ig**ger
There is/There are...	Der er...	dair air
Is there/Are there...?	Er der...?	air dair
There isn't/There aren't...	Der er ikke...	dair air **ig**ger
There isn't any/ There aren't any.	Der er ingen.	dair air **ing**ern

A few common words

big/small	**stor/lille**	sdoar/**lil**ler
quick/slow	**hurtig/langsom**	**hoor**dee/**lahng**som
early/late	**tidlig/sen**	**teedh**lee/sayn
cheap/expensive	**billig/dyr**	**bil**lee/dewr
near/far	**nær/fjern**	nair/fyehrn
hot/cold	**varm/kold**	vahrm/kol
full/empty	**fuld/tom**	fool/tom
easy/difficult	**let/vanskelig**	lehd/**vahnss**gerlee
heavy/light	**tung/let**	toong/lehd
open/shut	**åben/lukket**	**aw**bern/**loo**gerd
right/wrong	**rigtig/forkert**	**rig**dee/for**kayrd**
old/new	**gammel/ny**	**gah**merl/new
old/young	**gammel/ung**	**gah**merl/oong
beautiful/ugly	**smuk/grim**	smoog/grim
good/bad	**god/dårlig**	goadh/**dawr**lee
better/worse	**bedre/værre**	**behdh**rer/**veh**rer

Some prepositions and a few more useful words

at	**ved**	vaydh
on	**på**	paw
in	**i**	ee
to	**til**	til
from	**fra**	frar
inside	**indeni**	**in**nernee
outside	**udenfor**	**oodh**ernfor
up	**op**	ob
down	**ned**	naydh
before	**før**	furr
after	**efter**	**ehf**derr
with	**med**	maydh
without	**uden**	**oodh**ern
through	**gennem**	**gehn**erm
towards	**imod**	**ee**moadh
until	**indtil**	intil
during	**i løbet af**	ee **lur**berd ahf
and	**og**	o
or	**eller**	**ehl**err
not	**ikke**	**ig**ger
nothing	**intet**	**in**derd
none	**ingen**	**ing**ern
very	**meget**	**migh**erd
also	**også**	**oss**er
soon	**snart**	snahrd
perhaps	**måske**	moss**gay**
here	**her**	hair

there	**der**	dair
now	**nu**	noo
then	**så**	saw

Arrival

Your passport, please.	**Deres pas!**	**deh**rerss pahss
Here it is.	**Værs'go.**	**vehr**sgoa
Have you anything to declare?	**Har De noget at for-tolde?**	harr dee **noa**gerd ahd for**tol**ler
No, nothing at all.	**Nej, intet.**	nigh **in**derd
Porter!	**Drager!**	**drah**gerr
Can you help me with my luggage, please?	**Vil De hjælpe mig med min bagage?**	vil dee **yehl**per migh maydh meen bah**gai**sher
That's my suitcase.	**Det er min kuffert.**	day air meen **koo**ferrd
Where's the bus to the centre of town, please?	**Hvor holder bussen til centrum?**	vor **hol**lerr **boo**ssern til **sehn**troam
This way, please.	**Denne vej.**	**deh**ner vigh

Changing money

| Can you change a traveller's cheque, please? | **Kan De indløse en rejsecheck?** | kahn dee **in**lursser ayn **righs**serchehg |
| Where's the nearest bank, please? | **Hvor er den nærmeste bank?** | vor air dehn **nair**mersder bahnk |

Car rental

I'd like a car.	**Jeg vil gerne leje en vogn.**	yay vil **gehr**ner **lig**her ayn **voa**(g)ern
For how long?	**Hvor længe?**	vor **lehn**ger
A day/Four days/A week/Two weeks.	**En dag/Fire dage/En uge/to uger.**	ayn dai/**fee**rer **dai**(g)er/ayn **oo**(g)er/toa **oo**(g)err

Taxi

| Where can I get a taxi? | **Hvor kan jeg få en taxa?** | vor kahn yay faw ayn **tahg**sah |
| What's the fare to . . . ? | **Hvad koster det til . . . ?** | vahdh **koss**derr day til |

DANISH

15

| Come in! The door's open. | Kom ind! Døren er åben. | kom in durrern air awbern |
| May we have breakfast in our room? | Kan vi få morgenmad på værelset? | kahn vee faw mor(g)ernmahdh paw vairaylserd |

Breakfast

I'll have...	Jeg vil gerne have...	yay vil gehrner hai(wer)
I'll have some fruit juice.	Jeg vil gerne have noget frugtsaft.	yay vil gehrner hai(wer) noa(g)erd froogdsahfd
a boiled egg	et kogt æg	ayd kogd ehg
a fried egg	et spejlæg	ayd sbighlehg
some bacon/some ham	noget bacon/noget skinke	noa(g)erd baykern/ noa(g)erd sginggerr
some toast	noget ristet brød	noa(g)erd risderd brurd
a pot of tea	en kande te	ayn kahner tay
a cup of tea	en kop te	ayn kob tay
some coffee	noget kaffe	noa(g)erd kahfer
some chocolate	noget chokolade	noa(g)erd shoagoalardher
more butter	mere smør	mayrer smurr
some hot water	noget varmt vand	noa(g)erd vahrmd vahn

Difficulties

The central heating doesn't work.	Centralvarmen virker ikke.	sehntrarlvahrmen veergerr igger
the light/the socket the tap/the toilet	lyset/stikkontaken vandhanen/toilettet	lewsserd/sdiggondahgdern vahnharnern/toilehderd
There's no hot water.	Der er ikke noget varmt vand.	dair air igger noa(g)erd vahrmd vahn
May I see the manager, please?	Jeg vil gerne tale med direktøren.	yay vil gehrner tailer maydh direhgturrern

Telephone—Mail

There's a call for you.	Der er telefon til Dem.	dair air taylayfoan til dehm
Hold the line, please.	Et øjeblik.	ayd oierblig
Operator, I've been cut off.	Frøken, jeg er blevet afbrudt.	frurgern yay air blayverd owbrood

DANISH

Take me to this address, please.	**Kør mig til denne adresse.**	kurr migh til **deh**ner ah-**dreh**sser
I'm in a hurry.	**Jeg har travlt.**	yay harr trowlt
Could you drive more slowly, please?	**Vil De være venlig at køre lidt langsommere?**	vil dee **vai**rer **vehn**lee ahd **kurr**er let **lahng**somerrer

Hotel and other accommodation

My name is...	**Mit navn er...**	mid nown air
Have you a reservation?	**Har De reserveret?**	harr di raysehr**vai**rerd
Yes, here's the confirmation.	**Ja, her er bekræftelsen.**	yar hair air ber**krehf**derl-sern
I'd like...	**Jeg vil gerne have...**	yay vil **gehr**ner **hai**(wer)
I'd like a single room/a double room.	**Jeg vil gerne have et enkeltværelse/et dobbeltværelse.**	yay vil **gehr**ner **hai**(wer) ayd **ehng**gerld**vai**raylser/ayd **do**berld**vai**raylser
a room with a bath/ with a shower	**et værelse med bad/med brusebad**	ayd **vai**raylser maydh bardh/maydh **broos**ser-bardh

How much?

What's the price per night/per week/per month?	**Hvor meget koster det pr. nat/pr. uge/ pr. måned?**	vor **migh**erd **koss**derr day pehr nahd/pehr **oo**(g)er/ pehr **maw**nerdh
May I see the room?	**Må jeg se værelset?**	maw yay say **vai**raylserd
I'm sorry, I don't like it.	**Jeg synes ikke om det.**	yay **sew**nerss **ig**ger om day
Yes, that's fine. I'll take it.	**Ja, det er godt. Det tager jeg.**	yar day air god day **tar**(g)err yay
What's my room number, please?	**Hvilket nummer har mit værelse?**	**vil**kerd **noo**merr harr mid **vai**raylser
Number 123.	**Nummer 123.**	**noo**merr 123

Service, please

Who is it?	**Hvem er det?**	vehm air day
Just a minute.	**Et øjeblik.**	ayd **oi**erblig

Did anyone telephone me?	**Er der blevet ringet til mig?**	air dair **blay**verd **ring**erd til migh
Is there any mail for me?	**Er der post til mig?**	air dair possd til migh
Are there any messages for me?	**Er der en besked til mig?**	air dair ayn ber**sgaydh** til migh

Checking out

May I have my bill, please?	**Må jeg bede om regningen?**	maw yay **bay**dher om **righ**ningern
We're in a great hurry.	**Vi skal skynde os.**	vee sgahl **sgur**ner oss
It's been a very enjoyable stay.	**Det har været et meget behageligt ophold.**	day harr **vai**rerd ayd **migh**erd ber**har**gerligd **ob**hol

Eating out

Good evening, sir/ Good evening, madam.	**Godaften hr./ Godaften frue.**	goad**hahf**dern hehr/ goad**hahf**dern **froo**er
Good evening. I'd like a table for two, please.	**Godaften. Jeg vil gerne have et bord til to.**	goad**hahf**dern. yay vil **gehr**ner **hai**(wer) ayd bord til toa
Do you have a fixed-price menu?	**Har De en "dagens middag"?**	harr dee ayn **dai**(g)ernss **mi**ddar(g)
May I see the à la carte menu?	**Må jeg se spisekortet?**	maw yay say **sbee**serkor-derd
May we have an ashtray, please?	**Må vi tå et askebæger?**	maw vee faw ayd **ahss**gerbeh(g)err
some bread	**noget brod**	**noa**(g)erd brurdh
a fork	**en gaffel**	ayn **gahf**erl
a knife	**en kniv**	ayn kneeoo
a spoon	**en ske**	ayn sgay
a plate	**en tallerken**	ayn **tahlehr**gern
a glass	**et glas**	ayd glahss
a napkin	**en serviet**	ayn **sehrvie**hd
another chair	**en stol til**	ayn sdoal til
Where's the gentlemen's toilet (men's room)?	**Hvor er her-retoilettet?**	vor air **heh**rer-toaahlehderd
Where's the ladies' toilet (ladies' room)?	**Hvor er dametoilettet?**	vor air **darmer**-toaahlehderd

DANISH

DANISH

Appetizers

I'd like some ...	**Jeg vil gerne have ...**	yay vil **geh**rner **hai**(wer)
I'd like some assorted appetizers.	**Jeg vil gerne have forskellig hors d'oeuvre.**	yay vil **geh**rner **hai**(wer) foss**geh**lee or**durv**r
orange juice	**noget orangesaft**	**noa**gert oa**rahng**shersahft
ham	**skinke**	**sging**ger
melon	**melon**	may**loan**
pâté	**postej**	poss**digh**
smoked salmon	**røget laks**	**rur**(g)ert lahgs
shrimps (shrimp)	**rejer**	**righ**er

Soup

Have you any ... ?	**Har De ...?**	harr dee
Have you any chicken soup?	**Har De hønsekodssuppe?**	harr dee **hurnss**(g)er-**gurds**sooper
vegetable soup	**grønsagssuppe**	**grurn**sar(gs)soaber
onion soup	**løgsuppe**	**lurg**soaber

Fish

I'd like some ...	**Jeg vil gerne have ...**	yay vil **geh**rner **hai**(wer)
I'd like some fish.	**Jeg vil gerne have fisk.**	yay vil **geh**rner **hai**(wer) fisg
sole	**sotunge**	**sur**doanger
trout	**orred**	**urr**erd
lobster	**hummer**	**hoa**merr
crayfish	**krebs**	**krehb**ss
prawns	**store rejer**	**stoa**rer **righ**err
I'd like it ...	**Jeg vil gerne have den ...**	yay vil **geh**rner **hai**(wer) dehn
I'd like it steamed.	**Jeg vil gerne have den dampkogt.**	yay vil **geh**rner **hai**(wer) dehn **dahmp**kogd
grilled	**grilleret**	gri**lay**rerd
boiled	**kogt**	kogd
baked	**stegt i ovnen**	**sdehgd** ee **oaoo**nern
fried	**stegt**	sdehgd

Meat—Poultry—Game

I'd like some ...	**Jeg vil gerne have ...**	yay vil **geh**rner **hai**(wer)
I'd like some beef.	**Jeg vil gerne have oksekød.**	yay vil **geh**rner **hai**(wer) **og**serkurd
a beef steak	**en engelsk bøf**	ayn **ehng**erlsk burf
some roast beef	**roastbeef**	**rossd**bif
a veal cutlet	**en kalvekotelet**	ayn **kahl**verkoaterlehd
mutton	**fårekød**	**faw**rerkurdh
lamb	**lammekød**	**lah**morkurdh
a pork chop	**en svinekotelet**	ayn **svee**nerkoaterlehd
roast pork	**flæskesteg**	**flehss**gersdigh
hare	**hare**	**har**rer
chicken	**kylling**	**kew**ling
roast chicken	**stegt kylling**	sdehgd **kew**ling
duck	**and**	ahn
How do you like your meat?	**Hvordan vil De gerne have Deres kød tilberedt?**	vor**dahn** vil dee **geh**rner **hai**(wer) **day**rerss kurdh **til**berrayd
rare	**rødt**	rurd
medium	**medium**	**may**deeom
well done	**gennemstegt**	**geh**nermsdehgd

Vegetables

What vegetables have you got?	**Hvilke grønsager har De?**	**vil**ger **grurn**sar(g)err harr dee
I'd like some ...	**Jeg vil gerne have ...**	yay vil **geh**rner **hai**(wer)
I'd like some asparagus.	**Jeg vil gerne have asparges.**	yay vil **geh**rner **hai**(wer) ahss**rah**rerss
green beans	**grønne bønner**	**grur**ner **bur**nerr
mushrooms	**champignoner**	**shahng**pinyongnerr
carrots	**gulerødder**	**goo**lerrurderr
onions	**løg**	lurg
red cabbage	**rødkål**	**rurdh**kawl
spinach	**spinat**	sbin**aid**
rice	**ris**	reess
peas	**ærter**	**air**terr
tomatoes	**tomater**	toa**mai**derr
green salad	**grøn salat**	grurn sah**laid**
potatoes	**kartofler**	kahr**tof**lerr

Desserts

Nothing more, thanks.	**Tak, ikke mere.**	tahk igger **may**rer
Just a small portion, please.	**Kun en lille portion.**	koon ayn **lil**ler por**sy**oan
Have you any ice-cream?	**Har De is?**	harr dee eess
fruit salad	**frugtsalat**	**froagd**sahlaid
fresh fruit	**frisk frugt**	frisg froogd
cheese	**ost**	oossd

Drink

What would you like to drink?	**Hvad ønsker De at drikke?**	vahdh **urn**skerr dee ahd **dri**gger
I'll have a beer, please.	**Jeg vil gerne have en øl.**	yay vil **gehr**ner **hai**(wer) ayn url
I'll have a whisky, please.	**Jeg vil gerne have en whisky.**	yay vil **gehr**ner **hai**(wer) ayn **wiss**kee

Wine

I'd like a bottle of wine.	**Jeg vil gerne have en flaske vin.**	yay vil **gehr**ner **hai**(wer) ayn **flahss**ger veen
red wine	**rødvin**	**rurdh**veen
rosé wine	**rosé-vin**	roa**say**veen
white wine	**hvidvin**	**vidh**veen
Cheers!	**Skål!**	skawl

The bill (check)

May I have the bill (check) please?	**Jeg vil gerne have regningen.**	yay vil **gehr**ner **hai**(wer) **righ**ningern
Is service included?	**Er det med be-tjening?**	air day mehdh ber-**tyay**ning
Everything's included.	**Alt er iberegnet.**	ahlt air **ee**berrighnert
Thank you, that was a very good meal.	**Mange tak, det smagte fortræffeligt.**	**mahng**er tahk day **smarg**der for**treh**ferligd

Travelling

Where's the railway station, please?	**Hvor er banegården?**	vor air **bai**nergawr(d)ern

DANISH

Where's the ticket office, please?	**Hvor er billet-kontoret?**	vor air bilehdkontoarerd
I'd like a ticket to ...	**Jeg vil gerne have en billet til ...**	yay vil gehrner hai(wer) ayn bilehd til
First or second class?	**Første eller anden klasse?**	furrster ehlerr ahndern klahsser
First class, please.	**Første klasse.**	furrster klahsser
Single or return (one way or round-trip)?	**Enkelt eller retur?**	ehnggerld ehlerr rertoor
Do I have to change trains?	**Skal jeg skifte tog?**	sgahl yigh sgifder taw(g)
What platform does the train leave from?	**Fra hvilken perron afgår toget?**	frar vilgern pehrong ow-gawr tawgerd
Where's the nearest underground (subway) station?	**Hvor er den nærmeste undergrundsstation?**	vor air dehn nairmersder oanerrgroansssdahshoan
Where's the bus station, please?	**Hvor er rutebil-stationen?**	vor air rooderbeelsdah-shoanern
When's the first bus to ...?	**Hvornår kører den første bus til ...?**	vornawr kurrerr dehn fursder booss til
the last bus	**den sidste bus**	dehn see(d)sder booss
the next bus	**den næste bus**	dehn nehsder booss
Please let me off at the next stop.	**Jeg vil gerne af ved næste stoppested.**	yay vil gehrner ahv vaydh nehsder sdobbersdehdh

Relaxing

What's on at the cinema (movies)?	**Hvad går der i bio-grafen?**	vahdh gawr dair ee bioa-grarfern
What's on at the theatre?	**Hvad går der på teatret?**	vahdh gawr dair paw tayaidrerd
What time does the film begin? And the play?	**Hvornår begynder filmen? Og stykket?**	vornawr bergewnerr fil-mern? o stewgerd
Are there any tickets for tonight?	**Er der flere billetter til i aften?**	air dair flayrer bilehderr til ee ahfdern
Where can we go dancing?	**Hvor kan vi gå ud og danse?**	vor kahn vee gaw oodh o dahnser
Would you like to dance?	**Vil De danse?**	vil dee dahnser

DANISH

Introductions

How do you do?	**Goddag.**	goadh**dai**
How are you?	**Hvordan har De det?**	vor**dahn** harr dee day
Very well, thank you. And you?	**Godt, tak. Og De?**	god tahk. o dee
May I introduce Miss Philips?	**Må jeg præsentere Dem for frøken Philips?**	maw yigh praisern**tayrer** dehm for **frurgern** Philips
My name is ...	**Mit navn er ...**	mid nown air
I'm very pleased to meet you.	**Det glæder mig at træffe Dem.**	day **glaidherr** migh ahd **trehfer** dehm
How long have you been here?	**Hvor længe har De været her?**	vor **lahng**er harr dee **vai**rerd hair
It was nice meeting you.	**Det har glædet mig at træffe Dem.**	day harr **glaidherd** migh ahd **trehfer** dehm

Dating

Would you like a cigarette?	**Må jeg byde Dem en cigaret?**	maw yay **bew**dher dehm ayn sigah**rehd**
May I get you a drink?	**Må jeg byde Dem en drink?**	maw yay **bew**dher dehm ayn drink
Do you have a light, please?	**Undskyld, kan De give mig ild?**	**oon**sgewl kahn dee **gee**ver migh il
Are you waiting for someone?	**Venter De på nogen?**	**vehn**derr dee paw **noa**gern
Are you free this evening?	**Er De ledig i aften?**	air dee **lay**dhee ee **ahf**dern
Where shall we meet?	**Hvor skal vi mødes?**	vor sgahl vee **murdherss**
What time shall I meet you?	**Hvornår skal vi mødes?**	vor**nawr** sgahl vee **mur**dherss
May I take you home?	**Må jeg følge Dem hjem?**	maw yay **furl**ger dehm yehm
Thank you, it's been a wonderful evening.	**Tusind tak, det har været en vidunderlig aften.**	**toos**sin tahg day harr **vai**rerd ayn vidhoa**nerr**lee **ahf**dern
What's your telephone number?	**Hvad er Deres telefonnummer?**	vahdh air **day**rerss tayler**foann**noomerr
Do you live alone?	**Bor De alene?**	**boar** dee ah**lay**ner

| What time is your last train? | Hvornår går Deres sidste tog? | vornawr gawr dayrerss seessder tawg |
| Good-night . . . | Godnat . . . | goadhnahd |

Banks

Where's the nearest bank, please?	Hvor er den nærmeste bank?	vor air dehn nairmersder bahnk
Where can I cash some traveller's cheques?	Hvor kan jeg indløse rejsechecks?	vor kahn yay inlursser righssershehks
What time does the bank open/What time does it close?	Hvornår åbner banken/Hvornår lukker den?	vornawr awbnerr bahnggern/vornawr loagerr dehn
I'm expecting some money from home. Has it arrived?	Jeg venter nogle penge hjemmefra. Er de kommet?	yay vehnderr no(g)ler pehnger yehmerfrar. air dee kommerd
Can you give me some small change, please?	Vil De give mig nogle småpenge?	vill dee gee(ver) migh no(g)ler smawpehnger

Shops, stores and services

Where is the nearest chemist's (pharmacy)?	Hvor er det nærmeste apotek?	vor air day nairmersder ahpoatayg
the nearest hair-dresser's	den nærmeste frisør	dehn nairmersder frisurr
the photo shop	fotoforretningen	foatoaforehdningern
the jeweller's	guldsmeden	goolsmaydhern
the department store	stormagasinet	sdoarmahgahsseenerd
the police station	politistationen	poleeteestahshoanern
the garage	parkeringshuset	pahrkayringsshoosserd
How do I get there?	Hvordan kommer jeg derhen?	vordahn kommerr yay dehrhehn
Is it within walking distance?	Kan man nemt gå derhen?	kahn mahn nehmd gaw dehrhehn

Service

Can you help me, please?	Vil De hjælpe mig?	vil dee yehlber migh
Can you show me this? And that, too.	Vil De vise mig den her? Og den der.	vil dee veeser migh dehn hair? o dehn dair
It's too expensive/too big/too small.	Den er for dyr/for stor/for lille.	dehn air for dewr/for stoar/for liller

Can you show me some more?	**Kan De vise mig nogle flere?**	kahn dee **vee**sser migh **no(g)**ler flayrer
something better something cheaper	**noget bedre noget billigere**	**noa**(g)erd **beh**dhrer **noa**(g)erd **billig**gerrer
How much is this? And that?	**Hvor meget koster den her? Og den der?**	vor **migh**erd **koss**derr dehn hair? o dehn dair
It's not quite what I want.	**Det er ikke helt det, jeg gerne vil have.**	day air **ig**ger hayld day yay **gehr**ner vil **hai**(wer)
I like it.	**Den kan jeg lide.**	dehn kahn yay **lee**(dher)

Chemist's (Pharmacy)

| I'd like something for a cold/for a cough/for travel sickness. | **Jeg vil gerne have noget mod for-kølelse/mod hoste/ mod køresyge.** | yay vil **gehr**ner **hai**(wer) **noa**(g)erd moadh for**kur**lerlser/moadh **hoass**der/ moadh **kurr**ersew(g)er |
| Can you recommend something for hay-fever/for sunburn? | **Kan De anbefale noget mod høfeber/mod solforbrænding?** | kahn dee **ahn**berfailer **noa**(g)erd moadh **hur**fayberr/moadh **soal**for-brehning |

Toiletry

May I have some razor blades?	**Må jeg få nogle barberblade?**	maw yay faw **no**(g)ler bahr**bayr**blaidher
some shaving cream some toothpaste	**noget barbercreme noget tandpasta**	**noa**gerd bahr**bay**kraym **noa**gerd **tahn**pahsdah
I'd like some soap.	**Jeg vil gerne have noget håndsæbe.**	yay vil **gehr**ner **hai**(wer) **noa**(g)erd **hon**saiber
some suntan oil	**noget sololie**	**noa**(g)erd **soal**oalyer

At the barber's

I'd like a haircut, please.	**Jeg vil gerne klippes.**	yay vil **gehr**ner **klib**berss
Short/Leave it long.	**Kort/Lad det være langt.**	kord/lahdh day **vai**rer lahngd
A razor cut, please.	**Skåret med bar-berblad.**	**sgaw**rerd maydh bahr-**bayr**blahdh

At the hairdresser's

I'd like a shampoo and set, please.	**Jeg vil gerne have en vask og vandon-dulation.**	yay vil **gehr**ner **hai**(wer) ayn vahsg o **vahn**on-doolahshoan
I'd like a bleach.	**Jeg vil gerne have en blegning.**	yay vil **gehr**ner **hai**(wer) ayn **bligh**ning
a permanent	**en permanent**	ayn pehr**mah**nehnd
a colour rinse	**en skylning**	ayn **sgewl**ning
a manicure	**en manicure**	ayn mahni**kewr**

Photography

I'd like a film for this camera.	**Jeg vil gerne have en film til dette apparat.**	yay vil **gehr**ner **hai**(wer) ayn film til **deh**der ahbah**rard**
This camera doesn't work.	**Dette apparat virker ikke.**	**deh**der ahbah**rard veer**ger **ig**ger

At the post office

Where's the nearest post office, please?	**Hvor er det nærmeste posthus?**	vor air day **nair**mersder **possd**hooss
I'd like to send this by express (special delivery)/by air mail.	**Jeg vil gerne sende dette ekspres/som luftpost.**	yay vil **gehr**ner **seh**ner **deh**der ehks**brehss**/som **loofd**possd

Service stations

Where is the nearest service station, please?	**Hvor er den nærmeste service-station?**	vor air dehn **nair**mersder **surr**visssdahshoan
Fill her up, please.	**Vil De fylde den op?**	vil dee **few**ler dehn ob
Check the oil, please.	**Vil De kontrollere oliestanden?**	vil dee kontroa**lay**rer **oal**yersdahnern
Would you check the tyres?	**Vil De kontrollere dækkene?**	vil dee kontroa**lay**rer **deh**gerner

Street directions

Can you show me on the map where I am?	**Vil De vise mig på kortet, hvor jeg er?**	vil dee **vee**ser migh paw **kor**terd vor yay air
You're on the wrong road.	**De er ikke på den rigtige vej.**	dee air **ig**ger paw dehn **rayg**di(g)er vigh

DANISH

Go back to...	**Kør tilbage til ...**	kurr tilbai(g)er til
Go straight ahead.	**Kør ligeud.**	kurr lee(g)eroodh
It's on the left/on the right.	**Det er til venstre/til højre.**	day air til **vehn**strer/til **hol**rer

Accidents

May I use your telephone?	**Må jeg låne Deres telefon?**	maw yay **lawner dayr**erss tayler**foan**
Call a doctor quickly.	**Tilkald straks en læge.**	**til**kahl sdrahgs ayn **lai**ger
Call an ambulance.	**Tilkald en ambulance.**	**til**kahl ayn ahmboo**lahng**ser
Please call the police.	**Tilkald politiet.**	**til**kahl poleet**eeerd**

Numbers

one	**en**	ayn
two	**to**	toa
three	**tre**	tray
four	**fire**	**fee**rer
five	**fem**	fehm
six	**seks**	sehgs
seven	**syv**	sewoo
eight	**otte**	**odd**er
nine	**ni**	nee
ten	**ti**	tee
eleven	**elleve**	**ehl**ver
twelve	**tolv**	tol
thirteen	**tretten**	**treh**tern
fourteen	**fjorten**	**fyor**tern
fifteen	**femten**	**fehm**tern
sixteen	**seksten**	**sehgs**tern
seventeen	**sytten**	**sew**tern
eighteen	**atten**	**ah**tern
nineteen	**nitten**	**nit**tern
twenty	**tyve**	**tew**ver
twenty-one	**en og tyve**	ayn o **tew**ver
thirty	**tredive**	**trehd**ver
forty	**fyrre**	**few**rer
fifty	**halvtreds**	hahl**trayss**
sixty	**tres**	trayss
seventy	**halvfjerds**	hahl**fyehrss**
eighty	**firs**	feerss
ninety	**halvfems**	hahl**fehmss**

one hundred	**hundrede**	**hoon**rerdher
one thousand	**tusind**	**too**ssin
ten thousand	**ti tusind**	tee **too**ssin

Days

It's Sunday.	**Det er søndag.**	day air **surn**dai
Monday	**mandag**	**mahn**dai
Tuesday	**tirsdag**	**teerss**dai
Wednesday	**onsdag**	**oanss**dai
Thursday	**torsdag**	**torss**dai
Friday	**fredag**	**fray**dai
Saturday	**lørdag**	**lurr**dai
yesterday	**i går**	ee gawr
today	**i dag**	ee dai
tomorrow	**i morgen**	ee **mor**(g)ern
morning/afternoon	**formiddag/** **eftermiddag**	**for**middai/**ehf**derrmiddai
evening/night	**aften/nat**	**ahf**dern/nahd

Months

January	**januar**	yahnoo**arr**
February	**februar**	faybroo**arr**
March	**marts**	**mahr**dss
April	**april**	ah**preel**
May	**maj**	migh
June	**juni**	**yoo**nee
July	**juli**	**yoo**lee
August	**august**	ow**goo**ssd
September	**september**	sehb**tehm**berr
October	**oktober**	og**toa**berr
November	**november**	noa**vehm**berr
December	**december**	day**sehm**berr
Merry Christmas!	**Glædelig jul! Godt**	**glai**dherlee yool! goad
Happy New Year!	**nytår!**	**new**dawr

DUTCH

Guide to Pronunciation

Letter	Approximate pronunciation	Symbol	Example	
Consonants				
c, f, h, k, l, m, n, p, q, t, v, y, z	as in English			
b	as in English, but when at the end of a word, like **p** in cup	b	**ben**	behn
		p	**heb**	hehp
ch	1) generally like **ch** in Scottish loch	kh	**nacht**	nahkht
	2) in words of French origin like **sh** in **sh**ut	sh	**cheque**	shehk
chtj	like Dutch **ch** followed by Dutch **j**	khy	**nichtje**	nikhyer
d	as in English, but, when at the end of a word, like **t** in hit	d	**doe**	doo
		t	**bed**	beht
g	1) generally like **ch** in Scottish loch, but often slightly softer and voiced	ǵ	**goed**	ǵoot
	2) in a few words of French origin, like **s** in pleasure	zh	**genie**	zhernee
	3) like **ch** in Scottish loch when at the end of a word	kh	**deeg**	daykh

DUTCH

j	like **y** in **y**es	y	**ja**	yar
nj	like **ñ** in Spanish se**ñ**or or like **ni** in o**ni**on	ñ	**oranje**	oarah**ñ**er
r	always trilled, either in the front or the back of the mouth	r	**warm**	vahrm
s	always like **s** in **s**it	s/ss	**roos**	roass
sj, stj	like **sh** in **sh**ut	sh	**meisje**	may**sh**er
sch	like **s** followed by a Dutch **ch**	skh	**schrijven**	**skh**rayver(n)
th	like **t**	t	**thee**	tay
tj	like **ty** in hi**t y**ou	ty	**katje**	**kah**tyer
w	something like **v**, but with the bottom lip raised a little higher	v	**water**	**v**arterr

Vowels

In Dutch a vowel is *short* when followed by two consonants, or by one consonant at the end of a word. It is *long* when it is at the end of a word, or before a consonant followed by a vowel, or when written double.

a	1) when short, between **a** in c**a**t and **u** in c**u**t, or like **o** in American c**o**llege	ah	**kat**	kaht
	2) when long, like **a** in c**a**rt	ar	**vader**	**va**rderr
e	1) when short, like **e** in b**e**d	eh	**bed**	beht
	2) when long, like **a** in l**a**te, but a pure vowel	ay	**zee**	zay
	3) in unstressed syllables, like **a** in **a**bove	er	**zitten**	**zit**tern
eu	(long) like **eu** in French f**eu**; approximately like **u** in f**u**r, said with rounded lips	ur	**deur**	durr
i	1) when short, like **i** in b**i**t	i	**kind**	kint
	2) when long (also spelt *ie*), like **ee** in b**ee**	ee	**bier**	beer
	3) sometimes, in unstressed syllables, like **a** in **a**bove	er	**monnik**	**mon**nerk
ij	sometimes, in unstressed syllables, like **a** in **a**bove	er	**lelijgk**	**lay**lerk
o	1) when short, like a very short version of **aw** in l**aw**n	o	**pot**	pot
	2) when long, something like **oa** in r**oa**d, but a pure vowel and with more rounded lips	oa	**boot**	boat
oe	(long) like **oo** in m**oo**n and well rounded	oo	**hoe**	hoo

u	1) when short, something like **u** in h**u**rt, but with rounded lips	er	**bus**	berss
	2) when long, like **u** in French s**u**r or **ü** in German f**ü**r; say **ee**, and without moving your tongue, round your lips. The resulting "rounded **ee**" should be the correct sound	ew	**nu**	new

Diphthongs

ai	like **igh** in s**igh**	igh	**ai**	igh
ei, ij	like **a** in l**a**te	ay	**reis**	rayss
au, ou	Dutch short **o** followed by a weak, short **u**-sound; can sound very much like **ow** in n**ow**	ow	**koud**	kowt

The following diphthongs have a long vowel as their first element:

aai	like **a** in c**a**t followed by a short **ee** sound	aree	**draai**	draree
eeuw	like **a** in l**a**te followed by a short **oo** sound	ayoo	**leeuw**	layoo
ieuw	like **ee** in fr**ee**, followed by a short **oo** sound	eeoo	**nieuw**	neeoo
ooi	like **o** in wr**o**te followed by a short **ee** sound	oaee	**nooit**	noaeet
oei	like **oo** in s**oo**n, followed by a short **ee** sound	ooee	**roeit**	rooeet
ui	like **u** in f**u**r, followed by a short Dutch **u** sound, as described in **u** number 2)	urew	**huis**	hurewss
uw	like the sound described in **u** number 2), followed by a weak **oo** sound	ewoo	**duw**	dewoo

DUTCH

N.B.
1) When two consonants are next to each other, one will often influence the other even if it is not in the same word, e.g., *ziens* is pronounced **zeenss**, but in the expression *tot ziens*, it is pronounced **seenss** under the influence of the **t** before it.
2) In the **-en** ending of verbs and plural nouns, the **n** is generally dropped in everyday speech.

DUTCH

Some basic expressions

Yes.	**Ja.**	yar
No.	**Nee.**	nay
Please.	**Alstublieft.**	ahlsstew**bleeft**
Thank you.	**Dank U.**	dahngk ew
Thank you very much.	**Hartelijk dank.**	**hahr**terlerk dahngk
That's all right.	**Niets te danken.**	neets ter **dahng**kern

Greetings

Good morning.	**Goedemorgen.**	ġooder**mor**ġern
Good afternoon.	**Goedemiddag.**	ġooder**midd**ahkh
Good evening.	**Goedenavond.**	ġooden**ar**vernt
Good night.	**Goedenacht.**	ġooder**nahkht**
Good-bye.	**Tot ziens.**	tot seenss
See you later.	**Tot straks.**	tot strahks
This is Mr. ...	**Dit is Mijnheer ...**	dit iss mer**nayr**
This is Mrs. ...	**Dit is Mevrouw ...**	dit iss mer**vrow**
This is Miss ...	**Dit is Juffrouw ...**	dit iss yer**frow**
I'm very pleased to meet you.	**Aangenaam kennis te maken.**	**arn**ġernarm **keh**nerss ter **mak**ern
How are you?	**Hoe gaat het?**	hoo **ġar**tert
Very well, thank you.	**Heel goed, dank U.**	hayl ġoot dahngk ew
And you?	**En U?**	ehn ew
Fine.	**Uitstekend.**	urewt**stay**kernt
Excuse me.	**Neemt U me niet kwalijk.**	naymt ew mer neet **kva**rlerk

Questions

Where?	**Waar?**	varr
Where is ...?	**Waar is ...?**	varr iss
Where are ...?	**Waar zijn ...?**	varr zayn
When?	**Wanneer?**	vahn**nayr**
What?	**Wat?**	vaht
How?	**Hoe?**	hoo
How much?	**Hoeveel?**	hoo**vayl**
How many?	**Hoeveel?**	hoo**vayl**

Who?	**Wie?**	vee
Why?	**Waarom?**	**var**rom
Which?	**Welk/Welke?**	vehlk/**vehl**ker
What do you call this?	**Hoe noemt U dit?**	hoo noomt ew dit
What do you call that?	**Hoe noemt U dat?**	hoo noomt ew daht
What does this mean?	**Wat betekent dit?**	vaht ber**tay**kernt dit
What does that mean?	**Wat betekent dat?**	vaht ber**tay**kernt daht

Do you speak ... ?

Do you speak English?	**Spreekt U Engels?**	spraykt ew **ehng**erlss
Do you speak German?	**Spreekt U Duits?**	spraykt ew durewts
Do you speak French?	**Spreekt U Frans?**	spraykt ew frahnss
Do you speak Spanish?	**Spreekt U Spaans?**	spraykt ew sparnss
Do you speak Italian?	**Spreekt U Italiaans?**	spraykt ew itahli**arnss**
Could you speak more slowly, please?	**Kunt U wat langzamer spreken, alstublieft?**	kernt ew vaht **lahng**zarmerr **spray**kern ahlsstew**bleeft**
Please point to the phrase in the book.	**Wijs me de zin aan in het boek, alstublieft.**	vayss mer der zin arn in heht book ahlsstew**bleeft**
Just a minute. I'll see if I can find it in this book.	**Een ogenblik. Ik zal proberen het in dit boek op te zoeken.**	een **oa**gernblik. ik zahl proa**bay**rern heht in dit book op te **zoo**kern
I understand.	**Ik begrijp het.**	ik ber**grayp**heht
I don't understand.	**Ik begrijp het niet.**	ik ber**grayp**heht neet

Can ... ?

Can I have ... ?	**Mag ik ... hebben?**	mahkh ik ... **heh**bern
Can we have ... ?	**Mogen wij ... hebben?**	**moa**gern vay ... **heh**bern

DUTCH

Can you show me...?	Kunt U me... tonen?	kernt ew mer...**toa**nern
Can you tell me...?	Kunt U mij zeggen...?	kernt ew may **zeh**gern
Can you help me, please?	Kunt U mij helpen, alstublieft?	kernt ew may **hehl**pern ahlsstew**bleeft**

Wanting

I'd like...	Ik wil graag...	ik vil **g**rarkh
We'd like...	Wij willen graag...	vay **vi**llern **g**rarkh
Please give me...	Geeft U me..., alstublieft.	**g**ayft ew mer...ahlssteebleeft
Give it to me, please.	Geeft U het me, alstublieft.	**g**ayft ew heht mer ahlsstew**bleeft**
Please bring me...	Brengt U me..., alstublieft.	**breh**ngt ew mer...ahlsstew**bleeft**
Bring it to me, please.	Brengt U het me, alstublieft.	**breh**ngt ew heht mer ahlsstew**bleeft**
I'm hungry.	Ik heb honger.	ik hehp **hong**err
I'm thirsty.	Ik heb dorst.	ik hehp dorst
I'm tired.	Ik ben moe.	ik behn moo
I'm lost.	Ik ben verdwaald.	ik behn vęrr**dvarlt**
It's important.	Het is belangrijk.	heht iss berl**ahng**rayk
It's urgent.	Het is dringend.	heht iss **dring**ernt
Hurry up!	Vlug!	vlęrkh

It is/There is...

It is/It's...	Het is...	heht iss
Is it...?	Is het...?	iss heht
It isn't...	Het is niet...	heht iss neet
There is/There are...	Er is/Er zijn...	ehr iss/ehr zayn
Is there/Are there...?	Is er/Zijn er...?	iss ehr/zayn ehr
There isn't/There aren't...	Er is geen/Er zijn geen...	ehr iss **g**ayn/ehr zayn **g**ayn
There isn't any/There aren't any.	Er is er geen/Er zijn er geen.	ehr iss ehr **g**ayn/ehr zayn ehr **g**ayn

DUTCH

A few common words

big/small	groot/klein	ğroat/klayn
quick/slow	snel/langzaam	snehl/**lahng**zarm
early/late	vroeg/laat	vrookh/lart
cheap/expensive	goedkoop/duur	ğoot**koap**/dewr
near/far	dichtbij/ver	dikht**bay** vehr
hot/cold	warm/koud	vahrm/kowt
full/empty	vol/leeg	vol/laykh
easy/difficult	gemakkelijk/moeilijk	ğer**mah**kerlerk/**mooee**lerk
heavy/light	zwaar/licht	zvarr/likht
open/shut	open/dicht	**oa**pern/dikht
right/wrong	juist/verkeerd	yurewst/ver**kayrt**
old/new	oud/nieuw	owt/neeoo
old/young	oud/jong	owt/yong
beautiful/ugly	mooi/lelijk	moaee/**lay**lerk
good/bad	goed/slecht	ğoot/slehkht
better/worse	beter/slechter	**bay**ter/**slehkh**terr

Some prepositions and a few more useful words

at	te	ter
on	op	op
in	in	in
to	naar	narr
from	van	vahn
inside	binnen	**bin**nern
outside	buiten	**burew**tern
up	op	op
down	neer	nayr
before	voor	voar
after	na	nar
with	met	meht
without	zonder	**zon**derr
through	door	doar
towards	naar	narr
until	tot	tot
during	tijdens	**tay**dernss
and	en	ehn
or	of	off
not	niet	neet
nothing	niets	neets
none	geen	ğayn
very	zeer	zayr
also	ook	oak
soon	spoedig	**spoo**derkh
perhaps	misschien	miss**kheen**

here	**hier**	heer
there	**daar**	darr
now	**nu**	new
then	**dan**	dahn

DUTCH

Arrival

Your passport, please.	**Uw paspoort, alstublieft.**	ewoo **pahss**poart ahlsstew**bleeft**
Here it is.	**Alstublieft.**	ahlsstew**bleeft**
Have you anything to declare?	**Hebt U iets aan te geven?**	hehpt ew eets arn ter **ğay**vern
No, nothing at all.	**Nee, helemaal niets.**	nay **hay**lermarl neets
Porter!	**Kruier!**	**krue**wer
Can you help me with my luggage, please?	**Kunt U me met mijn bagage helpen, alstublieft?**	kernt ew mer meht mayn bah**ğa**rzher **hehl**pern ahlsstew**bleeft**
That's my suitcase.	**Dat is mijn koffer.**	daht iss mayn **kof**ferr
Where's the bus to the centre of town, please?	**Waar is de bus naar het centrum, alstublieft?**	varr iss der berss narr heht **sehn**trerm ahlsstew**bleeft**
This way, please.	**Hierlangs, alstublieft.**	**heer**lahngss ahlsstew**bleeft**

Changing money

| Can you change a traveller's cheque, please? | **Kunt U een traveller's cheque wisselen, alstublieft?** | kernt ew ern "traveller's cheque" **vis**serlern ahlsstew**bleeft** |
| Where's the nearest bank, please? | **Waar is de dichtstbijzijnde bank, alstublieft?** | varr iss der **dikhtst**bayzaynder bahngk ahlsstew**bleeft** |

Car rental

I'd like a car.	**Ik wil graag een auto huren.**	ik vil **ğrarkh** ern **ow**toa **hew**rern
For how long?	**Voor hoe lang?**	voar hoo lahng
A day/Four days/A week/Two weeks.	**Een dag/Vier dagen/Een week/Twee weken.**	ayn dahkh/veer **dah**ğer(n)/ayn vayk/tvay **vay**kern

Taxi

Where can I get a taxi?	**Waar kan ik een taxi krijgen?**	varr kahn ik ern **tak**see **kray**ĝern
What's the fare to . . . ?	**Wat kost het naar . . . ?**	vaht kost heht narr
Take me to this address, please.	**Breng me naar dit adres, alstublieft.**	brehng mer narr dit ah-**drehss** ahlsstew**bleeft**
I'm in a hurry.	**Ik heb haast.**	ik hehp harst
Could you drive more slowly, please?	**Wilt U wat langzamer rijden, alstublieft?**	vilt ew vaht **lahng**zarmerr **ray**dern ahlsstew**bleeft**

Hotel and other accommodation

My name is . . .	**Mijn naam is . . .**	mayn narm iss
Have you a reservation?	**Hebt U gereserveerd?**	hehpt ew ĝerrayserr**vayrt**
Yes, here's the confirmation.	**Ja, hier is de bevestiging.**	yar heer iss der ber-**vehss**stiĝing
I'd like . . .	**Ik wil graag . . .**	ik vil ĝrarkh
I'd like a single room/a double room.	**Ik wil graag een éénpersoonskamer/ een tweepersoons kamer.**	ik vil ĝrarkh een ayn**perr**soansskarmerr/ern **tvay**perrsoansskarmerr
a room with a bath/with a shower	**een kamer met bad/met douche**	ern **kar**merr meht baht/meht **doo**sher

How much?

What's the price per night/per week/per month?	**Hoeveel is het per nacht/per week/per maand?**	hoo**vayl** iss heht pehr nahkht/pehr vayk/pehr marnt
May I see the room?	**Mag ik de kamer zien?**	mahkh ik der **kar**merr zeen
I'm sorry, I don't like it.	**Het spijt me, hij bevalt me niet.**	heht spayt mer hay ber-**vahlt** mer neet
Yes, that's fine. I'll take it.	**Ja, dat is goed. Die neem ik.**	yar daht iss ĝoot. dee naym ik
What's my room number, please?	**Wat is mijn kamernummer, alstublieft?**	vaht iss mayn **kar**merrner-merr ahlsstew**bleeft**
Number 123.	**Nummer 123.**	**ner**merr 123.

DUTCH

DUTCH

Service, please

Who is it?	Wie is daar?	vee iss darr
Just a minute.	Een ogenblikje.	ern oaģernblikyer
Come in! The door's open.	Binnen! De deur is open.	binern. der durr iss oapern
May we have breakfast in our room?	Kunnen we in onze kamer ontbijten?	kernern ver in onzer karmerr ontbaytern

Breakfast

I'll have . . .	Ik neem . . .	ik naym
I'll have some fruit juice.	Ik neem vruchtensap.	ik naym vrerkhternsahp
a boiled egg	een gekookt ei	ern ģerkoakt ay
a fried egg	een gebakken ei	ern ģerbahkern ay
some bacon/some ham	spek/ham	spehk/hahm
some toast	toast	toast
a pot of tea	een kannetje thee	ern kahnertyer tay
a cup of tea	een kopje thee	ern kopyer tay
some coffee	koffie	kofee
some chocolate	chocola	shoakoalar
more butter	nog wat boter	nokh vaht boaterr
some hot water	wat warm water	vaht vahrm varterr

Difficulties

The central heating doesn't work.	De centrale verwarming werkt niet.	der sehntrarler verrvahrming vehrkt neet
the light/the socket	het licht/het stopcontact	heht likht/heht stopkontahkt
the tap/the toilet	de kraan/het toilet	der krarn/heht tvahleht
There's no hot water.	Er is geen warm water.	ehr iss ģayn vahrm varterr
May I see the manager, please?	Mag ik de direkteur spreken, alstublieft?	mahkh ik der deererkturr spraykern ahlsstewbleeft

Telephone—Mail

| There's a call for you. | Er is telefoon voor U. | ehr iss taylerfoan voar ew |
| Hold the line, please. | Blijft U aan het toestel, alstublieft. | blayft ew arn heht toosterl ahlsstewbleeft |

Operator, I've been cut off.	**Juffrouw, mijn ge-sprek is verbroken.**	yerfrow mayn ğersprehk iss verrbroakern
Did anyone tele-phone me?	**Heeft er iemand voor mij opgebeld?**	hayft ehr eemahnt voar may opğerbehlt
Is there any mail for me?	**Is er post voor mij?**	iss ehr post voar may
Are there any messages for me?	**Heeft iemand een boodschap voor mij achtergelaten?**	hayft eemahnt ern boatskhahp voar may ahkhterrğerlartern

Checking out

May I have my bill, please?	**Mag ik de rekening, alstublieft?**	mahkh ik der raykerning ahlsstewbleeft
We're in a great hurry.	**Wij hebben erge haast.**	vay hehbern ehrğer harst
It's been a very en-joyable stay.	**Wij hebben het hier erg prettig gehad.**	vay hehbern het heer ehrkh prehterkh ğerhaht

Eating out

Good evening, sir/ Good evening, madam.	**Goedenavond, Mijnheer/Goeden-avond Mevrouw.**	ğoodernarvernt mernayr ğoodernarvernt mervrow
Good evening. I'd like a table for two, please.	**Goedenavond. Ik wil graag een tafel voor twee per-sonen.**	ğoodernarvernt. ik vil ğrarkh ern tarferl voar tvay perrsoanern
Do you have a fixed-price menu?	**Hebt U een menu à prix fixe?**	hehpt ew ern mernewah pree feeks
May I see the à la carte menu?	**Mag ik het menu à la carte?**	mahkh ik heht mernew ah lah kahrt
May we have an ashtray, please?	**Kunt U ons een asbak brengen, alstublieft?**	kernt ew onss ern ahssbahk brehngern ahlsstewbleeft
some bread	**wat brood**	vat broat
a fork	**een vork**	ern vork
a knife	**een mes**	ern mehss
a spoon	**een lepel**	ern layperl
a plate	**een bord**	ern bort
a glass	**een glas**	ern ğlahss
a napkin	**een servet**	ern sehrveht
another chair	**nog een stoel**	nokh ern stool

DUTCH

DUTCH

| Where's the gentle-men's toilet (men's room)? | **Waar is het heren-toilet?** | varr iss heht **hay**rern-tvahleht |
| Where's the ladies' toilet (ladies' room)? | **Waar is het dames-toilet?** | varr iss heht **darmers**s-tvahleht |

Appetizers

I'd like some ...	**Ik wil graag ...**	ik vil ǧrarkh
I'd like some assorted appetizers.	**Ik wil graag hors-d'oeuvre varié.**	ik vil ǧrarkh or durvr vahreeay
orange juice	**sinaasappelsap**	**see**narsahperlsahp
ham	**ham**	hahm
melon	**meloen**	mer**loon**
pâté	**paté**	pah**tay**
smoked salmon	**gerookte zalm**	ǧer**roak**ter zahlm
shrimps (shrimp)	**garnalen**	ǧah**rnar**lern

Soup

Have you any ... ?	**Hebt U ... ?**	hehpt ew
Have you any chicken soup?	**Hebt U kippesoep?**	hehpt ew **ki**persoop
vegetable soup	**groentesoep**	ǧroontersoop
onion soup	**uiensoep**	**ure**wernsoop

Fish

I'd like some ...	**Ik wil graag ...**	ik vil ǧrarkh
I'd like some fish.	**Ik wil graag vis.**	ik vil ǧrarkh viss
sole	**zeetong**	**zay**tong
trout	**forel**	foa**rehl**
lobster	**kreeft**	krayft
crayfish	**rivierkreeft**	ree**veer**krayft
prawns	**steurgarnalen**	**sturr**ǧahrnarlern
I'd like it ...	**Ik heb hem graag ...**	ik hehp hehm ǧrarkh
I'd like it steamed.	**Ik heb hem graag gestoomd.**	ik hehp hehm ǧrarkh ǧer-stoamt
grilled	**gegrilleerd**	ǧer**ǧri**layrt
boiled	**gekookt**	ǧer**koakt**
baked	**in de oven ge-bakken**	in der **oa**vern ǧer**bah**kern
fried	**gebakken**	ǧer**bah**kern

Meat—Poultry—Game

I'd like some . . .	**Ik wil graag . . .**	ik vil ġrarkh
I'd like some beef.	**Ik wil graag rundvlees.**	ik vil ġrarkh **rernt**vlayss
a beef steak	**een biefstuk**	ern **beef**sterk
some roast beef	**rosbief**	**ross**beef
a veal cutlet	**een kalfskotelet**	ern **kahlfs**koaterleht
mutton	**schapevlees**	**skhah**pervlayss
lamb	**lamsvlees**	**lahmss**vlayss
a pork chop	**een varkenskotelet**	ayn **vahr**kernsskoaterleht
roast pork	**varkensfricandeau**	**vahr**kernssfreekahndoa
hare	**haas**	harss
chicken	**kip**	kip
roast chicken	**gebraden kip**	ġer**brar**dern kip
duck	**eend**	aynt
How do you like your meat?	**Hoe wenst U het vlees?**	hoo vehnst ew heht vlayss
rare	**rood**	roat
medium	**lichtgebakken**	**likht**ġerbahkern
well done	**doorgebakken**	**doar**ġerbahkern

Vegetables

What vegetables have you got?	**Wat voor groenten hebt U?**	vaht voar **ġroon**tern hehpt ew
I'd like some . . .	**Ik wil graag . . .**	ik vil ġrarkh
I'd like some asparagus.	**Il wil graag asperges.**	ik vil ġrarkh ahss**pehr**zherss
green beans	**sperziebonen**	spehr**zee**boanern
mushrooms	**champignons**	shahmpee**ñongss**
carrots	**worteltjes**	**vorterl**tyehss
onions	**uien**	**ure**wern
red cabbage	**rode kool**	**roa**der koal
spinach	**spinazie**	spee**nar**zee
rice	**rijst**	rayst
peas	**doperwtjes**	**dop**ehrtyerss
tomatoes	**tomaten**	toa**mar**tern
green salad	**sla**	slar
potatoes	**aardappelen**	**arr**dahperlern

Desserts

| Nothing more, thanks. | **Niets meer, dank U.** | neets mayr dangk ew |

DUTCH

DUTCH

Just a small portion, please.	**Een kleine portie, alstublieft.**	ern **klayner porsee** ahlsstew**bleeft**
Have you any ice-cream?	**Hebt U ijs?**	hehpt ew ayss
fruit salad	**vruchtensla**	**vrerkh**ternslar
fresh fruit	**vers fruit**	vehrss frurewt
cheese	**kaas**	karss

Drink

What would you like to drink?	**Wat wilt U drinken?**	vaht vilt ew **dring**kern
I'll have a beer, please.	**Een pils, alstublieft.**	ern pilss ahlsstew**bleeft**
I'll have a whisky, please.	**Een whisky, alstublieft.**	ern **viss**kee ahlsstew**bleeft**

Wine

I'd like a bottle of wine.	**Ik wil graag een fles wijn.**	ik vil ġrarkh ern flehss vayn
red wine	**rode wijn**	**roa**der vayn
rosé wine	**rosé**	**roa**zay
white wine	**witte wijn**	**vit**er vayn
Cheers!	**Proost!**	proast

The bill (check)

May I have the bill (check) please?	**Mag ik de rekening, alstublieft?**	mahkh ik der **ray**kerning ahlsstew**bleeft**
Is service included?	**Is de bediening inbegrepen?**	iss der ber**dee**ning inberġraypern
Everything's included.	**Alles inclusief.**	**ahl**erss inklew**zeef**
Thank you, that was a very good meal.	**Dank U, het was een uitstekende maaltijd.**	dangk ew heht vahss ern **urewt**staykernder **marl**tayt

Travelling

| Where's the railway station, please? | **Waar is het station, alstublieft?** | varr iss heht stah**shon** ahlsstew**bleeft** |
| Where's the ticket office, please? | **Waar is het loket, alstublieft?** | varr iss heht loa**keht** ahlsstew**bleeft** |

I'd like a ticket to ...	**Ik wil graag een kaartje naar ...**	ik vil ğrarkh ern **karr**tyer narr
First or second class?	**Eerste of tweede klas?**	**ayr**ster off **tvay**der klahss
First class, please.	**Eerste klas, alstublieft.**	**ayr**ster klahss ahlsstew**bleeft**
Single or return (one way or round-trip)?	**Enkele reis of retour?**	**ehng**kerler rayss off rer**toor**
Do I have to change trains?	**Moet ik overstappen?**	moot ik **oa**verrstahpern
What platform does the train leave from?	**Van welk perron vertrekt de trein?**	vahn vehlk peh**ron** verr**trehkt** der trayn
Where's the nearest underground (subway) station?	**Waar is het dichtstbijzijnde metrostation?**	varr iss hert **dikhtst**bayzaynder **meh**troastah**shon**
Where's the bus station, please?	**Waar is het busstation, alstublieft?**	varr iss heht **berss**stahshon ahlsstew**bleeft**
When's the first bus to ... ?	**Om hoe laat vertrekt de eerste bus naar ... ?**	om hoo lart verr**trehkt** der **ayr**ster berss narr
the last bus the next bus	**de laatste bus de volgende bus**	der **lart**ster berss der **vol**ğernder berss
Please let me off at the next stop.	**Wilt U me bij de volgende halte laten uitstappen?**	vilt ew mer bay der **vol**ğernder **hahl**ter **lar**tern **urewt**stahpern

Relaxing

What's on at the cinema (movies)?	**Wat wordt er in de bioscoop gegeven?**	vaht vort ehr in der beeo**skoap** ğerğayvern
What's on at the theatre?	**Wat wordt er in de schouwburg gegeven?**	vahr vort ehr in der **skhow**berkh ğerğayvern
What time does the film begin? And the play?	**Om hoe laat begint de film? En het toneelstuk?**	om hoo lart ber**ğint** der film? ehn hert toa**nayl**sterk
Are there any tickets for tonight?	**Zijn er nog plaatsen vrij voor vanavond?**	zayn ehr nokh **plart**sern vray voar vahn**ar**vont
Where can we go dancing?	**Waar kunnen we gaan dansen?**	varr **ker**nern ver ğarn **dahn**sern
Would you like to dance?	**Mag ik deze dans van U?**	mahkh ik **day**zer dahnss vahn ew

Introductions

How do you do?	**Hoe maakt U het?**	hoo markt ew heht
How are you?	**Hoe gaat het?**	hoo ġart heht
Very well, thank you. And you?	**Uitstekend, dank U. En U?**	urewtstaykernt dahngk ew. ehn ew
May I introduce Miss Philips?	**Mag ik U Juffrouw Philips voorstellen?**	mahkh ik ew yerfrow Philips voarstehlern
My name is . . .	**Mijn naam is . . .**	mayn narm iss
I'm very pleased to meet you.	**Prettig kennis met U te maken.**	prehterkh kehnerss meht ew ter markern
How long have you been here?	**Hoelang bent U al hier?**	hoolahng behnt ew ahl heer
It was nice meeting you.	**Het was mij een genoegen.**	heht vahss may ayn ġernooġern

Dating

Would you like a cigarette?	**Mag ik U een sigaret aanbieden?**	mahkh ik ew ern seeġarreht arnbeedern
May I get you a drink?	**Mag ik U iets te drinken aanbieden?**	mahkh ik ew eets ter dringkern arnbeedern
Do you have a light, please?	**Hebt U een vuurtje, alstublieft?**	hehpt ew ern vewrtyer ahlsstewbleeft
Are you waiting for someone?	**Wacht U op iemand?**	vahkht ew op eemahnt
Are you free this evening?	**Bent U vanavond vrij?**	behnt ew vahnarvont vray
Where shall we meet?	**Waar spreken we af?**	varr spraykern ver ahf
What time shall I meet you?	**Hoe laat spreken we af?**	hoo lart spraykern ver ahf
May I take you home?	**Mag ik U naar huis brengen?**	mahkh ik ew narr hurewss brehngern
Thank you, it's been a wonderful evening.	**Dank U, het was een heerlijke avond.**	dahngk ew heht vahss ern hayrlerker arvernt
What's your telephone number?	**Wat is uw telefoonnummer?**	vaht iss ewoo taylerfoannermerr
Do you live alone?	**Woont U alleen?**	voant ew ahleen
What time is your last train?	**Om hoe laat gaat uw laatste trein?**	om hoo lart ġart ewoo lartster trayn
Good-night . . .	**Tot ziens . . .**	tot seenss

Banks

Where's the nearest bank, please?	**Waar is de dichtstbijzijnde bank, alstublieft?**	varr iss der **dikhtst**bayzaynder bahngk ahlsstew**bleeft**
Where can I cash some traveller's cheques?	**Waar kan ik traveller's cheques inwisselen?**	varr kahn ik "traveller's cheques" **inv**iserlern
What time does the bank open? What time does it close?	**Om hoe laat gaat de bank open? Om hoe laat gaat hij dicht?**	om hoo lart ġart der bahngk **oa**pern? om hoo lart ġart hay dikht
I'm expecting some money from home. Has it arrived?	**Ik verwacht geld van thuis. Is het aangekomen?**	ik verr**vahkht** ġehlt vahn turewss. iss heht **arn**ġerkoamern
Can you give me some small change, please?	**Kunt U me wat kleingeld geven, alstublieft?**	kernt ew mer vaht **klayn**ġehlt **ġay**vern ahlsstew**bleeft**

Shops, stores and services

Where is the nearest chemist's (pharmacy)?	**Waar is de dichtstbijzijnde apotheek?**	varr iss der **dikhtst**bayzaynder arpoa**tayk**
the nearest hairdresser's	**de dichtstbijzijnde kapper**	der **dikhtst**bayzaynder **kah**perr
the photo shop	**de fotowinkel**	der **foat**oavingkerl
the jeweller's	**de juwelier**	der yewver**leer**
the department store	**het warenhuis**	heht **var**trrnhurewss
the police station	**het politiebureau**	heht polee(t)seebewroa
the garage	**de garage**	der ġah**rar**zher
How do I get there?	**Hoe kom ik daar?**	hoo kom ik darr
Is it within walking distance?	**Is het te lopen?**	iss heht ter **loa**pern

Service

Can you help me, please?	**Kunt U mij helpen, alstublieft?**	kernt ew may **heh**lpern ahlsstew**bleeft**
Can you show me this? And that, too.	**Kunt U me dit laten zien? En dat ook.**	kernt ew mer dit **lar**tern zeen ehn dat oak
It's too expensive/ too big/too small.	**Het is te duur/te groot/te klein.**	heht iss ter dewr/ter ġroat/ter klayn

DUTCH

DUTCH

Can you show me some more?	**Kunt U me er nog wat laten zien?**	kernt ew mer ehr mokh vaht lartern zeen
something better	**iets beters**	eets **bay**terrss
something cheaper	**iets goedkopers**	eets ǵoot**koa**perss
How much is this? And that?	**Hoeveel is dit? En dat?**	hoovayl iss dit? ehn daht
It's not quite what I want.	**Het is niet precies wat ik zoek.**	heht iss neet prer**seess** vaht ik zook
I like it.	**Het bevalt me.**	heht ber**vahlt** mer

Chemist's (Pharmacy)

| I'd like something for a cold/for a cough/for travel sickness. | **Ik wil graag iets tegen een verkoudheid/tegen hoesten/tegen misselijkheid.** | ik vil ǵrarkh eets **tay**ǵern ern ver**kowt**hayt/**tay**ǵern **hoo**stern/**tay**ǵern miserlerkhayt |
| Can you recommend something for hay-fever/for sunburn? | **Kunt U mij iets tegen hooikoorts aanbevelen/tegen zonnebrand?** | kernt ew may eets **tay**ǵern **hoa**eekoarts **arn**bervaylern/**tay**ǵern **zo**nerbrahnt |

Toiletry

May I have some razor blades?	**Mag ik scheermesjes?**	mahkh ik **skhayr**mehsherss
some shaving cream	**scheercrème**	**skhayr**kraim
some toothpaste	**tandpasta**	**tahnt**pahstarr
I'd like some soap.	**Ik wil graag zeep.**	ik vil ǵrarkh zayp
some suntan oil	**zonne-olie**	**zo**neroalee

At the barber's

I'd like a haircut, please.	**Knippen, alstublieft.**	kni**pern** ahlsstew**bleeft**
Short/Leave it long.	**Kort/Laat het lang.**	kort/lart heht lahng
A razor cut, please.	**Met het mes, alstublieft.**	meht heht mehss ahlsstew**bleeft**

At the hairdresser's

| I'd like a shampoo and set, please. | **Wassen en watergolven, alstublieft.** | **vah**sern ehn **var**terrǵolvern ahlsstew**bleeft** |

I'd like a bleach.	**Ik wil het laten bleken.**	ik vil heht lartern **blay**kern
a permanent	**een permanent**	ern pehrmar**nehnt**
a colour rinse	**een kleurspoeling**	ern **klurr**spooling
a manicure	**een manicure**	ern marnee**kew**rer

Photography

| I'd like a film for this camera. | **Ik wil graag een film voor dit toestel.** | ik vil ğrarkh ern film voar dit **toos**terl |
| This camera doesn't work. | **Deze camera doet het niet.** | **day**zer **kar**merrah doot heht neet |

At the post office

| Where's the nearest post office, please? | **Waar is het dichtstbijzijnde postkantoor, alstublieft?** | varr iss heht **dikhtst**bayzaynder **post**kahntoar ahlsstew**bleeft** |
| I'd like to send this by express (special delivery)/by air mail. | **Ik wil dit per express versturen/per luchtpost.** | ik vil pehr ehks**prehss** verstewrern/pehr **lerkht**post |

Service stations

Where is the nearest service station, please?	**Waar is het dichtstbijzijnde benzinestation, alstublieft?**	varr iss heht **dikhtst**bayzaynder behn**zee**nerstahshon ahlsstew**bleeft**
Fill her up, please.	**Vol, alstublieft.**	vol ahlsstew**bleeft**
Check the oil, please.	**Wilt U de olie controleren, alstublieft?**	vilt ew der **oa**lee kontroalayrern ahlsstew**bleeft**
Would you check the tyres?	**Wilt U de banden controleren?**	vilt ew der **bahn**dern kontroa**lay**rern

Street directions

Can you show me on the map where I am?	**Kunt U mij op de kaart aanwijzen waar ik ben?**	kern ew may op der karrt **arn**vayzern varr ik behn
You're on the wrong road.	**U bent verkeerd gereden.**	ew behnt verr**kayrt** ğer**ray**dern
Go back to ...	**Rijd terug naar ...**	rayt ter**rerkh** narr

DUTCH

DUTCH

| Go straight ahead. | **Rijd rechtuit.** | rayt **rehkh**turewt |
| It's on the left/on the right. | **Het is aan de linkerkant/aan de rechterkant.** | heht iss arn der **ling**kerkahnt/arn der **rehkh**terkahnt |

Accidents

May I use your telephone?	**Mag ik van uw telefoon gebruik maken?**	mahkh ik vahn ewoo tayler**foan** ğer**brurewk** markern
Call a doctor quickly.	**Roep vlug een dokter.**	roop vlerkh ern **dok**terr
Call an ambulance.	**Roep een ambulance.**	roop ern ahmbew**lahn**ser
Please call the police.	**Roep de politie, alstublieft.**	roop de polee(t)see ahlsstew**bleeft**

Numbers

one	**een**	ayn
two	**twee**	tvay
three	**drie**	dree
four	**vier**	veer
five	**vijf**	vayf
six	**zes**	zehss
seven	**zeven**	**zay**vern
eight	**acht**	ahkht
nine	**negen**	**nay**ğern
ten	**tien**	teen
eleven	**elf**	ehlf
twelve	**twaalf**	tvarlf
thirteen	**dertien**	**dehr**teen
fourteen	**veertien**	**vayr**teen
fifteen	**vijftien**	**vayf**teen
sixteen	**zestien**	**zehss**teen
seventeen	**zeventien**	**zay**vernteen
eighteen	**achttien**	**ahkh**teen
nineteen	**negentien**	**nay**ğernteen
twenty	**twintig**	**tvin**terkh
twenty-one	**eenentwintig**	**ay**nerntvinterkh
thirty	**dertig**	**dehr**terkh
forty	**veertig**	**vayr**terkh
fifty	**vijftig**	**vayf**terkh
sixty	**zestig**	**zehss**terkh
seventy	**zeventig**	**zay**vernterkh
eighty	**tachtig**	**tahkh**terkh
ninety	**negentig**	**nay**ğernterkh

one hundred	**honderd**	**hon**derrt
one thousand	**duizend**	**durew**zernt
ten thousand	**tienduizend**	**teen**durewzernt

Days

It's Sunday.	**Het is zondag.**	heht iss **zon**dahkh
Monday	**maandag**	**marn**dahkh
Tuesday	**dinsdag**	**dinss**dahkh
Wednesday	**woensdag**	**voonss**dahkh
Thursday	**donderdag**	**donderr**dahkh
Friday	**vrijdag**	**vray**dahkh
Saturday	**zaterdag**	**zar**terrdahkh
yesterday	**gisteren**	**g**isterrern
today	**vandaag**	vahn**darkh**
tomorrow	**morgen**	**morg**ern
morning/afternoon	**ochtend/namiddag**	**okh**ternt/narmi**dankh**
evening/night	**avond/nacht**	**ar**vernt/**nahkht**

Months

January	**januari**	yahne**warr**ee
February	**februari**	fehre**warr**ee
March	**maart**	marrt
April	**april**	ah**pril**
May	**mei**	may
June	**juni**	**yew**nee
July	**juli**	**yew**lee
August	**augustus**	ow**g**erss**sterss
September	**september**	sehp**tehm**berr
October	**oktober**	ok**toa**berr
November	**november**	noa**vehm**berr
December	**december**	day**sehm**berr
Merry Christmas!	**Prettig Kerstfeest!**	**preh**terkh **kehrst**fayst! er-
Happy New Year!	**Gelukkig Nieuwjaar!**	**ler**kerkh **neeoo**yarr

DUTCH

FINNISH

Guide to Pronunciation

Letter	Approximate pronunciation	Symbol	Example	

Consonants

Letter	Approximate pronunciation	Symbol	Example	
k, m, n, p, t, v	as in English			
d	as in ready, but sometimes very weak	d	taide	tighday
g	only found after n; ng is pronounced as in singer	ng	sangen	sahngayn
h	as in hot, whatever its position in the word	h	Lahti	lahhti
j	like y in you	y	ja	yah
l	as in let	l	talo	tahloa
r	always rolled	r	raha	rahhah
s	always as in set	s/ss	sillä	sillæ
			kiitos	keetoass

Vowels

a	like **a** in c**a**r, but shorter	ah	**matala**	**mah**tahlah
e	like **a** in l**a**te	ay	**kolme**	**ko**almay
i	like **i** in p**i**n	i	**takki**	**tah**kki
o	like **aw** in l**aw**, but shorter	oa	**olla**	**oa**llah
u	like **u** in p**u**ll	oo	**hupsu**	**hoo**psoo
y	like **u** in French s**u**r or **ü** in German **ü**ber; say **ee** as in s**ee** and round your lips while still trying to pronounce **ee**	ew	**yksi**	**ew**ksi
ä	like **a** in h**a**t	æ	**äkkiä**	**æ**kkiæ
ö	like **ur** in f**ur**, but with the lips rounded	ur	**tyttö**	**tew**ttur

N.B. The letters **b, c, f, q, ś, sh, x, z, ž** and **å** are only found in words borrowed from foreign languages, and they are pronounced as in the language of origin.

Diphthongs

In Finnish, diphthongs occur only in the first syllable of a word, except for those ending in **-i**, which can occur anywhere. They should be pronounced as a combination of the two vowel sounds represented by the spelling. The first vowel is pronounced louder in the following diphthongs: **ai, ei, oi, ui, yi, äi, öi, au, eu, ou, ey, äy, öy, iu**; the second vowel is louder in: **ie, uo, yö**.

Double letters

Remember that in Finnish *every* letter is pronounced, therefore a letter written double is pronounced long. Thus, the **kk** in ku**kk**a should be pronounced like the two k-sounds in the words thi**ck c**oat. Similarly, the **aa** in k**aa**tua should be pronounced long (like **a** in English c**a**r). These distinctions are important, not least because ku**k**a has a different meaning from ku**kk**a and k**a**tua a different meaning from k**aa**tua.

Stress

A strong stress always falls on the first syllable of a word.

Some basic expressions

Yes.	Kyllä.	kewllæ
No.	Ei.	ay
Please.	Olkaa hyvä.	oalkar hewvæ
Thank you.	Kiitos.	keetoass
Thank you very much.	Kiitoksia paljon.	keetoaksiah pahlyoan
That's all right.	Ei kestä.	ay kaysstæ

Greetings

Good morning.	Hyvää huomenta.	hewvææ hoooamayntah
Good afternoon.	Hyvää päivää.	hewvææ pæivææ
Good evening.	Hyvää iltaa.	hewvææ iltar
Good night.	Hyvää yötä.	hewvææ ewurtæ
Good-bye.	Näkemiin.	nækaymeen
See you later.	Pikaisiin näkemiin.	pikighsseen nækaymeen
This is Mr. . . .	Tämä on herra . . .	tæmæ oan hayrrah
This is Mrs. . . .	Tämä on rouva . . .	tæmæ oan roavah
This is Miss . . .	Tämä on neiti . . .	tæmæ oan nayti
I'm very pleased to meet you.	Hauska tutustua.	howsskah tootoosstooah
How are you?	Mitä kuuluu?	mitæ kooloo
Very well, thank you.	Erittäin hyvää, kiitos.	ayrittæin hewvææ keetoass
And you?	Entä teille?	ayntæ tayllay
Fine.	Kiitos hyvää.	keetoass hewvææ
Excuse me.	Anteeksi.	ahntayksi

Questions

Where?	Missä?	misssæ
Where is . . . ?	Missä on . . . ?	misssæ oan
Where are . . . ?	Missä ovat . . . ?	misssæ oavaht
When?	Milloin?	milloyn
What?	Mikä?	mikæ
How?	Kuinka?	kooingkah
How much?	Kuinka paljon?	kooingkah pahlyoan

54

How many?	Kuinka monta?	kooingkah moantah
Who?	Kuka?	kookah
Why?	Miksi?	miksi
Which?	Mikä?	mikæ
What do you call this?	Miksi tätä kutsutaan?	miksi tætæ kootsootarn
What do you call that?	Miksi tuota kutsutaan?	miksi toooatah kootsootarn
What does this mean?	Mitä tämä tarkoittaa?	mitæ tæmæ tahrkoyttar
What does that mean?	Mitä tuo tarkoittaa?	mitæ toooa tahrkoyttar

Do you speak . . . ?

Do you speak English?	Puhutteko englantia?	poohoottaykoa aynglahntiah
Do you speak German?	Puhutteko saksaa?	poohoottaykoa sahksah
Do you speak French?	Puhutteko ranskaa?	poohoottaykoa rahnskar
Do you speak Spanish?	Puhutteko espanjaa?	poohoottaykoa aysspahnyar
Do you speak Italian?	Puhutteko italiaa?	poohoottaykoa italiar
Could you speak more slowly, please?	Voisitteko puhua hitaammin?	voysittaykoa poohooah hitarmmin
Please point to the phrase in the book.	Olkaa hyvä ja näyttäkää lause kirjasta.	oalkar hewvæ yah næewttækææ lowsay kiryahsstah
Just a minute. I'll see if I can find it in this book.	Hetkinen. Katson löydänkö sen tästä kirjasta.	haytkinayn. kahtsoan lurewdængkur sayn tæsstæ kiryahsstah
I understand.	Ymmärrän.	ewmmærræn
I don't understand.	En ymmärrä.	ayn ewmmærræ

Can . . . ?

Can I have . . . ?	Voinko saada . . . ?	voyngkoa sardah
Can we have . . . ?	Voimmeko saada . . . ?	voymmaykoa sardah
Can you show me . . . ?	Voitteko näyttää minulle . . . ?	voyttaykoa næewttææ minoollay

| Can you tell me . . . ? | **Voitteko sanoa minulle . . . ?** | **voyt**taykoa **sah**noaah minoollay |
| Can you help me, please? | **Voitteko auttaa minua?** | **voyt**taykoa **owt**tar minooah |

Wanting

I'd like . . .	**Haluaisin . . .**	**hah**looighssin
We'd like . . .	**Haluaisimme . . .**	**hah**looighssimmay
Please give me . . .	**Olkaa hyvä ja antakaa minulle . . .**	**oal**kar **hew**væ yah **ahn**tahkar minoollay
Give it to me, please.	**Antakaa se minulle.**	**ahn**tahkar say minoollay
Please bring me . . .	**Tuokaa minulle . . .**	**tooo**akar minoollay
Bring it to me, please.	**Tuokaa se minulle.**	**tooo**akar say minoollay
I'm hungry.	**Minun on nälkä.**	minoon oan **næl**kæ
I'm thirsty.	**Minun on jano.**	minoon oan **yah**noa
I'm tired.	**Olen väsynyt.**	**oa**layn **væ**sewnewt
I'm lost.	**Olen eksyksissä.**	**oa**layn **ayk**sewksisssæ
It's important.	**Se on tärkeää.**	say oan **tær**kayæ æ
It's urgent.	**Sillä on kiire.**	**sil**læ oan **kee**ray
Hurry up!	**Pitäkää kiirettä!**	**pi**tækæ æ **kee**rayttæ

It is/There is . . .

It is/It's . . .	**Se on . . .**	say oan
Is it . . . ?	**Onko se . . . ?**	**oang**koa say
It isn't . . .	**Se ei ole . . .**	say ay **oa**lay
There is/There are . . .	**Siellä on . . .**	**siayl**læ oan
Is there/Are there . . . ?	**Onko siellä . . . ?**	**oang**koa **siayl**læ
There isn't/There aren't . . .	**Siellä ei ole . . .**	**siayl**læ ay **oa**lay
There isn't any/There aren't any.	**Ei ole yhtään.**	ay **oa**lay **ewh**tææn

A few common words

big/small	**suuri/pieni**	**soo**ri/**pee**ayni
quick/slow	**nopea/hidas**	**noa**payah/**hi**dahss
early/late	**aikaisin/myöhään**	**igh**kighssin/**mew**urhææn

cheap/expensive	halpa/kallis	hahlpah/kahlliss
near/far	lähellä/kaukana	læhayllæ/kowkahnah
hot/cold	kuuma/kylmä	koomah/kewlmæ
full/empty	täysi/tyhjä	tæewsi/tewhyæ
easy/difficult	helppo/vaikea	haylppoa/vighkayah
heavy/light	painava/kevyt	pighnahvah/kayvewt
open/shut	avoin/suljettu	ahvoyn/soolyayttoo
right/wrong	oikea/väärä	oykayah/vææræ
old/new	vanha/uusi	vahnhah/oosi
old/young	vanha/nuori	vahnhah/noooari
beautiful/ugly	kaunis/ruma	kowniss/roomah
good/bad	hyvä/huono	hewvæ/hoooanoa
better/worse	parempi/huonompi	pahraympi/hoooanoampi

Some prepositions and a few more useful words

at	-lla, -llä	-llah, -llæ
on	päällä	pæællæ
in	-ssa, -ssä	-ssah, -ssæ
to	-lle	-llay
from	-sta, -stä	-stah, -stæ
inside	sisällä	sisællæ
outside	ulkopuolella	oolkaopoooalayllah
up	ylos	ewlurss
down	alas	ahlahss
before	ennen	aynnayn
after	jälkeen	yælkayn
with	kanssa	kahnssah
without	ilman	ilmahn
through	läpi	læpi
towards	kohti	koahti
until	asti	ahssti
during	aikana	ighkahnah
and	ja	yah
or	tai	tigh
not	ei	ay
nothing	ei mitään	ay mitææn
none	ei yhtään	ay ewhtææn
very	erittäin	ayrittæin
also	myös	mewurss
soon	pian	piahn
perhaps	ehkä	ayhkæ
here	tässä	tæsssæ
there	tuossa	toooasssah
now	nyt	newt
then	sitten	sittayn

Arrival

Your passport, please.	Passinne, olkaa hyvä.	pahsssinnay oalkar hewvæ
Here it is.	Tässä.	tæsssæ
Have you anything to declare?	Onko teillä mitään tullattavaa?	oangkoa tayllä mitææn toollahttahvar
No, nothing at all.	Ei, ei mitään.	ay ay mitææn
Porter!	Kantaja!	kahntahyah
Can you help me with my luggage, please?	Voitteko auttaa minua kantamaan matkatavarani?	voyttaykoa owttar minooah kahntahmarn mahtkahtahvahrahni
That's my suitcase.	Tuo on minun matkalaukkuni.	toooa oan minoon matkahlowkkooni
Where's the bus to the centre of town, please?	Mistä lähtee bussi keskikaupungille?	misstæ læhtay boosssi kaysskikowpoonggillay
This way, please.	Tätä tietä, olkaa hyvä.	tætæ tiaytæ oalkar hewvæ

Changing money

Can you change a traveller's cheque, please?	Voitteko vaihtaa matkašekin?	voyttaykoa vighhtar mahtkahshaykin
Where's the nearest bank, please?	Missä on lähin pankki?	misssæ oan læhin pahnkki

Car rental

I'd like a car.	Haluaisin auton.	hahlooighsin owtoan
For how long?	Kuinka pitkäksi aikaa?	kooingkah pitkæksi ighkar
A day/Four days/ A week/Two weeks.	Päiväksi/Neljäksi päiväksi/Viikoksi/ Kahdeksi viikoksi.	pæivæksi/naylyæksi pæivæksi/veekoaksi/ kahhdayksi veekoaksi

Taxi

Where can I get a taxi?	Mistä voin saada taksin?	misstæ voyn sardah tahksin
What's the fare to...?	Paljonko se maksaa...n?	pahlyoangkoa say mahksar...n

FINNISH

Take me to this address, please.	Viekää minut tähän osoitteeseen.	viaykææ minoot tæhæn oasoyttayssayn
I'm in a hurry.	Minulla on kiire.	minoollah oan keeray
Could you drive more slowly, please?	Voisitteko ajaa hitaammin?	voysittaykoa ahyar hitarmmin

Hotel and other accommodation

My name is...	Nimeni on...	nimayni oan
Have you a reservation?	Onko teillä varaus?	oangkoa tayllæ vahrahooss
Yes, here's the confirmation.	Kyllä, tässä on vahvistus.	kewllæ tæsssæ oan vahhvisstooss
I'd like...	Haluaisin...	hahlooighsin
I'd like a single room/a double room.	Haluaisin yhden hengen huoneen/kahden hengen huoneen.	hahlooighssin ewhdayn hayngayn hoooanayn/kahhdayn hayngayn hoooanayn
a room with a bath/with a shower	huoneen jossa on kylpy/jossa on suihku	hoooanayn yoasssah oan kewlpew/yoasssah oan sooihkoo

How much?

What's the price per night/per week/per month?	Paljonko hinta on yöltä/viikolta/kuukaudelta?	pahlyoangkoa hintah oan ewurltæ/veekoaltah/kookowdayltah
May I see the room?	Saanko nähdä huoneen?	sarngkoa næhdæ hoooanayn
I'm sorry, I don't like it.	Valitan mutta en pidä siitä.	vahlitahn moottah ayn pidæ seetæ
Yes, that's fine. I'll take it.	Kyllä, se sopii mainiosti. Otan sen.	kewllæ say soapee mighnioassti. oatahn sayn
What's my room number, please?	Mikä on huoneeni numero?	mikæ oan hoooanayni noomayroa
Number 123.	Numero 123.	noomayroa 123

Service, please

Who is it?	Kuka siellä?	kookah siayllæ
Just a minute.	Hetkinen.	haytkinayn
Come in! The door's open.	Sisään! Ovi on auki.	sissææn! oavi oan owki
May we have breakfast in our room?	Voimmeko saada varhaisaamiaisen huoneeseemme?	voymmaykoa sardah vahrhighssarmiighssayn hooanayssaymmay

59

Breakfast

I'll have...	Haluaisin...	hahlooighssin
I'll have some fruit juice.	Haluaisin hedelmätuoremehua.	hahlooighssin haydaylmætoooaraymayhooah
a boiled egg	keitetyn munan	kaytaytewn moonahn
a fried egg	paistetun munan	pighsstaytoon moonahn
some bacon/some ham	pekonia/kinkkua	paykoaniah/kinkkooah
some toast	paahtoleipää	parhtoalaypææ
a pot of tea	annoksen teetä	ahnnoaksayn taytæ
a cup of tea	kupin teetä	koopin taytæ
some coffee	kahvia	kahhviah
some chocolate	kaakaota	karkahoatah
more butter	lisää voita	lisææ voytah
some hot water	kuumaa vettä	koomar vayttæ

Difficulties

The central heating doesn't work.	Keskuslämmitys ei toimi.	kaysskoosslæmmitewss ay toymi
the light/the socket the tap/the toilet	valo/pistorasia hana/wc	vahloa/pisstoarahssiah hahnah/vay say
There's no hot water.	Kuumaa vettä ei tule.	koomar vayttæ ay toolay
May I see the manager, please?	Haluaisin tavata johtajan.	hahlooighssin tahvahtah yoahtahyahn

Telephone—Mail

There's a call for you.	Teille on puhelu.	tayllay oan poohayloo
Hold the line, please.	Hetkinen, olkaa hyvä.	haytkinayn oalkar hewvæ
Operator, I've been cut off.	Keskus, puhelu katkesi.	kaysskooss poohayloo kahtkayssi
Did anyone telephone me?	Onko kukaan soittanut minulle?	oangkoa kookarn soyttahnoot minoollay
Is there any mail for me?	Onko minulle mitään postia?	oangkoa minoollay mitæææn poasstiah
Are there any messages for me?	Onko minulle mitään viestejä?	oangkoa minoollay mitæææn viaysstayyæ

Checking out

May I have my bill, please?	**Saisinko laskuni?**	sighsingkoa lahsskooni
We're in a great hurry.	**Meillä on kova kiire.**	mayllæ oan koavah keeray
It's been a very enjoyable stay.	**Nautimme kovasti oleskelustamme.**	nowtimmay koavahsti oalaysskayloosstahmmay

Eating out

Good evening, sir/ Good evening, madam.	**Hyvää iltaa.**	hewvææ iltar
Good evening. I'd like a table for two, please.	**Hyvää iltaa. Haluaisin pöydän kahdelle.**	hewvææ iltar. hahlooighsin purewdæn kahhdayllay
Do you have a fixed-price menu?	**Onko teillä päivän ateriaa?**	oangkoa tayllæ pæivæn ahtayriar
May I see the à la carte menu?	**Saanko à la carte ruokalistan?**	sarngkoa ah lah kahrt roooakahlisstahn
May we have an ashtray, please?	**Saisimmeko tuhkakupin?**	sighsimmaykoa toohkahkoopin
some bread	**leipää**	laypææ
a fork	**haarukan**	harrookahn
a knife	**veitsen**	vaytsayn
a spoon	**lusikan**	loosikahn
a plate	**lautasen**	lowtahsayn
a glass	**lasin**	lahsin
a napkin	**lautasliinan**	lowtahsleenahn
another chair	**vielä yhden tuolin**	viaylay ewhdayn toooalin
Where's the gentlemen's toilet (men's room)?	**Missä on miestenhuone?**	misssæ oan miaystaynhoooanay
Where's the ladies' toilet (ladies' room)?	**Missä on naistenhuone?**	misssæ oan nighstaynhoooanay

Appetizers

I'd like some...	**Haluaisin...**	hahlooighssin
I'd like some assorted appetizers.	**Haluaisin alkupala-valikoiman.**	hahlooighssin ahlkoopah-lahvahlikoymahn
orange juice	**appelsiinimehun**	ahppaylseenimayhoon
ham	**kinkkua**	kinkkooah

melon	melonia	mayloaniah
pâté	tahnaa	tahhnar
smoked salmon	savustettua lohta	sahvoosstayttooah loahtah
shrimps (shrimp)	katkarapuja	kahtkahrahpooyah

Soup

Have you any...?	Onko teillä...?	oangkoa tayllæ
Have you any chicken soup?	Onko teillä kanakeittoa?	oangkoa tayllæ kahnah- kayttoaah
vegetable soup	vihanneskeittoa	vihahnnaysskayttoaah
onion soup	sipulikeittoa	sipoolikayttoaah

Fish

I'd like some...	Haluaisin...	hahlooighssin
I'd like some fish.	Haluaisin kalaa.	hahlooighssin kahlar
sole	kampelaa	kahmpaylar
trout	taimenta	tighmayntah
lobster	hummeria	hoommayiah
crayfish	rapuja	rahpooyah
prawns	isoja katkarapuja	isoayah kahtkahrah- pooyah
I'd like it...	Haluaisin sen...	hahlooighssin sayn
I'd like it steamed.	Haluaisin sen höyrytettynä.	hahlooighssin sayn hurew- rewtayttewnæ
grilled	pariloituna	pahriloytoonah
boiled	keitettynä	kayttayttewnæ
baked	uunissa paistettuna	oonisssah pighsstayt- toonah
fried	paistettuna	pighsstayttoonah

Meat—Poultry—Game

I'd like some...	Haluaisin...	hahlooighssin
I'd like some beef.	Haluaisin naudan- lihaa.	hahlooighssin nowdahn- lihar
a beef steak	pihvin	pihvin
some roast beef	paahtopaistia	parhtoapighsstiah
a veal cutlet	vasikanleikkeen	vahsikahnlaykkayn
mutton	lammasta	lahmmahsstah
lamb	nuorta lammasta	noooartah lahmmahsstah
a pork chop	porsaankyljyksen	porsarngkewlyewksayn

roast pork	porsaanpaistia	porsaanpighsstiah
hare	jäniksenlihaa	yæniksaynlihar
chicken	kanaa	kahnar
roast chicken	kanapaistia	kahnahpighsstiah
duck	ankkaa	ahnkkar

How do you like your meat?	Miten valmistettuna haluatte lihan?	mitayn vahlmisstayttoonah hahlooahttay lihahn
rare	verisenä	vayrissaynæ
medium	puolikypsänä	poooalikewpsænæ
well done	hyvin paistettuna	hewvin pighsstayttoonah

Vegetables

What vegetables have you got?	Mitä vihanneksia teillä on?	mitæ vihahnnayksiah tayllah oan
I'd like some . . .	Haluaisin . . .	hahlooighssin
I'd like some asparagus.	Haluaisin parsaa.	hahlooighssin pahrsar
green beans	vihreitä papuja	vihraytæ pahpooyah
mushrooms	sieniä	siayniæ
carrots	porkkanaa	porkkahnar
onions	sipulia	sipooliah
red cabbage	punakaalia	poonahkarliah
spinach	pinaattia	pinarttiah
rice	riisiä	reesiæ
peas	herneitä	hayrnaytæ
tomatoes	tomaatteja	toamarttayyah
green salad	vihreätä sekasalaattia	vihrayætæ saykahssahlarttiah
potatoes	perunoita	payroonoitah

Desserts

Nothing more, thanks.	Ei muuta, kiitos.	ay mootah keetoass
Just a small portion, please.	Vain pieni annos.	vighn piayni ahnnoass
Have you any ice-cream?	Onko teillä jäätelöä?	oangkoa tayllæ yææ-tayluræ
fruit salad	hedelmäsalaattia	haydaylmæsahlarttiah
fresh fruit	tuoreita hedelmiä	toooaraytah haydaylmiæ
cheese	juustoa	yoosstoa

Drink

What would you like to drink?	**Mitä haluaisitte juoda?**	mitæ hahlooighssittay joooadah
I'll have a beer, please.	**Haluaisin oluen.**	hahlooighssin oalooayn
I'll have a whisky, please.	**Haluaisin viskin.**	hahlooighssin visskin

Wine

I'd like a bottle of wine.	**Haluaisin pullon viiniä.**	hahlooighssin poolloan veeniæ
red wine	**punaviiniä**	poonahveeniæ
rosé wine	**rosé-viiniä**	roasayveeniæ
white wine	**valkoviiniä**	vahlkoaveeniæ
Cheers!	**Terveydeksenne!**	tayrvayewdayksaynnay

The bill (check)

May I have the bill (check) please?	**Saisinko laskun?**	sighsingkoa lahsskoon
Is service included?	**Sisältyykö siihen palvelu?**	sisæltewkur seehayn pahlvayloo
Everything's included.	**Kaikki on mukana.**	kighkki oan mookahnah
Thank you, that was a very good meal.	**Kiitoksia, se oli erittäin hyvä ateria.**	keetoaksiah say oali ayrittæin hewvæ ahtayriah

Travelling

Where's the railway station, please?	**Missä on rautatieasema?**	misssæ oan rowtahtiay-ahssaymah
Where's the ticket office, please?	**Missä on lipun-myynti?**	misssæ oan lipoonmewnti
I'd like a ticket to . . .	**Haluaisin lipun . . . n.**	hahlooighssin lipoon . . . n
First or second class?	**Ensimmäinen vai toinen luokka?**	aynsimmæinayn vigh toynayn loooakkah
First class, please.	**Ensimmäinen.**	aynsimmæinayn
Single or return (one way or round-trip)?	**Yhdensuuntainen vai edestakainen?**	ewhdaynsoontighnayn vigh aydaysstahkighnayn

Do I have to change trains?	**Täytyykö minun vaihtaa junaa?**	tæewtewkur minoon vighhtar yoonar
What platform does the train leave from?	**Miltä laiturilta juna lähtee?**	miltæ lightooriltah yoonah læhtay
Where's the nearest underground (subway) station?	**Missä on lähin maanalaisen asema?**	misssæ oan læhin marnhahlighssayn ahsaymah
Where's the bus station, please? /	**Missä on linja-autoasema?**	misssæ oan linyah owtoa-ahssaymah
When's the first bus to . . . ?	**Milloin lähtee ensimmäinen bussi . . . n?**	milloyn læhtay aynsimmæinayn boosssi . . . n
the last bus the next bus	**viimeinen bussi/ seuraava bussi**	veemaynayn boosssi/ sayoorarvah boosssi
Please let me off at the next stop.	**Päästäisittekö minut pois seuraavalla pysäkillä?**	pææsstæissittaykur minoot poyss sayoo-rarvahllah pewsækillæ

Relaxing

What's on at the cinema (movies)?	**Mitä elokuvissa esitetään?**	mitæ ayloakoovisssah aysitaytææn
What's on at the theatre?	**Mitä teatterissa esitetään?**	mitæ tayahttayrisssah aysitaytææn
What time does the film begin? And the play?	**Mihin aikaan elokuva alkaa? Entä näytelmä?**	mihin ighkarn ayloakoovah ahlkarr? ayntæ næewtaylmæ
Are there any tickets for tonight?	**Onko täksi illaksi vielä lippuja?**	oangkoa tæksi illaksi viayæ lippooyah
Where can we go dancing?	**Mihin voimme mennä tanssimaan?**	mihin voymmay maynnæ tahnsssimarn
Would you like to dance?	**Haluaisitteko tanssia?**	hahlooighssittaykoa tahnsssiah

Introductions

How do you do?	**Hyvää päivää.**	hewvææ pæivææ
How are you?	**Mitä kuuluu?**	mitæ kooloo
Very well, thank you. And you?	**Kiitos, erittäin hyvää. Entä teille?**	keetoass ayrrittæin hewvææ. ayntæ tayllay
May I introduce Miss Philips?	**Saanko esitellä neiti Philipsin?**	sarngkoa aysitayllæ nayti filipsin

My name is...	Minun nimeni on...	minoon nimayni oan
I'm very pleased to meet you.	Hauska tavata.	howsskah tahvahtah
How long have you been here?	Kauanko olette ollut täällä?	kowahngkoa oalayttay oalloot tæællæ
It was nice meeting you.	Oli hauska tavata.	oali howsskah tahvahtah

Dating

Would you like a cigarette?	Haluaisitteko savukkeen?	hahlooighssittaykoa savookkayn
May I get you a drink?	Saanko tarjota teille lasillisen?	sarngkoa tahryoatah tayllay lahsillissayn
Do you have a light, please?	Onko teillä tulta?	oangkoa tayllæ tooltah
Are you waiting for someone?	Odotatteko jotakuta?	oadoatahttaykoa yoatahkootah
Are you free this evening?	Oletteko vapaa tänä iltana?	oalayttaykoa vahpar tænæ iltahnah
Where shall we meet?	Missä tapaamme?	misssæ tahparmmay
What time shall I meet you?	Mihin aikaan tapaan teidät?	mihin ighkarn tahparn taydæt
May I take you home?	Saanko saattaa teidät kotiin?	sarngkoa sarttar taydæt koateen
Thank you, it's been a wonderful evening.	Kiitos, oli ihana ilta.	keetoass oali ihahnah iltah
What's your telephone number?	Mikä on puhelinnumeronne?	mikæ oan poohaylinnoomayroannay
Do you live alone?	Asutteko yksin?	ahsoottaykoa ewksin
What time is your last train?	Mihin aikaa viimeinen junanne lähtee?	mihin ighkar veemaynayn yoonahnnay læhtay
Good-night...	Hyvää yötä...	hewvæ æ ewurtæ

Banks

| Where's the nearest bank, please? | Missä on lähin pankki? | misssæ oan læhin pahnkki |
| Where can I cash some traveller's cheques? | Missä voin vaihtaa matkašekkejä? | misssæ voyn vighhtar mahtkahshaykkayyæ |

What time does the bank open? What time does it close? | **Mihin aikaan pankki avataan? Mihin aikaan se suljetaan?** | mihin ighkarn pahnkki ahvahtarn? mihin ighkarn say soolyaytarn

I'm expecting some money from home. Has it arrived? | **Odotan rahaa kotoa. Onkohan se jo tullut?** | oadoatahn rahhar koatoaah. oangkoahahn say yoa toolloot

Can you give me some small change, please? | **Voitteko antaa minulle hiukan vaihtorahaa?** | voyttaykoa ahntar minoollay hiookahn vighhtoarahhar

Shops, stores and services

Where is the nearest chemist's (pharmacy)? | **Missä on lähin apteekki?** | misssæ oan læhin ahptaykki

the nearest hairdresser's | **lähin kampaamo** | læhin kahmparmoa

the photo shop | **valokuvausliike** | vahloakoovahoossleekay
the jeweller's | **kultaseppä** | kooltassayppæ
the department store | **tavaratalo** | tahvahrahtahloa
the police station | **poliisiasema** | poaleessiahssaymah
the garage | **pysäköintitalo** | pewsækurintitahloa

How do I get there? | **Miten sinne pääsee?** | mitayn sinnay pææsay

Is it within walking distance? | **Onko se kävelymatkan päässä?** | oangkoa say kævaylewmahtkahn pæssssæ

Service

Can you help me, please? | **Voitteko auttaa minua?** | voyttaykoa owttaa minooah

Can you show me this? And that, too. | **Voitteko näyttää minulle tätä? Ja myös tuota.** | voyttaykoa næewttææ minoollay tætæ? yah mewurss toooatah

It's too expensive/too big/too small. | **Se on liian kallis/liian suuri/liian pieni.** | say oan leeahn kahllis/leeahn soori/leeahn piayni

Can you show me some more? | **Voitteko näyttää minulle vielä joitakin muita?** | voyttaykoa næewtiææ minoollay viaylæ yoytahkin mooitah

something better | **jotakin parempaa** | yoatahkin pahraympar
something cheaper | **jotakin halvempaa** | yoatahkin hahlvaympar

67

How much is this? And that?	Paljonko tämä maksaa? Entä tuo?	pahlyoangkoa tæmæ mahksar? ayntæ toooa
It's not quite what I want.	Se ei ole aivan sitä mitä haluan.	say ay oalay ighvahn sitæ mitæ hahlooahn
I like it.	Pidän siitä.	pidæn seetæ

Chemist's (Pharmacy)

| I'd like something for a cold/for a cough/for travel sickness. | Haluaisin jotakin vilustumiseen/yskään/matkapahoinvointiin. | hahlooighssin yoatahkin viloosstoomissayn/ewsskææn/mahtkahpahhoynvoynteen |
| Can you recommend something for hayfever/for sunburn? | Voitteko suositella jotakin heinänuhaan/auringonpolttamaan? | voyttaykoa soooasitayllah yoatahkin haynænooharn/owringoanpoalttahmarn |

Toiletry

May I have some razor blades?	Saisinko parranajokoneenteriä?	sighsingkoa pahrrahnahyoakoanaayntayriæ
some shaving cream some toothpaste	partavaahdoketta hammastahnaa	pahrtahvarhdoakayttah hahmmahsstahhnar
I'd like some soap. some suntan oil	Haluaisin saippuaa. aurinkoöljyä	hahlooighssin sighppooar owringkoaurlyewæ

At the barber's

I'd like a haircut, please.	Haluaisin hiustenleikkuun.	hahlooighssin hioosstaynlaykkoon
Short/Leave it long.	Lyhyiksi/Jättäkää ne pitkiksi.	lewhewiksi/yættækææ nay pitkiksi
A razor cut, please.	Veitsellä, olkaa hyvä.	vaytsayllæ oalkar hewvæ

At the hairdresser's

I'd like a shampoo and set, please.	Haluaisin pesun ja kampauksen.	hahlooighssin paysoon yah kahmpahooksayn
I'd like a bleach.	Haluaisin vaalennuksen.	hahlooighssin varlaynnook sayn
a permanent a colour rinse a manicure	permanentin värihuuhtelun käsienhoidon	payrmahnayntin værihoohtayloon kæsiaynhoydoan

68

Photography

| I'd like a film for this camera. | Haluaisin filmin tähän kameraan. | hahlooighssin filmin tæhæn kahmayrarn |
| This camera doesn't work. | Tämä kamera ei toimi. | tæmæ kahmayrah ay toymi |

At the post office

| Where's the nearest post office, please? | Missä on lähin postitoimisto? | misssæ oan læhin poasstitoymisstoa |
| I'd like to send this by express (special delivery)/by air mail. | Haluaisin lähettää tämän pikakirjeenä/lentopostitse. | hahlooighssin læhayttææ tæmæn pikahkiryaynæ/layntoapoasstitsay |

Service stations

Where is the nearest service station, please?	Missä on lähin huoltoasema?	misssæ oan læhin hoooaltoaahssaymah
Fill her up, please.	Täyteen, olkaa hyvä.	tæewtayn oalkar hewvæ
Check the oil, please.	Tarkistakaa öljy.	tahrkisstahkar urlyew
Would you check the tyres?	Tarkistaisitteko renkaat?	tahrkisstighssittaykoa rayngkart

Street directions

Can you show me on the map where I am?	Voitteko näyttää minulle kartalla missä olen?	voyttaykoa næewttæ minoollay kahrtahltah misssæ oalayn
You're on the wrong road.	Olette väärällä tiellä.	oalayttay væærællæ teeayllæ
Go back to ...	Menkää takaisin ...	mayngkææ tahkighssin
Go straight ahead.	Ajakaa suoraan eteenpäin.	ahyahkar soooaraan aytaynpæin
It's on the left/on the right.	Se on vasemmalla/oikealla.	say oan vahsaymmahllah/oykayahllah

Accidents

| May I use your telephone? | Saanko käyttää puhelintanne? | sarngkoa kæewttææ poohaylintahnnay |
| Call a doctor quickly. | Kutsukaa nopeasti lääkäri. | kootsookar noapayahssti læækæri |

Call an ambulance.	**Kutsukaa am-bulanssi.**	koot sookar ahm-boolahnsssi
Please call the police.	**Olkaa hyvä ja kut-sukaa poliisi.**	oalkar hewvæ yah koot-sookar poaleessi

Numbers

one	**yksi**	ewksi
two	**kaksi**	kahksi
three	**kolme**	koalmay
four	**neljä**	naylyæ
five	**viisi**	veesi
six	**kuusi**	koosi
seven	**seitsemän**	sayt saymæn
eight	**kahdeksan**	kahh dayksahn
nine	**yhdeksän**	ewh dayksæn
ten	**kymmenen**	kewm maynayn
eleven	**yksitoista**	ewksitoysstah
twelve	**kaksitoista**	kahksitoysstah
thirteen	**kolmetoista**	koalmaytoysstah
fourteen	**neljätoista**	naylyætoysstah
fifteen	**viisitoista**	veesitoysstah
sixteen	**kuusitoista**	koositoysstah
seventeen	**seitsemäntoista**	sayt saymæntoysstah
eighteen	**kahdeksantoista**	kahh dayksahntoysstah
nineteen	**yhdeksäntoista**	ewh dayksæntoysstah
twenty	**kaksikymmentä**	kahksikewmmayntæ
twenty-one	**kaksikymmentäyksi**	kahksikewmmayntæewksi
thirty	**kolmekymmentä**	koalmaykewmmayntæ
forty	**neljäkymmentä**	naylyækewmmayntæ
fifty	**viisikymmentä**	veesikewmmayntæ
sixty	**kuusikymmentä**	koosikewmmayntæ
seventy	**seitsemänkymmentä**	sayt saymængkewmmayntæ
eighty	**kahdeksankymmentä**	kahh dayksahngkewmmayntæ
ninety	**yhdeksänkymmentä**	ewh dayksængkewmmayntæ
one hundred	**sata**	sahtah
one thousand	**tuhat**	toohat
ten thousand	**kymmenentuhatta**	kewm maynayntoohahttah

Days

It's Sunday.	**On sunnuntai.**	oan soon noontigh
Monday	**maanantai**	marnahntigh
Tuesday	**tiistai**	teesstigh
Wednesday	**keskiviikko**	kayss kiveekkoa

Thursday	**torstai**	**toars**stigh
Friday	**perjantai**	**payr**ryayntigh
Saturday	**lauantai**	**low**ahntigh
yesterday	**eilen**	**ay**layn
today	**tänään**	**tæ**næ**æ**n
tomorrow	**huomenna**	**hoo**oamaynnah
morning/afternoon	**aamupäivä/iltapäivä**	**ar**moopæivæ/**ilt**ahpæivæ
evening/night	**ilta/yö**	**ilt**ah/ewur

Months

January	**tammikuu**	**tahm**mikoo
February	**helmikuu**	**hayl**mikoo
March	**maaliskuu**	**mar**lisskoo
April	**huhtikuu**	**hooh**tikoo
May	**toukokuu**	**toaoo**koakoo
June	**kesäkuu**	**kays**ækoo
July	**heinäkuu**	**hayn**ækoo
August	**elokuu**	**ayl**oakoo
September	**syyskuu**	**sews**skoo
October	**lokakuu**	**loak**ahkoo
November	**marraskuu**	**mahr**rahsskoo
December	**joulukuu**	**yoaoo**lookoo
Merry Christmas!	**Hyvää joulua!**	**hew**væ**æ** **yoaoo**looah!
Happy New Year!	**Onnellista uutta**	**oan**naylIisstah **oott**ah
	vuotta!	**voo**attah

FRENCH

Guide to Pronunciation

Letter	Approximate pronunciation	Symbol	Example	

Consonants

b, c, d, f, k, as in English
l, m, n, p, s,
t, v, x, z

ch	like **sh** in **sh**ut	sh	**ch**ercher	she**rsh**ay
ç	like **s** in **s**it	s	**ç**a	sah
g	1) before **e**, **i**, **y**, like **s** in pleasure	zh	man**g**er	mah**ngzh**ay
	2) before **a**, **o**, **u**, like **g** in **g**o	g	**g**arçon	**g**ahrsawng
gn	like **ni** in o**ni**on	ñ	li**gn**e	lee**ñ**
h	always silent		**h**omme	om
j	like **s** in plea**s**ure	zh	**j**amais	**zh**ahmeh
qu	like **k** in **k**ill	k	**qu**i	**k**ee
r	rolled in the back of the mouth, rather like gargling	r	**r**ouge	roo**zh**
w	usually like **v** in **v**oice	v	**w**agon	**v**ahgawng

Vowels

a, à or â	between the a in hat and the a in father	ah	**mari**	mahree
é, er, et, e	like a in late	ay	**enchanté**	ahngshahngtay
è, ê, e + most consonants	like e in get	eh	**même**	mehm
e	sometimes (when at the end of a syllable or of a one-syllable word), like er in other (quite short)	er	**me**	mer
i	like ee in meet	ee	**il**	eel
o	generally like o in hot but sometimes like o in wrote	o	**donner**	donay
ô	like o in wrote	oa	**Rhône**	roan
u	no equivalent in English. Round your lips and try to say ee; this should sound more or less correct	ew	**cru**	krew

Sounds spelt with two or more letters

ai, ay	can be pronounced as a in late	ay	**j'ai**	zhay
aient, ais, ait, aî	like e in get	eh	**chaîne**	shehn
(e)au	similar to o in wrote	oa	**chaud**	shoa
ei	like e in get	eh	**peine**	pehn
eu	like ur in fur, but with lips rounded, not spread	ur	**peu**	pur
oi	like w followed by the a in hat	wah	**moi**	mwah
ou	like oo in look	oo	**nouveau**	noovoa
ui	approximately like wee in between	wee	**traduire**	trahdweer

Nasal sounds

The following sounds are pronounced through the mouth and the nose at the same time, very much like the twang found in speech in some parts of America or Britain.

an	something like arn in tarnish	ahng	**tante**	tahngt
en	generally like the previous sound	ahng	**enchanté**	ahngshahngtay
ien	sounds like yan in yank	yang	**bien**	byang
(a)in	approximately like ang in rang	ang	**instant**	angstahng
on	approximately like orn in corn	awng	**maison**	mayzawng
un	approximately like ang in rang	ang	**brun**	brang

Liaison

Normally, the final consonants are not pronounced in French. However, when a word ending in a consonant is followed by one beginning with a vowel, they are often run together, and the consonant is pronounced as if it began the following word. For instance, **nous** (*we*) is pronounced **noo**, but, in the sentence **"Nous avons un enfant"** (*We have a child*), the **s** of **nous** is pronounced, and the sentence sounds something like: **noozahvawngzangnahngfahng**. Another example: **"comment"** is pronounced **komahng**, but the **t** is pronounced in **"Comment allez-vous?"** (*How are you*), which sounds something like: **komahngtahlay voo**.

FRENCH

Some basic expressions

Yes.	**Oui.**	wee
No.	**Non.**	nawng
Please.	**S'il vous plaît.**	seel voo play
Thank you.	**Merci.**	mehrsee
Thank you very much.	**Merci beaucoup.**	mehrsee boakoo
That's all right.	**Il n'y a pas de quoi.**	eel nee ah pah der kwah

Greetings

Good morning.	**Bonjour.**	bawngzhoor
Good afternoon.	**Bonjour.**	bawngzhoor
Good evening.	**Bonsoir.**	bawngswahr
Good night.	**Bonne nuit.**	bon nwee
Good-bye.	**Au revoir.**	oa rervwahr
See you later.	**A bientôt.**	ah byangtoa
This is Mr....	**Voici Monsieur...**	vwahssee merssyur
This is Mrs....	**Voici Madame...**	vwahssee mahdahm
This is Miss...	**Voici Mademoiselle...**	vwahssee mahdmwahzehl
I'm very pleased to meet you.	**Enchanté.**	ahngshahngtay
How are you?	**Comment allez-vous?**	komahngtahlayvoo
Very well, thank you. And you?	**Très bien, merci. Et vous?**	treh byang mehrsee. ay voo
Fine.	**Bien.**	byang
Excuse me.	**Excusez-moi.**	ehkskewzaymwah

Questions

Where?	**Où?**	oo
Where is...?	**Où se trouve...?**	oo ser troov
Where are...?	**Où se trouvent...?**	oo ser troov
When?	**Quand?**	kahng

What?	**Quoi?**	kwah
How?	**Comment?**	komahng
How much?	**Combien?**	kawngbyang
How many?	**Combien?**	kawngbyang
Who?	**Qui?**	kee
Why?	**Pourquoi?**	poorkwah
Which?	**Lequel/Laquelle?**	lerkehl/lahkehl
What do you call this?	**Comment appelez-vous ceci?**	komahng ahperlayvoo serssee
What do you call that?	**Comment appelez-vous cela?**	komahng ahperlayvoo serlah
What does this mean?	**Que veut dire ceci?**	ker vur deer serssee
What does that mean?	**Que veut dire cela?**	ker vur deer serlah

Do you speak ... ?

Do you speak English?	**Parlez-vous anglais?**	pahrlayvoo ahngglay
Do you speak German?	**Parlez-vous allemand?**	pahrlayvoo ahlmahng
Do you speak French?	**Parlez-vous français?**	pahrlayvoo frahngsay
Do you speak Spanish?	**Parlez-vous espagnol?**	pahrlayvoo ehspahñol
Do you speak Italian?	**Parlez-vous italien?**	pahrlayvoo eetahlyang
Could you speak more slowly, please?	**Pourriez-vous parler plus lentement, s'il vous plaît?**	pooreeayvoo pahrlay plew lahngtermahng seelvooplay
Please point to the phrase in the book.	**Montrez-moi la phrase dans le livre, s'il vous plaît.**	mawngtraymwah lah frahz dahng ler leevr seelvooplay
Just a minute. I'll see if I can find it in this book.	**Un instant. Je vais voir si je la trouve dans ce livre.**	angnangstahng. zher vay vwahr see zher lah troov dahng ser leevr
I understand.	**Je comprends.**	zher kawngprahng
I don't understand.	**Je ne comprends pas.**	zher ner kawngprahng pah

FRENCH

Can...?

Can I have...?	**Puis-je avoir...?**	pweezh ahvwahr
Can we have...?	**Pouvons-nous avoir...?**	poovawngnoo ahvwahr
Can you show me...?	**Pouvez-vous m'indiquer...?**	poovayvoo mangdeekay
Can you tell me...?	**Pouvez-vous me dire...?**	poovayvoo mer deer
Can you help me, please?	**Pouvez-vous m'aider, s'il vous plaît?**	poovayvoo mayday seelvooplay

Wanting

I'd like...	**Je voudrais...**	zher voodray
We'd like...	**Nous voudrions...**	noo voodreeawng
Please give me...	**S'il vous plaît, donnez-moi...**	seelvooplay donaymwah
Give it to me, please.	**Donnez-le moi, s'il vous plaît.**	donaylermwah seelvooplay
Please bring me...	**S'il vous plaît, apportez-moi...**	seelvooplay ahportaymwah
Bring it to me, please.	**Apportez-le moi, s'il vous plaît.**	ahportayler mwah seelvooplay
I'm hungry.	**J'ai faim.**	zhay fang
I'm thirsty.	**J'ai soif.**	zhay swahf
I'm tired.	**Je suis fatigué.**	zher swee fahteegay
I'm lost.	**Je me suis perdu.**	zher mer swee pehrdew
It's important.	**C'est important.**	saytangportahng
It's urgent.	**C'est urgent.**	saytewrzhahng
Hurry up!	**Dépêchez-vous!**	daypayshayvoo

It is/There is...

It is/It's...	**C'est...**	say
Is it...?	**Est-ce...?**	ehss
It isn't...	**Ce n'est pas...**	ser nay pah

There is/There are ...	Il y a ...	eel ee ah
Is there/Are there ... ?	Y a-t-il ...?	ee ahteel
There isn't/There aren't ...	Il n'y a pas ...	eel nee ah pah
There isn't any/ There aren't any.	Il n'y en a pas.	eel nee ahngnah pah

A few common words

big/small	**grand/petit**	grahng/pertee
quick/slow	**rapide/lent**	rahpeed/lahng
early/late	**tôt/tard**	toa/tahr
cheap/expensive	**bon marché/cher**	bawng mahrshay/shehr...
near/far	**près/loin**	pray/lwang
hot/cold	**chaud/froid**	shoa/frwah
full/empty	**plein/vide**	plang/veed
easy/difficult	**facile/difficile**	fahsseel/deefeesseel
heavy/light	**lourd/léger**	loor/layzhay
open/shut	**ouvert/fermé**	oovair/fehrmay
right/wrong	**juste/faux**	zhewst/foa
old/new	**ancien/nouveau**	ahngsyang/noovoa
old/young	**vieux/jeune**	vyur/zhurn
beautiful/ugly	**beau/laid**	boa/lay
good/bad	**bon/mauvais**	bawng/movay
better/worse	**meilleur/pire**	mayyurr/peer

Some prepositions and a few more useful words

at	**à**	ah
on	**sur**	sewr
in	**dans**	dahng
to	**à**	ah
from	**de**	der
inside	**dedans**	derdahng
outside	**dehors**	derawr
up	**en haut**	ahng oa
down	**en bas**	ahng bah
before	**avant**	ahvahng
after	**après**	ahpray
with	**avec**	ahvehk
without	**sans**	sahng
through	**à travers**	ah trahvehr
towards	**vers**	vehr
until	**jusqu'à**	zhewskah
during	**pendant**	pahngdahng
and	**et**	ay

FRENCH

or	où	oo
not	ne ... pas	ner ... pah
nothing	rien	ryang
none	aucun	oakang
very	très	tray
also	aussi	oasee
soon	bientôt	byangtoa
perhaps	peut-être	purtehtr
here	ici	eesee
there	là	lah
now	maintenant	mangternahng
then	alors	ahlawr

Arrival

Your passport, please.	**Votre passeport, s'il vous plaît.**	votr pahsspawr seelvooplay
Here it is.	**Le voici.**	lervwahsee
Have you anything to declare?	**Avez-vous quelque chose à déclarer?**	ahvayvoo kehlkershoaz ah dayklahray
No, nothing at all.	**Non, rien du tout.**	nawng ryang dew too
Porter!	**Porteur!**	porturr
Can you help me with my luggage, please?	**Pouvez-vous prendre mes bagages, s'il vous plaît?**	poovayvoo prahngdr may bahgahzh seelvooplay
That's my suitcase.	**C'est ma valise.**	say mah vahleez
Where's the bus to the centre of town, please?	**Où est le bus qui va en ville, s'il vous plaît?**	oo ay ler bewss kee vah ahng veel seelvooplay
This way, please.	**Par ici, s'il vous plaît.**	pahr eessee seelvooplay

Changing money

Can you change a traveller's cheque, please?	**Pouvez-vous changer un chèque de voyage, s'il vous plaît?**	poovayvoo shanhngzhay ang shekh der vwahyahzh seelvooplay
Where's the nearest bank, please?	**Où est la banque la plus proche, s'il vous plaît?**	oo ay lah bahngk lah plew prosh seelvooplay

Car rental

I'd like a car.	**Je voudrais une voiture.**	zher voodray ewn vwahtewr
For how long?	**Pour combien de temps?**	poor kawngbyang der tahng
A day/Four days/ A week/Two weeks.	**Un jour/Quatre jours/ Une semaine/Deux semaines.**	ang zhoor/kahtr zhoor/ewn sermehn/dur sermehn

Taxi

Where can I get a taxi?	**Où puis-je avoir un taxi?**	oo pweezh ahvwahr ang tahksee
What's the fare to ...?	**Quel est le tarif pour ...?**	kehl ay ler tahreef poor
Take me to this address, please.	**Conduisez-moi à cette adresse, s'il vous plaît.**	kawngdweezaymwah ah seht ahdrehss seel-vooplay
I'm in a hurry.	**Je suis pressé.**	zher swee prehssay
Could you drive more slowly, please?	**Pourriez-vous conduire plus lentement, s'il vous plaît?**	pooreeayvoo kawngdweer plew lahngtermahng seel-vooplay

Hotel and other accommodation

My name is ...	**Je m'appelle ...**	zher mahpehl
Have you a reservation?	**Avez-vous fait réserver?**	ahvayvoo fay rayzehrvay
Yes, here's the confirmation.	**Oui, voici la confirmation.**	wee, vwahsee lah kawngfeermahsyawng
I'd like ...	**J'aimerais ...**	zhehmerray
I'd like a single room/a double room.	**J'aimerais une chambre pour une personne/pour deux personnes.**	zhehmerray ewn shahngbr poor ewn pehrson/poor dur pehrson
a room with a bath/with a shower	**une chambre avec bain/avec douche**	ewn shahngbr ahvehk bang/ahvehk doosh

How much?

What's the price per night/per week/per month?	**Quel est le prix pour une nuit/pour une semaine/pour un mois?**	kehl ay ler pree poor ewn nwee/poor ewn sermehn/poor ang mwah
May I see the room?	**Puis-je voir la chambre?**	pweezh vwahr lah shahngbr
I'm sorry, I don't like it.	**Je regrette, elle ne me plaît pas.**	zher rergreht ehl ner mer play pah
Yes, that's fine. I'll take it.	**Oui, c'est bien. Je la prends.**	wee say byang. zher lah prahng
What's my room number, please?	**Quel est le numéro de ma chambre, s'il vous plaît?**	kehl ay ler newmayroa der mah shahngbr seel-vooplay
Number 123.	**Numéro 123.**	newmayroa 123.

Service, please

Who is it?	**Qui est-ce?**	kee ehss
Just a minute.	**Un instant, s'il vous plaît.**	angnangstahng seel-vooplay
Come in! The door's open.	**Entrez! La porte est ouverte.**	ahngtray! lah port aytoovairt
May we have breakfast in our room?	**Pouvons-nous prendre le petit déjeuner dans notre chambre?**	poovawngnoo prahngdr le pertee dayzhurnay dahng notr shahngbr

Breakfast

I'll have . . .	**Je voudrais . . .**	zher voodray
I'll have some fruit juice.	**Je voudrais un jus de fruit.**	zher voodray ang zhew der frwee
a boiled egg	**un œuf à la coque**	angnurf ah lah kok
a fried egg	**un œuf sur le plat**	angnurf sewr ler plah
some bacon/some ham	**du bacon/du jambon**	dew baykern/dew zhahngbawng
some toast	**des toasts**	day toast
a pot of tea	**du thé**	dew tay
a cup of tea	**une tasse de thé**	ewn tahss der tay
some coffee	**du café**	dew kahfay
some chocolate	**du chocolat**	dew shokolah
more butter	**davantage de beurre**	dahvahngtahzh der burr
some hot water	**de l'eau chaude**	der loa shoad

Difficulties

The central heating doesn't work.	**Le chauffage central ne marche pas.**	ler shoafahzh sahngtrahl ner mahrsh pah
the light/the socket the tap/the toilet	**la lumière/la prise le robinet/les toilettes**	lah lewmyair/lah preez ler robeenay/lay twahleht
There's no hot water.	**Il n'y a pas d'eau chaude.**	eel nee ah pah doa shoad
May I see the manager, please?	**Puis-je voir le directeur, s'il vous plaît?**	pweezh vwahr ler deerehkturr seelvooplay

Telephone—Mail

There's a call for you.	**Il y an un appel pour vous.**	eel ee ah angnahpehl poor voo
Hold the line, please.	**Ne quittez pas, s'il vous plaît.**	ner keetay pah seelvooplay
Operator, I've been cut off.	**Mademoiselle, la communication a été coupée.**	mahdmwahzehl lah komewneekahsyawng ah aytay koopay
Did anyone telephone me?	**Est-ce qu'on m'a appelé?**	ehss kawng mah ahperlay
Is there any mail for me?	**Y a-t-il du courrier pour moi?**	ee ahteel dew kooreeay poor mwah
Are there any messages for me?	**Y a-t-il un message pour moi?**	ee ahteel ang mehssahzh poor mwah

Checking out

May I have my bill, please?	**Puis-je avoir ma note, s'il vous plaît?**	pweezh ahvwahr mah not seelvooplay
We're in a great hurry.	**Nous sommes très pressés.**	noh som tray prehssay
It's been a very enjoyable stay.	**Le séjour a été très agréable.**	ler sayzhoor ah aytay trayzahgrayahbl

Eating out

Good evening, sir/ Good evening, madam.	**Bonsoir, Monsieur/ Bonsoir, Madame.**	bawngswahr mersyur/ bawngswahr mahdahm

FRENCH

FRENCH

Good evening, I'd like a table for two, please.	**Bonsoir. Je voudrais une table pour deux personnes, s'il vous plaît.**	bawngswahr. zher voodray ewn tahbl poor dur pehrson seelvooplay
Do you have a fixed-price menu?	**Avez-vous un menu?**	ahvayvoo ang mernew
May I see the à la carte menu?	**Puis-je voir la carte?**	pweezh vwahr lah kahrt
May we have an ashtray, please?	**Pouvons-nous avoir un cendrier, s'il vous plaît?**	poovawngnoo ahvwahr ang sahngdreeay seelvooplay
some bread	**du pain**	dew pang
a fork	**une fourchette**	ewn foorsheht
a knife	**un couteau**	ang kootoa
a spoon	**une cuillère**	ewn kweeyair
a plate	**une assiette**	ewn ahssyeht
a glass	**un verre**	ang vair
a napkin	**une serviette**	ewn sehrvyeht
another chair	**une autre chaise**	ewn oatr shaiz
Where's the gentlemen's toilet (men's room)?	**Où sont les toilettes pour messieurs?**	oo sawng lay twahleht poor maysyur
Where's the ladies' toilet (ladies' room)?	**Où sont les toilettes pour dames?**	oo sawng lay twahleht poor dahm

Appetizers

I'd like some . . .	**Je voudrais . . .**	zher voodray
I'd like some assorted appetizers.	**Je voudrais des hors-d'œuvre variés.**	zher voodray day ordurvr vahreeay
orange juice	**un jus d'orange**	ang zhew dorahngzh
ham	**du jambon**	dew zhahngbawng
melon	**du melon**	der merlawng
pâté	**du pâté**	dew pahtay
smoked salmon	**du saumon fumé**	dew soamawng fewmay
shrimps (shrimp)	**des crevettes**	day krerveht

Soup

Have you any . . . ?	**Avez-vous . . . ?**	ahvayvoo
Have you any chicken soup?	**Avez-vous du potage au poulet?**	ahvayvoo dew potahzh oa poolay
vegetable soup	**une soupe de légumes**	ewn soop der laygewm
onion soup	**de la soupe à l'oignon**	der lah soop ah loñawng

Fish

I'd like some . . .	**J'aimerais . . .**	zhehmerray
I'd like some fish.	**J'aimerais du poisson.**	zhehmerray dew pwahssawng
sole	**de la sole**	der lah sol
trout	**de la truite**	der lah trweet
lobster	**du homard**	dew omahr
crayfish	**des écrevisses**	day aykrerveess
prawns	**des langoustines**	day lahnggoosteen
I'd like it . . .	**Je l'aimerais . . .**	zher lehmerray
I'd like it steamed.	**Je l'aimerais cuit à la vapeur.**	zher lehmerray kwee ah lah vahpurr
grilled	**grillé**	greeyay
boiled	**au court-bouillon**	oa koor booyawng
baked	**cuit au four**	kwee oa foor
fried	**frit**	free

Meat—Poultry—Game

I'd like some . . .	**Je voudrais . . .**	zher voodray
I'd like some beef.	**Je voudrais du bœuf.**	zher voodray dew burf
a beef steak	**un bifteck**	ang beeftehk
some roast beef	**du rosbif**	dew roazbeef
a veal cutlet	**une côtelette de veau**	ewn koatleht de voa
mutton	**du mouton**	dew mootawng
lamb	**de l'agneau**	der lahñoa
a pork chop	**une côtelette de porc**	ewn koatleht der pawr
roast pork	**du rôti de porc**	dew roatee der pawr
hare	**du lièvre**	dew lyehvr
chicken	**du poulet**	dew poolay
roast chicken	**du poulet rôti**	dew poolay roatee
duck	**du canard**	dew kahnahr
How do you like your meat?	**Comment désirez-vous la viande?**	komahng dayzeerayvoo lah vyahngd
rare	**saignante**	sehñahngt
medium	**à point**	ah pwang
well done	**bien cuite**	byang kweet

Vegetables

What vegetables have you got?	Quels légumes servez-vous?	kehl laygewm sehrvayvoo
I'd like some ...	Je voudrais ...	zher voodray
I'd like some asparagus.	Je voudrais des asperges.	zher voodray dayzahspehrzh
green beans	des haricots verts	day ahreekoa vair
mushrooms	des champignons	day shahngpeeñawng
carrots	des carottes	day kahrot
onions	des oignons	dayzoñawng
red cabbage	du chou rouge	dew shoo roozh
spinach	des épinards	dayzaypeenahr
rice	du riz	dew ree
peas	des petits pois	day pertee pwah
tomatoes	des tomates	day tomaht
green salad	de la salade verte	der lah sahlahd vairt
potatoes	des pommes de terre	day pom der tair

Desserts

Nothing more, thanks.	Je ne veux plus rien, merci.	zher ner vur plew ryang mehrsee
Just a small portion, please.	Juste une petite portion, s'il vous plaît.	zhewst ewn perteet porsyawng seelvooplay
Have you any icecream?	Avez-vous des glaces?	ahvayvoo day glahss
fruit salad	une salade de fruits	ewn sahlahd der frwee
fresh fruit	des fruits frais	day frwee fray
cheese	du fromage	dew fromahzh

Drink

What would you like to drink?	Qu'aimeriez-vous boire?	kehmerreeayvoo bwahr
I'll have a beer, please.	J'aimerais une bière, s'il vous plaît.	zhehmerray ewn byair seelvooplay
I'll have a whisky, please.	Je voudrais un whisky, s'il vous plaît.	zher voodray ang weeskee seelvooplay

Wine

I'd like a bottle of wine.	**Je voudrais une bouteille de vin.**	zher voodray ewn bootay der vang
red wine	**vin rouge**	vang roozh
rosé wine	**vin rosé**	vang roazay
white wine	**vin blanc**	vang blahng
Cheers!	**A votre santé!**	ah votr sahngtay

The bill (check)

May I have the bill (check) please?	**Puis-je avoir l'addition, s'il vous plaît?**	pweezh ahvwahr lahdee-ssyawng seelvooplay
Is service included?	**Le service est-il compris?**	ler sehrveess ayteel kawngpree
Everything's included.	**Tout est compris.**	tootay kawngpree
Thank you, that was a very good meal.	**Merci, c'était très bon.**	mehrsee saytay tray bawng

Travelling

Where's the railway station, please?	**Où se trouve la gare, s'il vous plaît?**	oo ser troov lah gahr seelvooplay
Where's the ticket office, please?	**Où est le guichet, s'il vous plaît?**	oo ay ler geeshay seelvooplay
I'd like a ticket to...	**J'aimerais un billet pour...**	zhehmerray ang beeyay poor
First or second class?	**Première ou deuxième classe?**	prermyair oo durzyehm klahss
First class, please.	**Première classe, s'il vous plaît.**	prermyair klahss seelvooplay
Single or return (one way or round-trip)?	**Aller simple ou aller et retour?**	ahlay sangpl oo ahlay ay rertoor
Do I have to change trains?	**Est-ce que je dois changer de train?**	ehss ker zher dwah shahngzhay der trang
What platform does the train leave from?	**De quel quai le train part-il?**	der kehl kay ler trang pahrteel
Where's the nearest underground (subway) station?	**Où est la station de métro la plus proche?**	oo ay lah stahsyawng der maytroa la plew prosh
Where's the bus station, please?	**Où est la gare routière, s'il vous plaît?**	oo ay lah gahr rootyair seelvooplay

FRENCH

When's the first bus to ...?	A quelle heure est le premier autobus pour ...?	ah kehl urr ay ler prer-myayroatoabewss poor
the last bus	le dernier autobus	ler dehrnyayroatoabewss
the next bus	le prochain autobus	ler proshehnoatoabewss
Please let me off at the next stop.	S'il vous plaît, déposez-moi au prochain arrêt.	seelvooplay daypoazay-mwah oa proshehnahray

Relaxing

What's on at the cinema (movies)?	Que donne-t-on au cinéma?	ker dontawng oa see-naymah
What's on at the theatre?	Que joue-t-on au théâtre?	ker zhootawng oa tayahtr
What time does the film begin?	A quelle heure commence le film?	ah kehl urr komahngss ler feelm
And the play?	Et la pièce?	ay lah pyehss
Are there any tickets for tonight?	Reste-t-il encore des places pour ce soir?	rehstteel ahngkawr day plahss poor ser swahr
Where can we go dancing?	Où pouvons-nous aller danser?	oo poovawngnoo ahlay dahngsay
Would you like to dance?	Voulez-vous danser?	voolayvoo dahngsay

Introductions

How do you do?	Bonjour.	bawngzhoor
How are you?	Comment allez-vous?	komahngtahlayvoo
Very well, thank you. And you?	Très bien, merci. Et vous?	tray byang mehrsee. ay voo
May I introduce Miss Philips?	Puis-je vous présenter Mademoiselle Philips?	pweezh voo prayzahngtay mahdmwahzehl feeleeps
My name is ...	Je m'appelle ...	zher mahpehl
I'm very pleased to meet you.	Je suis ravi de vous connaître.	zher swee rahvee der voo konaitr

| How long have you been here? | Depuis combien de temps êtes-vous ici? | derpwee kawngbyang der tahng ehtvoo eesee |
| It was nice meeting you. | Enchanté d'avoir fait votre connaissance. | ahngshahngtay dahvwahr fay votr konaysahngss |

Dating

Would you like a cigarette?	Voulez-vous une cigarette?	voolayvoo ewn seegahreht
May I get you a drink?	Puis-je vous offrir un verre?	pweezh vooz offreer ang vair
Do you have a light, please?	Avez-vous du feu, s'il vous plaît?	ahvayvoo dew fur seelvooplay
Are you waiting for someone?	Attendez-vous quelqu'un?	ahtahngdayvoo kehlkang
Are you free this evening?	Etes-vous libre ce soir?	ehtvoo leebr ser swahr
Where shall we meet?	Où nous retrouverons-nous?	oo noo rertroover-rawngnoo
What time shall I meet you?	A quelle heure vous verrai-je?	ah kehl urr voo vairayzh
May I take you home?	Puis-je vous ramener chez vous?	pweezh voo rahmnay shay voo
Thank you, it's been a wonderful evening.	Merci pour cette merveilleuse soirée.	mehrsee poor seht mehrvayyurz swahray
What's your telephone number?	Quel est votre numéro de téléphone?	kehl ay votr newmayroa der taylayfon
Do you live alone?	Habitez-vous seule?	ahbeetayvoo surl
What time is your last train?	A quelle heure est votre dernier train?	ah kehl urr ay votr dairnyay trang
Good-night...	Bonne nuit...	bon nwee

FRENCH

Banks

| Where's the nearest bank, please? | Où se trouve la banque la plus proche, s'il vous plaît? | oo ser troov lah bahngk lah plew prosh seelvooplay |
| Where can I cash some traveller's cheques? | Où puis-je toucher des chèques de voyage? | oo pweezh tooshay day shehk der vwahyahzh |

FRENCH

What time does the bank open?	A quelle heure la banque ouvre-t-elle?	ah kehl urr lah bahngk oovrertehl
What time does it close?	A quelle heure ferme-t-elle?	ah kehl urr fairmtehl
I'm expecting some money from home. Has it arrived?	J'attends de l'argent de la maison. Est-il arrivé?	zhahtahng der lahrzhahng der lah mayzawng ayteel ahreevay
Can you give me some small change, please?	Pouvez-vous me donner de la monnaie, s'il vous plaît?	poovayvoo mer donay der lah monay seelvooplay

Shops, stores and services

Where is the nearest chemist's's (pharmacy)?	Où est la pharmacie la plus proche?	oo ay lah fahrmahssee lah plew prosh
the nearest hairdresser's	le coiffeur le plus proche	le kwahfurr ler plew prosh
the photo shop	le magasin de photographie	le mahgahzang der foatoagrahfee
the jeweller's	la bijouterie	lah beezhooterree
the department store	le grand magasin	ler grahng mahgahzang
the police station	le poste de police	ler post der poleess
the garage	le garage	ler gahrahzh
How do I get there?	Comment puis-je m'y rendre?	komahng pweezh mee rahngdr
Is it within walking distance?	Est-il possible d'y aller à pied?	ayteel posseebl dee ahlay ah pyay

Service

Can you help me, please?	Pouvez-vous m'aider, s'il vous plaît?	poovayvoo mayday seelvooplay
Can you show me this? And that, too.	Pouvez-vous me montrer ceci? Et cela aussi.	poovayvoo mer mawngtray serssee? ay serlah oasee
It's too expensive/too big/too small.	C'est trop cher/trop grand/trop petit.	say troa shair/troa grahng/troa pertee
Can you show me some more?	Pouvez-vous me montrer un plus grand choix?	poovayvoo mer mawngtray ang plew grahng shwah
something better	quelque chose de mieux	kehlker shoaz der myur
something cheaper	quelque chose de meilleur marché	kehlker shoaz der mayyurr mahrshay

How much is this? And that?	Combien coûte ceci? Et cela?	kawngbyang koot sersee ay serlah
It's not quite what I want.	Ce n'est pas exactement ce que je désire.	ser nay pah ehgzahktermahng ser ker zher dayzeer
I like it.	Cela me plaît.	serlah mer play

Chemist's (Pharmacy)

| I'd like something for a cold/for a cough/for travel sickness. | J'aimerais quelque chose contre le rhume/contre la toux/contre le mal de coeur. | zhehmerray kehlkershoaz kawngtr ler rewm/kawngtr lah too/kawngtr ler mahl der kurr |
| Can you recommend something for hayfever/for sunburn? | Pouvez-vous m'indiquer quelque chose contre le rhume des foins/contre un coup de soleil? | poovayvoo mangdeekay kehlker shoaz kawngtr ler rewm day fwang/kawngtr ang koo der solay |

Toiletry

May I have some razor blades?	Puis-je avoir des lames de rasoir?	pweezh ahvwahr day lahm de rahzwahr
some shaving cream some toothpaste	de la crème à raser du dentifrice	der lah krehm ah rahzay dew dahngteefreess
I'd like some soap.	Je voudrais du savon.	zher voodray dew sahvawng
some suntan oil	de l'huile solaire	der lweel solair

At the barber's

I'd like a haircut, please.	Je voudrais me faire couper les cheveux, s'il vous plaît.	zher voodray mer fair koopay lay shervur seelvooplay
Short/Leave it long.	Courts/Laissez-les longs.	koor/layssaylay lawng
A razor cut, please.	Une coupe au rasoir, s'il vous plaît.	ewn koop oa rahzwahr seelvooplay

At the hairdresser's

| I'd like a shampoo and set, please. | J'aimerais un shampooing-mise en plis, s'il vous plaît. | zhehmerray ang shahngpwangmeezahng plee seelvooplay |

FRENCH

FRENCH

I'd like a bleach.	**Je voudrais une dé-coloration.**	zher voodray ewn dayko-lorahsyawng
a permanent	**une permanente**	ewn pehrmahnahngt
a colour rinse	**un rinçage**	ang rangsahzh
a manicure	**une manucure**	ewn mahnewkewr

Photography

| I'd like a film for this camera. | **J'aimerais un film pour cet appareil.** | zhehmerray ang feelm poor seht ahpahray |
| This camera doesn't work. | **Cet appareil ne marche pas.** | seht ahpahray ner mahrsh pah |

At the post office

| Where's the nearest post office, please? | **Où est le bureau de poste le plus proche, s'il vous plaît?** | oo ay ler bewroa der post ler plew prosh seelvoo-play |
| I'd like to send this by express (special delivery)/by air mail. | **J'aimerais envoyer ceci par express/par avion.** | zhehmerray ahngvwahyay serssee pahr ehksprehss/pahr ahvyawng |

Service stations

Where is the nearest service station, please?	**Où est la station-service la plus proche, s'il vous plaît?**	oo ay lah stahs-syawngsehrveess lah plew prosh seelvooplay
Fill her up, please.	**Le plein, s'il vous plaît.**	ler plang seelvooplay
Check the oil, please.	**Contrôlez l'huile, s'il vous plaît.**	kawngtroalay lweel seel-vooplay
Would you check the tyres?	**Voudriez-vous véri-fier les pneus?**	voodreeayvoo vayreefeeay lay pnur

Street directions

Can you show me on the map where I am?	**Pouvez-vous me montrer sur le carte où je me trouve?**	poovayvoo mer mawngtray sewr lah kahrt oo zher mer troov
You're on the wrong road.	**Vous n'êtes pas sur la bonne route.**	voo neht pah sewr lah bon root
Go back to...	**Retournez à...**	rertoornay ah

Go straight ahead.	**Continuez tout droit.**	kawngteeneway too drwah
It's on the left/on the right.	**C'est à gauche/à droite.**	saytah goash/ah drwaht

Accidents

May I use your telephone?	**Puis-je utiliser votre téléphone?**	pweezh ewteeleezay votr taylayfon
Call a doctor quickly.	**Appelez vite un docteur.**	ahperlay veet ang dokturr
Call an ambulance.	**Appelez une ambulance.**	ahperlay ewn ahngbewlahngss
Please call the police.	**Appelez la police, s'il vous plaît.**	ahperlay lah poleess seel-vooplay

Numbers

one	**un**	ang
two	**deux**	dur
three	**trois**	trwah
four	**quatre**	kahtr
five	**cinq**	sangk
six	**six**	seess
seven	**sept**	seht
eight	**huit**	weet
nine	**neuf**	nurf
ten	**dix**	deess
eleven	**onze**	awngz
twelve	**douze**	dooz
thirteen	**treize**	traiz
fourteen	**quatorze**	kahtorz
fifteen	**quinze**	kangz
sixteen	**seize**	saiz
seventeen	**dix-sept**	deess-seht
eighteen	**dix-huit**	deez-weet
nineteen	**dix-neuf**	deez-nurf
twenty	**vingt**	vangt
twenty-one	**vingt et un**	vang-tay-ang
thirty	**trente**	trahngt
forty	**quarante**	kahrahngt
fifty	**cinquante**	sangkahngt
sixty	**soixante**	swahsahngt
seventy	**soixante-dix**	swahsahngtdeess
eighty	**quatre vingts**	kahtrervang
ninety	**quatre-vingt-dix**	kahtrervangdeess
one hundred	**cent**	sahng
one thousand	**mille**	meel
ten thousand	**dix mille**	dee meel

FRENCH

FRENCH

Days

It's Sunday.	**C'est dimanche.**	say deemahngsh
Monday	**lundi**	langdee
Tuesday	**mardi**	mahrdee
Wednesday	**mercredi**	mehrkrerdee
Thursday	**jeudi**	zhurdee
Friday	**vendredi**	vahngdrerdee
Saturday	**samedi**	sahmdee
yesterday	**hier**	eeair
today	**aujourd'hui**	oazhoordwee
tomorrow	**demain**	dermang
morning/afternoon	**matin/après-midi**	mahtang/ahpraymeedee
evening/night	**soir/nuit**	swahr/nwee

Months

January	**janvier**	zhahngveeay
February	**février**	fayvreeay
March	**mars**	mahrss
April	**avril**	ahvreel
May	**mai**	may
June	**juin**	zhwang
July	**juillet**	zhweeyay
August	**août**	oot
September	**septembre**	sehptahngbr
October	**octobre**	oktobr
November	**novembre**	novahngbr
December	**décembre**	daysahngbr
Merry Christmas!	**Joyeux Noël! Bonne**	zhwahyur noaehl! bon
Happy New Year!	**Année!**	ahnay

GERMAN

Guide to Pronunciation

Letter	Approximate pronunciation	Symbol	Example	
Consonants				
f, h, k, l, m n, p, t, x	normally pronounced as in English			
b	1) at the end of a word, or between a vowel and a consonant, like **p** in up	p	**ab**	ahp
	2) elsewhere as in English	b	**bis**	biss
c	1) before **e, i, ö,** and **ä,** like **ts** in hi**ts**	ts	**Celsius**	**tsehl**zeeuss
	2) elsewhere like **c** in cat	k	**Café**	kahfay
ch	like **ch** in Scottish lo**ch**	kh	**ich**	ikh
d	1) at the end of a word, or between a vowel and a consonant, like **t** in eat	t	**Rad**	rart
	2) elsewhere, like **d** in do	d	**durstig**	**dur**stikh
g	1) always hard as in go, but, at the end of a word, often more like **ck** in tack	g k	**gehen** **weg**	**gay**ern vehk
	2) when preceded by **i** at the end of a word, like Scottish lo**ch**	kh	**billig**	**bil**ikh
j	like **y** in yes	y	**ja**	yar
qu	like **k** followed by **v** in vat	kv	**Quark**	kvahrk
r	generally rolled in the back of the mouth	r	**warum**	vah**rum**

GERMAN

s	1) before or between vowels like **z** in **z**oo	z	**sie**	zee
	2) before **p** and **t**, at the beginning of a syllable like **sh** in **sh**ut	sh	**spät**	shpait
	3) elsewhere, like **s** in **s**it	s/ss	**es ist**	ehss ist
ß	always like **s** in **s**it	ss	**heiß**	highss
sch	like **sh** in **sh**ut	sh	**schnell**	shnehl
tsch	like **ch** in **ch**ip	ch	**deutsch**	doych
tz	like **ts** in hi**ts**	ts	**Platz**	plahts
v	like **f** in **f**or	f	**vier**	feer
w	like **v** in **v**ice	v	**wie**	vee
z	like **ts** in hi**ts**	ts	**zeigen**	tsighgern

Vowels

N.B. In German, vowels are generally long when followed by **h** or by one consonant and short when followed by two or more consonants.

a	1) short, like **u** in c**u**t	ah	**hat**	haht
	2) long, like **a** in c**a**r	ar	**Abend**	arbernt
ä	1) short, like **e** in l**e**t	eh	**nächst**	nehkhst
	2) long, like **ai** in h**ai**r	ai	**spät**	sphait
e	1) short, like **e** in l**e**t	eh	**sprechen**	shprehkhern
	2) long, like **a** in l**a**te	ay	**gehen**	gayern
	3) in unstressed syllables, it is generally pronounced like **a** in about	er	**bitte**	biter
			geben	gaybern
i	1) short, like **i** in h**i**t	i	**bis**	biss
	2) long, like **ee** in m**ee**t	ee	**ihm**	eem
ie	like **ee** in b**ee**	ee	**hier**	heer
o	1) short, like **o** in g**o**t	o	**voll**	fol
	2) long, like **o** in n**o**te	oa	**ohne**	oaner
ö	like **ur** in f**ur** (long or short)	ur	**können**	kurnern
u	1) short, like **oo** in f**oo**t	u	**Nuß**	nuss
	2) long, like **oo** in m**oo**n	oo	**gut**	goot
ü	like French **u** in une; no English equivalent. Round your lips and try to say **ea** as in m**ea**n (long or short)	ew	**über**	ewberr
y	like German **ü**	ew	**Symphonie**	zewmfoanee

Diphthongs

ai, ay, ei, ey	like **igh** in h**igh**	igh	**mein**	mighn
au	like **ow** in n**ow**	ow	**auf**	owf
äu, eu	like **oy** in b**oy**	oy	**neu**	noy

Some basic expressions

Yes.	**Ja.**	yar
No.	**Nein.**	nighn
Please.	**Bitte.**	biter
Thank you.	**Danke.**	**dahng**ker
Thank you very much.	**Vielen Dank.**	**fee**lern dahngk
That's all right.	**Gern geschehen.**	gairn ger**shay**ern

Greetings

Good morning.	**Guten Morgen.**	**goo**tern **mor**gern
Good afternoon.	**Guten Tag.**	**goo**tern targ
Good evening.	**Guten Abend.**	**goo**tern **ar**bernt
Good night.	**Gute Nacht.**	**goo**ter nahkht
Good-bye.	**Auf Wiedersehen.**	owf **vee**derrzayern
See you later.	**Auf bald.**	owf bahlt
This is Mr. . . .	**Das ist Herr . . .**	dahss ist hair
This is Mrs. . . .	**Das ist Frau . . .**	dahss ist frow
This is Miss . . .	**Das ist Fräulein . . .**	dahss ist **froy**lighn
I'm very pleased to meet you.	**Sehr erfreut.**	zair ehr**froyt**
How are you?	**Wie geht es Ihnen?**	vee gayt ehss **ee**nern
Very well, thank you. And you?	**Sehr gut, danke.** **Und Ihnen?**	zair goot **dahng**ker. unt **ee**nern
Fine.	**Gut.**	goot
Excuse me.	**Verzeihung.**	fehr**tsigh**ung

Questions

Where?	**Wo?**	voa
Where is . . . ?	**Wo ist . . . ?**	voa ist
Where are . . . ?	**Wo sind . . . ?**	voa zint
When?	**Wann?**	vahn
What?	**Was?**	vahss
How?	**Wie?**	vee
How much?	**Wieviel?**	vee**feel**
How many?	**Wie viele?**	vee**fee**ler

Who?	**Wer?**	vair
Why?	**Warum?**	vah**rum**
Which?	**Welcher/Welche/Welches?**	**vehl**kherr/**vehl**kher/**vehl**kherss
What do you call this?	**Wie heißt dies?**	vee highst deess
What do you call that?	**Wie heißt das?**	vee highst dahss
What does this mean?	**Was bedeutet dies?**	vahss ber**doy**tert deess
What does that mean?	**Was bedeutet das?**	vahss ber**doy**tert dahss

Do you speak...?

Do you speak English?	**Sprechen Sie Englisch?**	**shpreh**khern zee **ehn**glish
Do you speak German?	**Sprechen Sie Deutsch?**	**shpreh**khern zee doych
Do you speak French?	**Sprechen Sie Französisch?**	**shpreh**khern zee frahnt**sur**zish
Do you speak Spanish?	**Sprechen Sie Spanisch?**	**shpreh**khern zee **shpar**nish
Do you speak Italian?	**Sprechen Sie Italienisch?**	**shpreh**khern zee itahl**yay**nish
Could you speak more slowly, please?	**Könnten Sie bitte langsamer sprechen?**	**kurn**tern zee **bi**ter **lahng**zamerr **shpreh**khern
Please point to the phrase in the book.	**Bitte zeigen Sie mir den Satz im Buch.**	**bi**ter **tsigh**gern zee meer dayn zahts im bookh
Just a minute. I'll see if I can find it in this book.	**Einen Augenblick, ich sehe mal nach, ob ich es in diesem Buch finde.**	**igh**nern **ow**gernblik ikh **zay**er mahl nahkh op ikh ehss in **dee**zerm bookh **fin**der
I understand.	**Ich verstehe.**	ikh fehr**shtay**er
I don't understand.	**Ich verstehe nicht.**	ikh fehr**shtay**er nikht

Can...?

| Can I have...? | **Kann ich...haben?** | kahn ikh... **har**bern |
| Can we have...? | **Können wir...haben?** | **kur**nern veer... **har**bern |

GERMAN

Can you show me...?	Können Sie mir...zeigen?	kurnern zee meer...tsighgern
Can you tell me...?	Können Sie mir sagen...?	kurnern zee meer zargern
Can you help me, please?	Können Sie mir bitte helfen?	kurnern zee meer biter hehlfern

Wanting

I'd like...	Ich hätte gern...	ikh hehter gairn
We'd like...	Wir hätten gern...	veer hehtern gairn
Please give me...	Geben Sie mir bitte...	gaybern zee meer biter
Give it to me, please.	Bitte geben Sie es mir.	biter gaybern zee ehss meer
Please bring me...	Bringen Sie mir bitte...	bringern zee meer biter
Bring it to me, please.	Bitte bringen Sie es mir.	biter bringern zee ehss meer
I'm hungry.	Ich habe Hunger.	ikh harber hunger
I'm thirsty.	Ich habe Durst.	ikh harber durst
I'm tired.	Ich bin müde.	ikh bin mewder
I'm lost.	Ich habe mich verirrt.	ikh harber mikh fehrirt
It's important.	Es ist wichtig.	ehss ist vikhtikh
It's urgent.	Es ist dringend.	ehss ist dringernt
Hurry up!	Beeilen Sie sich!	berighlern zee zikh

It is/There is...

It is/It's...	Es ist...	ehss ist
Is it...?	Ist es...?	ist ehss
It isn't...	Es ist nicht...	ehss ist nikht
There is/There are...	Es gibt...	ehss gibt
Is there/Are there...?	Gibt es...?	gibt ehss
There isn't/There aren't...	Es gibt keinen/Es gibt keine/Es gibt kein...	ehss gibt kighnern/ehss gibt kighner/ehss gibt kighn

GERMAN

There isn't any/	**Es gibt keinen/Es**	ehss gibt **kigh**nern/ehss
There aren't any.	**gibt keine/Es gibt**	gibt **kigh**ner/ehss gibt
	keins.	kighnss

A few common words

big/small	**groß/klein**	groass/**klighn**
quick/slow	**schnell/langsam**	shnehl/**lahng**zarm
early/late	**früh/spät**	frew/shpait
cheap/expensive	**billig/teuer**	**bi**likh/**toy**err
near/far	**nah/weit**	nar/vight
hot/cold	**heiß/kalt**	highss/kahlt
full/empty	**voll/leer**	fol/layr
easy/difficult	**leicht/schwierig**	lighkht/**shvee**rikh
heavy/light	**schwer/leicht**	shvair/lighkht
open/shut	**offen/geschlossen**	**o**fern/ger**shlo**ssern
right/wrong	**richtig/falsch**	**rikh**tikh/fahlsh
old/new	**alt/neu**	ahlt/noy
old/young	**alt/jung**	ahlt/yung
beautiful/ugly	**schön/häßlich**	shurn/**hehss**likh
good/bad	**gut/schlecht**	goot/shlehkht
better/worse	**besser/schlechter**	**behss**err/**shleh**terr

Some prepositions and a few more useful words

at	**an**	ahn
on	**auf**	owf
in	**in**	in
to	**zu**	tsoo
from	**von**	fon
inside	**drinnen**	**dri**nern
outside	**draußen**	**drow**ssern
up	**hinauf**	hin**owf**
down	**hinunter**	hin**un**ter
before	**vor**	fawr
after	**nach**	nahkh
with	**mit**	mit
without	**ohne**	**oa**ner
through	**durch**	doorkh
towards	**gegen**	**gay**gern
until	**bis**	biss
during	**während**	**vai**rernt
and	**und**	unt
or	**oder**	**oa**derr
not	**nicht**	nikht
nothing	**nichts**	nikhts
none	**kein**	kighn

GERMAN

very	**sehr**	zair
also	**auch**	owkh
soon	**bald**	bahlt
perhaps	**vielleicht**	fee**lighkht**
here	**hier**	heer
there	**dort**	dort
now	**jetzt**	yehtst
then	**dann**	dahn

Arrival

Your passport, please.	**Ihren Paß, bitte.**	**ee**rern pahss **bit**er
Here it is.	**Hier, bitte.**	heer **bit**er
Have you anything to declare?	**Haben Sie etwas zu vorzollen?**	**har**bern zee **eht**vahss tsoo **fehr**tsolern
No, nothing at all.	**Nein, gar nichts.**	nighn garr nikhts
Porter!	**Gepäckträger!**	ger**pehk**traigerr
Can you help me with my luggage, please?	**Können Sie mir mit meinem Gepäck helfen, bitte?**	**kur**nern zee meer mit **migh**nerm ger**pehk hehl**fern **bit**er
That's my suitcase.	**Das ist mein Koffer.**	dahss ist mighn **kof**err
Where's the bus to the centre of town, please?	**Wo ist der Bus zum Stadtzentrum, bitte?**	voa ist dehr buss tsum **shtaht**tsehntrum **bit**er
This way, please.	**Hier durch, bitte.**	heer doorkh **bit**er

Changing money

| Can you change a traveller's cheque, please? | **Können Sie einen Reisescheck ein-lösen, bitte?** | **kur**nern zee **igh**nern **righ**zershehk **ighn**lurzern **bit**er |
| Where's the nearest bank, please? | **Wo ist die nächste Bank, bitte?** | voa ist dee **nehkh**ster **bahngk bit**er |

Car rental

I'd like a car.	**Ich möchte einen Wagen.**	ikh **murkh**ter **igh**nern **var**gern
For how long?	**Für wie lange?**	fewr vee **lahng**er
A day/Four days/ A week/Two weeks.	**Einen Tag/Vier Tage/Eine Woche/ Zwei Wochen.**	**igh**nern targ/feer **targ**er/**igh**ner **vo**kherr/ tsvigh **vo**khern

GERMAN

Taxi

Where can I get a taxi?	**Wo finde ich ein Taxi?**	voa **finder** ikh ighn **tahk**see
What's the fare to . . . ?	**Was kostet es bis . . . ?**	vahss **koss**tert ehss biss
Take me to this address, please.	**Fahren Sie mich bitte zu dieser Adresse.**	**farr**ern zee mikh **bit**er tsoo **dee**zerr ah**dreh**sser
I'm in a hurry.	**Ich habe es eilig.**	ikh **harb**er ehss **igh**likh
Could you drive more slowly, please?	**Können Sie bitte langsamer fahren?**	**kurn**tern zee **bit**er **lahng**zarmerr **farr**ern

Hotel and other accommodation

My name is . . .	**Mein Name ist . . .**	mighn **narm**er ist
Have you a reservation?	**Haben Sie vorbestellt?**	**harb**ern zee **for**bershtehlt
Yes, here's the confirmation.	**Ja, hier ist die Bestätigung.**	yar heer ist dee ber**shtait**igung
I'd like . . .	**Ich hätte gern . . .**	ikh **heh**ter gairn
I'd like a single room/a double room.	**Ich hätte gern ein Einzelzimmer/ein Doppelzimmer.**	ikh **heh**ter gairn ighn **ighnt**serltsimerr/ighn **dop**erltsimerr
a room with a bath/with a shower	**ein Zimmer mit Bad/mit Dusche**	ighn **tsim**err mit bart/mit **dush**er

How much?

What's the price per night/per week/per month?	**Wieviel kostet es pro Nacht/pro Woche/pro Monat?**	**vee**feel **koss**tert ehss proa nahkht/proa **vokh**err/proa **moa**nart
May I see the room?	**Kann ich das Zimmer sehen?**	kahn ikh dahss **tsim**err **zay**ern
I'm sorry, I don't like it.	**Bedaure, es gefällt mir nicht.**	ber**dow**rer ehss ger**fehlt** meer nikht
Yes, that's fine. I'll take it.	**Ja, sehr gut. Ich nehme es.**	yar zair goot. ikh **naym**er ehss
What's my room number, please?	**Welche Zimmernummer habe ich, bitte?**	**vehl**kher **tsim**errnumerr **harb**er ikh **bit**er
Number 123.	**Nummer 123.**	**num**err 123

GERMAN

Service, please

Who is it?	**Wer ist da?**	vair ist dar
Just a minute.	**Einen Augenblick, bitte.**	**igh**nern **ow**gernblik **bi**ter
Come in! The door's open.	**Herein! Die Tür ist offen.**	hair**ighn**! dee tewr ist **o**fern
May we have breakfast in our room?	**Können wir in unserem Zimmer frühstücken?**	**kur**nern veer in **un**zerrerm **tsi**merr **frew**shtewkern

Breakfast

I'll have . . .	**Ich möchte . . .**	ikh **murkh**ter
I'll have some fruit juice.	**Ich möchte einen Fruchtsaft.**	ikh **murkh**ter **igh**nern **frookht**zahft
a boiled egg	**ein gekochtes Ei**	ighn ger**kokh**terss igh
a fried egg	**ein Spiegelei**	ighn **shpee**gerligh
some bacon/some ham	**Speck/Schinken**	shpehk/**shing**kern
some toast	**Toast**	toast
a pot of tea	**ein Kännchen Tee**	ighn **kehn**khern tay
a cup of tea	**eine Tasse Tee**	**igh**ner **tah**sser tay
some coffee	**Kaffee**	**kah**fay
some chocolate	**Schokolade**	shoakoa**lar**der
more butter	**noch etwas Butter**	nokh **eht**vahss **bu**terr
some hot water	**etwas heißes Wasser**	**eht**vahss **high**sserss **vah**sserr

Difficulties

The central heating doesn't work.	**Die Zentralheizung funktioniert nicht.**	dee tsehn**trarl**hightsung fungktseeoa**neert** nikht
the light/the socket	**das Licht/die Steckdose**	dahss likht/dee **shtehk**doazer
the tap/the toilet	**der Wasserhahn/die Toilette**	dair **vah**sserrharn/dee toy**leh**ter
There's no hot water.	**Es kommt kein warmes Wasser.**	ehss komt kighn **vahr**merss **vah**sserr
May I see the manager, please?	**Kann ich bitte den Direktor sprechen?**	kahn ikh **bi**ter dayn dee**rehk**tawr **shpreh**khern

Telephone—Mail

There's a call for you.	**Hier ist ein Anruf für Sie.**	heer ist ighn **ahn**roof fewr zee

GERMAN

GERMAN

Hold the line, please.	**Bitte bleiben Sie am Apparat.**	biter **bligh**bern zee ahm ahpah**rart**
Operator, I've been cut off.	**Fräulein, ich bin unterbrochen worden.**	**froy**lighn ikh bin unterr**brokh**ern **vord**ern
Did anyone telephone me?	**Hat mich jemand angerufen?**	haht mikh **yay**mahnt **ahn**gerroofern
Is there any mail for me?	**Ist Post für mich da?**	ist post fewr mikh dar
Are there any messages for me?	**Hat jemand eine Nachricht für mich hinterlassen?**	haht **yay**mahnt **igh**ner **nahkh**rikht fewr mikh hinterlah**ssern**

Checking out

May I have my bill, please?	**Kann ich bitte meine Rechnung haben?**	kahn ikh biter **migh**ner **rehkh**nung **harb**ern
We're in a great hurry.	**Wir haben es sehr eilig.**	veer **harb**ern ehss **igh**likh
It's been a very enjoyable stay.	**Der Aufenthalt war sehr angenehm.**	dair **owf**ehnthahlt varr zair **ahn**gernaym

Eating out

Good evening, sir/ Good evening, madam.	**Guten Abend, mein Herr/Guten Abend, gnädige Frau.**	**goot**ern **arb**ernt mighn hair/**goot**ern **arb**ernt **gnai**diger frow
Good evening. I'd like a table for two, please.	**Guten Abend. Ich hätte gern einen Tisch für zwei Personen, bitte.**	**goot**ern **arb**ernt. ikh **heh**ter gairn **igh**nern tish fewr tsvigh pehr**zoa**nern biter
Do you have a fixed-price menu?	**Haben Sie ein Menü?**	**harb**ern zee ighn meh**new**
May I see the à la carte menu?	**Kann ich die Speisekarte sehen?**	kahn ikh dee **shpigh**zer-kahrter **zay**ern
May we have an ashtray, please?	**Können wir bitte einen Aschen-becher haben?**	**kurn**ern veer biter **igh**nern **ahshern**behkher **harb**ern
some bread	**etwas Brot**	**eht**vahss broat
a fork	**eine Gabel**	**igh**ner **garb**erl
a knife	**ein Messer**	ighn **mehss**err
a spoon	**einen Löffel**	**igh**nern **lurf**erl
a plate	**einen Teller**	**igh**nern **tehl**err

a glass	ein Glas	ighn glahss
a napkin	eine Serviette	ighner zairveeehter
another chair	noch einen Stuhl	nokh ighnern shtool
Where's the gentle-men's toilet (men's room)?	Wo ist die Herren-toilette?	voa ist dee hehrern-twahlehter
Where's the ladies' toilet (ladies' room)?	Wo ist die Damen-toilette?	voa ist dee darmern-twahlehter

Appetizers

I'd like some...	Ich hätte gern...	ikh hehter gairn
I'd like some assorted appetizers.	Ich hätte gern gemischte Vor-speisen.	ikh hehter gairn germish-ter fawrshpighzern
orange juice	Orangensaft	oarahngzhernzahft
ham	Schinken	shingkern
melon	Melone	mayloaner
pâté	Pastete	pahsstayter
smoked salmon	geräucherten Lachs	gerroykherrtern lahks
shrimps (shrimp)	Krevetten	krervehtern

Soup

Have you any...?	Haben Sie...?	harbern zee
Have you any chicken soup?	Haben Sie Hühner-suppe?	harbern zee hewnerrzuper
vegetable soup	Gemüsesuppe	germewzerzuper
onion soup	Zwiebelsuppe	tsveeberlzuper

Fish

I'd like some...	Ich hätte gern...	ikh hehter gairn
I'd like some fish.	Ich hätte gern Fisch.	ikh hehter gairn fish
sole	Seezunge	zaytsunger
trout	Forelle	forehler
lobster	Hummer	humerr
crayfish	Krebs	krayps
prawns	Garnelen	gahrnaylern
I'd like it...	Ich hätte es gern...	ikh hehter ehss gairn
I'd like it steamed.	Ich hätte es gern gedämpft.	ikh hehter ehss gairn ger-dehmpft
grilled	gegrillt	gergrillt
boiled	gekocht	gerkokht

GERMAN

| baked | **gebacken** | ger**bahk**ern |
| fried | **in der Pfanne gebraten** | in dair **pfahn**er ger**brar**tern |

Meat—Poultry—Game

I'd like some . . .	**Ich hätte gern . . .**	ikh **heh**ter gairn
I'd like some beef.	**Ich hätte gern Rindfleisch.**	ikh **heh**ter gairn **rint**flighsh
a beef steak	**ein Beefsteak**	ighn **beef**stayk
some roast beef	**Roastbeef**	**rost**beef
a veal cutlet	**ein Kalbskotelett**	ighn **kahlps**kaoterleht
mutton	**Hammelfleisch**	**hah**merlflighsh
lamb	**Lammfleisch**	**lahm**flighsh
a pork chop	**ein Schweinskotelett**	ighn **shvighns**kaoterleht
roast pork	**Schweinebraten**	**shvighn**erbrartern
hare	**Hase**	**har**zer
chicken	**Huhn**	hoon
roast chicken	**Brathühnchen**	**brat**hewnkhern
duck	**Ente**	**ehn**ter
How do you like your meat?	**Wie möchten Sie Ihr Fleisch?**	vee **murkh**tern zee eer flighsh
rare	**halbroh**	**hahl**proa
medium	**mittel**	**mit**erl
well done	**durchgebraten**	**doorkh**gerbrartern

Vegetables

What vegetables have you got?	**Was für Gemüse haben Sie?**	vahss fewr ger**mew**zer **har**bern zee
I'd like some . . .	**Ich hätte gern . . .**	ikh **heh**ter gairn
I'd like some asparagus.	**Ich hätte gern Spargeln.**	ikh **heh**ter gairn **shparr**gerln
green beans	**grüne Bohnen**	**grew**ner **boan**ern
mushrooms	**Pilze**	**pilt**ser
carrots	**Karotten**	kah**rot**ern
onions	**Zwiebeln**	**tsvee**berln
red cabbage	**Rotkohl**	**roat**koal
spinach	**Spinat**	shpi**nart**
rice	**Reis**	righss
peas	**Erbsen**	**airp**sern
tomatoes	**Tomaten**	toa**mar**tern
green salad	**grünen Salat**	**grew**nern zah**lart**
potatoes	**Kartoffeln**	kahr**tof**erln

Desserts

Nothing more, thanks.	**Nein danke, nichts mehr.**	nighn **dahng**ker nikhts mair
Just a small portion, please.	**Nur eine kleine Portion, bitte.**	noor **igh**ner **kligh**ner portsee**oan** bi**ter**
Have you any ice-cream?	**Haben Sie Eis?**	**har**bern zee ighss
fruit salad	**Obstsalat**	**oapst**zahlart
fresh fruit	**frisches Obst**	**frisher**ss oapst
cheese	**Käse**	**kai**zer

Drink

What would you like to drink?	**Was möchten Sie gern trinken?**	vahss **murkh**tern zee gairn **tring**kern
I'll have a beer, please.	**Ich nehme ein Bier, bitte.**	ikh **nay**mer ighn beer bi**ter**
I'll have a whisky, please.	**Ich möchte einen Whisky, bitte.**	ikh **murkh**te **igh**nern **viss**kee bi**ter**

Wine

I'd like a bottle of wine.	**Ich möchte eine Flasche Wein.**	ikh **murkh**ter **igh**ner **flah**sher vighn
red wine	**Rotwein**	**roat**vighn
rosé wine	**Roséwein**	roa**zay**vighn
white wine	**Weißwein**	**vighss**vighn
Cheers!	**Zum Wohl!**	tsum voal

The bill (check)

May I have the bill (check) please?	**Die Rechnung, bitte.**	dee **rehkh**nung bi**ter**
Is service included?	**Ist Bedienung inbegriffen?**	ist ber**dee**nung inber**grif**ern
Everything's included.	**Alles ist inbegriffen.**	**ahl**erss ist **in**bergrifern
Thank you, that was a very good meal.	**Danke, das Essen war sehr gut.**	**dang**ker dahss **ehss**ern varr zair goot

GERMAN

GERMAN

Travelling

Where's the railway station, please?	**Wo ist der Bahnhof, bitte?**	voa ist dair **barn**hoaf **bi**ter
Where's the ticket office, please?	**Wo ist der Fahrkartenschalter, bitte?**	voa ist dair **farr**kahrternshahlterr **bi**ter
I'd like a ticket to ...	**Ich möchte eine Fahrkarte nach ...**	ikh **murkh**ter **igh**ner **farr**kahrter nahkh
First or second class?	**Erste oder zweite Klasse?**	**airs**ter **oa**derr **tsvigh**ter **klah**sser
First class, please.	**Erste Klasse, bitte.**	**airs**ter **klah**sser **bi**ter
Single or return (one way or round-trip)?	**Einfach oder hin und zurück?**	**ighn**fahkh **oa**derr hin unt tsu**rewk**
Do I have to change trains?	**Muß ich umsteigen?**	muss ikh **um**shtighern
What platform does the train leave from?	**Auf welchem Bahnsteig fährt der Zug ab?**	owf **vehl**kherm **barn**shtighg fairt dair tsoog ahp
Where's the nearest underground (subway) station?	**Wo ist die nächste U-Bahnstation?**	voa ist dee **nehkh**ster **oo**barnshtahtsioan
Where's the bus station, please?	**Wo ist der Busbahnhof, bitte?**	voa ist dair **buss**barnhoaf **bi**ter
When's the first bus to ...?	**Wann fährt der erste Bus nach ...?**	vahn fairt dair **ehr**ster buss nahkh
the last bus	**der letzte Bus**	dair **leht**ster buss
the next bus	**der nächste Bus**	der **nehkh**ster buss
Please let me off at the next stop.	**Bitte lassen Sie mich an der nächsten Haltestelle aussteigen.**	**bi**ter **lah**ssern zee mikh ahn dair **nehkh**stern **hahl**tershtehler **owss**shtighern

Relaxing

What's on at the cinema (movies)?	**Was gibt es im Kino zu sehen?**	vahss gibt ehss im **kee**noa tsoo **zay**ern
What's on at the theatre?	**Was gibt es im Theater?**	vahss gibt ehss im tay**ar**terr
What time does the film begin? And the play?	**Wann beginnt der Film? Und das Stück?**	vahn ber**gint** dair film? unt dahss shtewk

Are there any tickets for tonight?	**Gibt es noch Karten für heute abend?**	gibt ehss nokh **kahr**tern fewr **hoy**ter **ar**bernt
Where can we go dancing?	**Wohin können wir tanzen gehen?**	voahin **kur**nern veer **tahnt**sern **gay**ern
Would you like to dance?	**Darf ich bitten?**	dahrf ikh **bi**tern

Introductions

How do you do?	**Guten Tag.**	**goo**tern targ
How are you?	**Wie geht es Ihnen?**	vee gayt ehss **ee**nern
Very well, thank you. And you?	**Sehr gut, danke. Und Ihnen?**	zair goot **dahng**ker, unt **ee**nern
May I introduce Miss Philips?	**Darf ich Fräulein Philips vorstellen?**	dahrf ikh **froy**lighn filips **for**shtehlern
My name is...	**Ich heiße...**	ikh **high**sser
I'm very pleased to meet you.	**Sehr erfreut.**	zair ehr**froyt**
How long have you been here?	**Wie lange sind Sie schon hier?**	vee **lahng**er zint zee shoan heer
It was nice meeting you.	**Es war mir ein Vergnügen.**	ehss varr meer ighn fehr**gnew**gern

Dating

Would you like a cigarette?	**Möchten Sie eine Zigarette?**	**murkh**tern zee **igh**ner tsiga**reh**ter
May I get you a drink?	**Darf ich Ihnen etwas zu trinken bestellen?**	dahrf ikh **ee**nern **eht**vahss; tsoo **tring**kern ber**shteh**lern
Do you have a light, please?	**Haben Sie Feuer, bitte?**	**har**bern zee **foy**err **bi**ter
Are you waiting for someone?	**Warten Sie auf jemanden?**	**vahr**tern zee owf **yay**mahndern
Are you free this evening?	**Sind Sie heute abend frei?**	zint zee **hoy**ter **ar**bernt frigh
Where shall we meet?	**Wo treffen wir uns?**	voa **treh**fern veer unss
What time shall I meet you?	**Wann treffe ich Sie?**	vahn **treh**fer ikh zee
May I take you home?	**Darf ich Sie nach Hause bringen?**	dahrf ikh zee nahkh **how**zer **bring**ern

GERMAN

Thank you, it's been a wonderful evening.	**Danke, es war ein wunderbarer Abend.**	**dahng**ker ehss varr ighn **vunderr**barrerr **arbernt**
What's your telephone number?	**Wie ist Ihre Telephonnummer?**	vee ist **eerer** tailai**foan**numerr
Do you live alone?	**Wohnen Sie alleine?**	**voa**nern zee ah**lighn**
What time is your last train?	**Wann fährt Ihr letzter Zug?**	vahn fairt eer **lehts**terr tsoog
Good-night...	**Gute Nacht...**	**goo**ter nahkht

Banks

Where's the nearest bank, please?	**Wo ist die nächste Bank, bitte?**	voa ist dee **nehk**ster bahngk **bi**ter
Where can I cash some traveller's cheques?	**Wo kann ich Reiseschecks einlösen?**	voa kahn ikh **righ**zershehks **ighn**lurzern
What time does the bank open? What time does it close?	**Wann öffnet die Bank? Wann schließt sie?**	vahn **urf**nert dee bahngk? vahn shleest zee
I'm expecting some money from home. Has it arrived?	**Ich erwarte Geld von zu Hause. Ist es eingetroffen?**	ikh air**vahr**ter gehlt fon tsoo **how**zer. ist ehss **ighn**gertrofern
Can you give me some small change, please?	**Können Sie mir bitte Kleingeld geben?**	**kur**nern zee meer **bi**ter **klighn**gehlt **gay**bern

Shops, stores and services

Where is the nearest chemist's (pharmacy)?	**Wo ist die nächste Apotheke?**	voa ist dee **nehk**ster ahpoa**tay**ker
the nearest hair-dresser's	**der nächste Friseur**	dair **nehk**ster fri**zurr**
the photo shop	**das Photogeschäft**	dahss **foa**toagershehft
the jeweller's	**der Juwelier**	dair yoover**leer**
the department store	**das Warenhaus**	dahss **varren**howss
the police station	**die Polizeiwache**	dee poalit**sigh**vahkher
the garage	**die Garage**	dee gah**rar**zher
How do I get there?	**Wie komme ich dorthin?**	vee **ko**mer ikh dort**hin**
Is it within walking distance?	**Kann man zu Fuß gehen?**	kahn mahn tsoo fooss **gay**ern

GERMAN

Service

Can you help me, please?	Können Sie mir helfen, bitte?	kurnern zee meer **hehl**fern **bi**ter
Can you show me this? And that, too.	Können Sie mir dies zeigen? Und das ebenfalls.	kurnern zee meer deess **tsigh**gern? unt dahss **ay**bernfahlss
It's too expensive/ too big/too small.	Es ist zu teuer/zu groß/zu klein.	ehss ist tsoo **toy**err/tsoo groass/tsoo klighn
Can you show me some more?	Können Sie mir noch mehr zeigen?	**kur**nern zee meer nokh mair **tsigh**gern
something better something cheaper	etwas Besseres etwas Billigeres	**eht**vahss **behs**serrerss **eht**vahss biligerrerss
How much is this? And that?	Wieviel kostet dies? Und das?	**vee**feel **kos**stert deess? unt dahss
It's not quite what I want.	Es ist nicht ganz das, was ich möchte.	ehss ist nikht gahnts dahss vahss ikh **murkh**ter
I like it.	Es gefällt mir.	ehss ger**fehlt** meer

Chemist's (Pharmacy)

| I'd like something for a cold/for a cough/for travel sickness. | Ich möchte etwas gegen eine Erkältung/gegen Husten/gegen Reisekrankheit. | ikh **murkh**ter **eht**vahss **gay**gern **igh**ner ehr**kehl**tung/**gay**gern **hoos**stern/**gay**gern **righ**zerkrahngkhight |
| Can you recommend something for hay-fever/for sunburn? | Können Sie mir etwas gegen Heufieber/gegen Sonnenbrand empfehlen? | **kur**nern zee meer **eht**vahss **gay**gern **hoy**feeberr/ **gay**gern **zo**nernbrahnt ehmp**fay**lern |

Toiletry

May I have some razor blades?	Kann ich Rasierklingen haben?	kahn ikh rah**zeer**klingern **har**bern
some shaving cream some toothpaste	Rasiercreme Zahnpasta	ra**zeer**kraym **tsarn**pahstah
I'd like some soap.	Ich hätte gern Seife.	ikh **heh**ter gairn **zigh**fer
some suntan oil	Sonnenöl	**zo**nernurl

At the barber's

| I'd like a haircut, please. | Ich möchte mir das Haar schneiden lassen, bitte. | ikh **murkh**ter meer dahss harr **shnigh**dern **lahs**sern |

GERMAN

| Short/Leave it long. | **Kurz/Lassen Sie es lang.** | koorts/**lahs**sern zee ehss lahng |
| A razor cut, please. | **Einen Messer-schnitt, bitte.** | **igh**nern **mehs**serrshnit **bi**ter |

At the hairdresser's

I'd like a shampoo and set, please.	**Waschen und legen, bitte.**	**vah**shern unt **lay**gern **bi**ter
I'd like a bleach.	**Ich möchte eine Aufhellung.**	ikh **murkh**ter **igh**ner **owf**hehllung
a permanent	**eine Dauerwelle**	**igh**ner **dow**errvehler
a colour rinse	**eine Farbspülung**	**igh**ner **fahrp**shpewlung
a manicure	**eine Maniküre**	**igh**ner **mahni**kewrer

Photography

| I'd like a film for this camera. | **Ich möchte einen Film für diese Kamera.** | ikh **murkh**ter **igh**nern film fewr **dee**zer **kah**merrah |
| This camera doesn't work. | **Diese Kamera ist defekt.** | **dee**zer **kah**merrah ist dai**fehkt** |

At the post office

| Where's the nearest post office, please? | **Wo ist das nächste Postamt, bitte?** | voa ist dahss **nehkh**ster **post**ahmt **bi**ter |
| I'd like to send this by express (special delivery)/by air mail. | **Ich möchte dies durch Eilboten/ mit Luftpost Schicken.** | ikh **murkh**ter deess doorkh **ighl**boatern/ mit **luft**post **shi**kern |

Service stations

Where is the nearest service station, please?	**Wo ist die nächste Tankstelle, bitte?**	voa ist dee **nehkh**ster **tahngk**shtehler **bi**ter
Fill her up, please.	**Voll, bitte.**	fol **bi**ter
Check the oil, please.	**Kontrollieren Sie bitte das Ölstand.**	kontro**leer**ern zee **bi**ter dayn **url**shtahnt
Would you check the tyres?	**Würden Sie bitte die Reifen prüfen?**	**vewr**dern zee **bi**ter dee **righ**fern **prew**fern

Street directions

Can you show me on the map where I am?	Können Sie mir auf der Karte zeigen, wo ich bin?	**kur**nern zee meer owf dair **kahr**ter **tsigh**gern voa ikh bin
You're on the wrong road.	Sie sind auf der falschen Straße.	zee zint owf dair **fahl**shern **shtrar**sser
Go back to...	Fahren Sie zurück nach...	farrern zee tsoo**rewk** nahkh
Go straight ahead.	Fahren Sie geradeaus.	farrern zee gerrarder**owss**
It's on the left/on the right.	Es ist linker Hand/rechter Hand.	ehss ist **ling**kerr hahnt/**rehkh**terr hahnt

Accidents

May I use your telephone?	Darf ich Ihr Telephon benutzen?	dahrf ikh eer tailai**foan** ber**newt**sern
Call a doctor quickly.	Rufen Sie schnell einen Arzt.	**roo**fern zee shnehl **igh**nern ahrtst
Call an ambulance.	Rufen Sie einen Krankenwagen.	**roo**fen zee **igh**nern **krahng**kernvargern
Please call the police.	Rufen Sie bitte die Polizei.	**roo**fen zee **bi**ter dee poalit**sigh**

Numbers

one	eins	ighnss
two	zwei	tsvigh
three	drei	drigh
four	vier	feer
five	fünf	fewnf
six	sechs	zehks
seven	sieben	**zee**bern
eight	acht	ahkht
nine	neun	noyn
ten	zehn	tsayn
eleven	elf	ehlf
twelve	zwölf	tsvurlf
thirteen	dreizehn	**drigh**tsayn
fourteen	vierzehn	**feer**tsayn
fifteen	fünfzehn	**fewnf**tsayn
sixteen	sechzehn	**zehkh**tsayn
seventeen	siebzehn	**zeep**tsayn
eighteen	achtzehn	**ahkh**tsayn
nineteen	neunzehn	**noyn**tsayn

GERMAN

twenty	**zwanzig**	tsvahntsikh
twenty-one	**einundzwanzig**	ighnunttsvahntsikh
thirty	**dreißig**	drighssikh
forty	**vierzig**	feertsikh
fifty	**fünfzig**	fewnftsikh
sixty	**sechzig**	zehkhtsikh
seventy	**siebzig**	zeeptsikh
eighty	**achtzig**	ahkhtsikh
ninety	**neunzig**	noyntsikh
one hundred	**hundert**	hunderrt
one thousand	**tausend**	towzernt
ten thousand	**zehntausend**	tsayntowzernt

Days

It's Sunday.	**Es ist Sonntag.**	ehss ist zontark
Monday	**Montag**	moantark
Tuesday	**Dienstag**	deensstark
Wednesday	**Mittwoch**	mitvokh
Thursday	**Donnerstag**	donerrsstark
Friday	**Freitag**	frightark
Saturday	**Sonnabend**	zonarbernt
yesterday	**gestern**	gehssterrn
today	**heute**	hoyter
tomorrow	**morgen**	morgern
morning/afternoon	**Vormittag/Nach-mittag**	formitark/nahkhmitark
evening/night	**Abend/Nacht**	arbernt/nahkht

Months

January	**Januar**	yahnooarr
February	**Februar**	faybrooarr
March	**März**	mairts
April	**April**	ahpril
May	**Mai**	migh
June	**Juni**	yoonee
July	**Juli**	yoolee
August	**August**	owgust
September	**September**	zehptehmberr
October	**Oktober**	oktoaberr
November	**November**	noavehmberr
December	**Dezember**	daytsehmberr
Merry Christmas!	**Fröhliche Weihnach-ten! Glückliches Neues Jahr!**	frurlikher vighnahkhtern!
Happy New Year!		glewklikherss noyerss yarr

GREEK

Guide to Pronunciation

Letter	Approximate pronunciation	Symbol	Example	
Vowels				
α	like the vowel in car, but pronounced further forward in the mouth	ah	αρωμα	**ah**romah
ε	like e in sell	eh	μέρα	**meh**rah
η, ι, υ	like ee in meet	ee	κύριος	**kee**reeoss
ο, ω	like o in got	o	παρακαλώ	pahrahkahl**o**
Consonants				
β	like v in vine	v	βιβλίο	vee**vleeo**
γ	1) before α, ο, ω, ου, and consonants, a voiced version of the ch sound in Scottish loch	ğ	μεγάλος	meh**ğah**loss
	2) before ε, αι, η, ι, υ, ει, οι, like y in yet	y	γεμᾶτος	**yehmah**toss
δ	like th in this	dh	δέν	**dhehn**
ζ	like z in zoo	z	ζεστός	zhe**stoss**
θ	like th in thing	th	θά	**thah**
κ	like k in kit	k	καλός	kah**loss**
λ	like l in lemon	l	λάθος	**lah**thoss
μ	like m in man	m	μέσα	**meh**ssah

114

υ	like **n** in new	n	νέος	**neh**oss
ξ	like **x** in si**x**	ks	ἔξω	**eh**kso
π	like **p** in **p**ot	p	πρός	pross
ρ	like **r** in **r**ed	r	πρίν	preen
σ, ς	1) before β, γ, δ, ζ, μ, ν, ρ, like **z** in **z**oo	z	κόσμος	**koz**moss
	2) elsewhere, like **s** in **s**ee	s/ss	στό	sto
τ	like **t** in **t**ea	t	τότε	**tot**eh
φ	like **f** in **f**ive	f	φέρτε	**fehr**teh
χ	like **ch** in Scottish lo**ch**	kh	ἄσχημος	ahss**kheem**oss
ψ	like **ps** in dro**psy**	ps	διψῶ	dheep**so**

Groups of letters

αι	like **e** in g**e**t	eh	εἶναι	**een**eh
ει, οι	like **ee** in s**ee**	ee	πεῖτε	**pee**teh
ου	like **oo** in r**oo**t	oo	μοῦ	moo
αυ	similar to **ave** in h**ave**	ahv	αὐτό	ahv**to**
ευ	like **ev** in l**ev**el	ehv	Εὐρώπη	ehv**rop**ee
γγ	like **ng** in li**ng**er	ngg	Ἀγγλία	ahng**glee**ah
γκ	1) at the beginning of a word like **g** in **g**o	g	γκαμήλα	gah**meel**ah
	2) in the middle of a word, like **ng** in li**ng**er	ngg	ἄγκυρα	**ahng**geerah
γξ	like **nks** in li**nks**	ngks	φάλαγξ	**fah**lahngks
γχ	like **ng** followed by the **ch** of Scottish lo**ch**	ngkh	μελαγ-χολία	mehlahng-**khol**eeah
μπ	1) at the beginning of a word like **b** in **b**eer	b	μπορεῖτε	bo**ree**teh
	2) in the middle of a word like **mb** in lu**mb**er	mb	Ὄλυμπος	o**leemb**oss
ντ	1) at the beginning of a word, like **d** in **d**ear	d	ντομάτα	do**mah**tah
	2) in the middle of a word, like **nd** in u**nd**er	nd	κέντρο	**kehn**dro
τζ	like **ds** in see**ds**	dz	τζάκι	**dzah**kee

Accent marks

These are written in various ways, e.g., ὰ, ά, or ᾶ, but all of them indicate the stressed syllable. The signs for the "breathing" of initial vowels (α, ἀ) can be ignored. A diaeresis (two dots) written over a letter means that the letter is pronounced separately from the previous one, e.g., καιρός is pronounced keh**ross**, but in Κάϊρο, the α and ι are pronounced separately, **kah**eero.

The alphabet

Here are the characters which comprise the Greek alphabet. The column at left shows the printed capital and small letters, while written letters are shown in the center column. The column at right gives you the name of these letters as pronounced by Greeks.

Printed		Written		Pronunciation
A	α	*A*	*a*	**ahl**fah
B	β	*B*	*b*	**vee**tah
Γ	γ	*Γ*	*γ*	**ghah**mah
Δ	δ	*Δ*	*δ*	**dheh**ltah
E	ε	*E*	*e*	**eh**pseelon
Z	ζ	*Z*	*z*	**zee**tah
H	η	*H*	*n*	**ee**tah
Θ	θ	*θ*	*θ*	**thee**tah
I	ι	*I*	*c*	yee**o**tah
K	κ	*K*	*u*	**kah**pah
Λ	λ	*Λ*	*λ*	**lahm**dhah
M	μ	*M*	*μ*	mee
N	ν	*N*	*ν*	nee
Ξ	ξ	*Ξ*	*ξ*	ksee
O	o	*O*	*o*	**o**meekron
Π	π	*Π*	*π*	pee
P	ρ	*P*	*ρ*	ro
Σ	σ	ς	*Σ*	*ς ς*	**seegh**mah
T	τ	*T*	*τ*	tahf
Y	υ	*Y*	*υ*	**ee**pseelon
Φ	φ	*φ*	*φ*	fee
X	χ	*X*	*χ*	khee
Ψ	ψ	*Ψ*	*ψ*	psee
Ω	ω	*ω*	*ω*	o**mehg**hah

Some basic expressions

Yes.	Ναί.	neh
No.	'Όχι.	okhee
Please.	Παρακαλῶ.	pahrahkahlo
Thank you.	Εὐχαριστῶ.	ehvkhahreesto
Thank you very much.	Εὐχαριστῶ πολύ.	ehvkhahreesto polee
That's all right.	Τίποτα.	teepotah

Greetings

Good morning.	Καλημέρα.	kahleemehrah
Good afternoon.	Καλησπέρα.	kahleespehrah
Good evening.	Καλησπέρα.	kahleespehrah
Good night.	Καληνύκτα.	kahleeneektah
Good-bye.	'Αντίο.	ahndeeo
See you later.	Εἰς τό ἐπανιδεῖν.	eess to ehpahneedheen
This is Mr....	Ὁ κύριος ...	o keereeoss
This is Mrs....	Ἡ κυρία ...	ee keereeah
This is Miss ...	Ἡ δεσποινίς ...	ee dhehspeeneess
I'm very pleased to meet you.	Χαίρομαι πού σᾶς γνωρίζω.	khehromeh poo sahss gnoreezo
How are you?	Τί κάνετε;	tee kahnehteh
Very well, thank you.	Πολύ καλά, εὐχαριστῶ.	polee kahlah ehvkhahreesto
And you?	Καί ἐσεῖς;	keh ehsseess
Fine.	Πολύ καλά.	polee kahlah
Excuse me.	Μέ συγχωρεῖτε.	meh seengkhoreeteh

Questions

Where?	Ποῦ;	poo
Where is ... ?	Ποῦ εἶναι ...;	poo eeneh
Where are ... ?	Ποῦ εἶναι ...;	poo eeneh
When?	Πότε;	poteh
What?	Τί;	tee

How?	Πῶς;	poss
How much?	Πόσο;	posso
How many?	Πόσα;	possah
Who?	Ποιός;	peeoss
Why?	Γιατί;	yeeahtee
Which?	Ποιός/Ποιά/Ποιό;	peeoss/peeah/peeo
What do you call this?	Πῶς λέγεται αὐτό;	poss lehyehteh ahvto
What do you call that?	Πῶς λέγεται ἐκεῖνο;	poss lehyehteh ehkeeno
What does this mean?	Τί σημαίνει αὐτό;	tee seemehnee ahvto
What does that mean?	Τί σημαίνει ἐκεῖνο;	tee seemehnee ehkeeno

Do you speak . . . ?

Do you speak English?	Μιλᾶτε 'Αγγλικά;	meelahteh ahnggleekah
Do you speak German?	Μιλᾶτε Γερμανικά;	meelahteh yehrmahneekah
Do you speak French?	Μιλᾶτε Γαλλικά;	meelahteh ġahleekah
Do you speak Spanish?	Μιλᾶτε 'Ισπανικά;	meelahteh eespahneekah
Do you speak Italian?	Μιλᾶτε 'Ιταλικά;	meelahteh eetahleekah
Could you speak more slowly, please?	Μπορεῖτε νά μιλᾶτε πιό ἀργά, παρακαλῶ;	boreeteh nah meelahteh peeo ahrġah pahrahkahlo
Please point to the phrase in the book.	Παρακαλῶ δεῖξτε τή φράση στό βιβλίο.	pahrahkahlo dheeksteh tee frahssee sto veevleeo
Just a minute. I'll see if I can find it in this book.	"Ενα λεπτό. Θά δῶ ἄν μπορῶ, νά τό βρῶ σ'αὐτό τό βιβλίο.	ehnah lehpto. thah dho ahn boro nah to vro s ahvto to veevleeo
I understand.	Καταλαβαίνω.	kahtahlahvehno
I don't understand.	Δέν καταλαβαίνω.	dhehn kahtahlahvehno

Can...?

Can I have...?	Μπορῶ νά ἔχω...;	boro nah **eh**kho
Can we have...?	Μπορούμε νά ἔχουμε...;	bor**oo**meh nah eh-**khoo**meh
Can you show me...?	Μπορεῖτε νά μοῦ δείξετε...;	bor**ee**teh nah moo **dheek**steh
Can you tell me...?	Μπορεῖτε νά μοῦ πῆτε...;	bor**ee**teh nah moo **pee**teh
Can you help me, please?	Μπορεῖτε νά μέ βοηθήσετε, παρακαλῶ;	bor**ee**teh nah meh voee-**thee**sehteh, pahrahkah**lo**

Wanting

I'd like...	Θά ἤθελα...	thah **ee**thehlah
We'd like...	Θά θέλαμε...	thah **theh**lahmeh
Please give me...	Παρακαλῶ δῶστε μου...	pahrahkah**lo dhoss**teh moo
Give it to me, please.	Δῶστε μοῦ το, παρακαλῶ.	**dhoss**teh moo to pahrahkah**lo**
Please bring me...	Παρακαλῶ, φέρτε μου...	pahrahkah**lo fehr**teh moo
Bring it to me, please.	Φέρτε μοῦ το, παρακαλῶ.	**fehr**teh moo to pahrahkah**lo**
I'm hungry.	Πεινῶ.	pee**no**
I'm thirsty.	Διψῶ.	dheep**so**
I'm tired.	Εἶμαι κουρασμένος.	**ee**meh koorah**smeh**noss
I'm lost.	Χάθηκα.	**kah**theekah
It's important.	Εἶναι σοβαρό.	**ee**neh sovah**ro**
It's urgent.	Εἶναι ἐπεῖγον.	**ee**neh eh**pee**ğon
Hurry up!	Γρήγορα!	**ğree**ğorah

It is/There is...

It is/It's...	Εἶναι...	**ee**neh
Is it...?	Εἶναι...;	**ee**neh
It isn't...	Δέν εἶναι...	dhehn **ee**neh
There is/There are...	Ὑπάρχει/ Ὑπάρχουν...	ee**pahr**khee/eepahr**khoon**

Is there/Are there . . . ?	Ὑπάρχει/ Ὑπάρχουν . . . ;	eepahrkhee/eepahrkhoon
There isn't/There aren't . . .	Δέν ὑπάρχει/Δέν ὑπάρχουν . . .	dhehn eepahrkhee/ dhehn eepahrkhoon
There isn't any/ There aren't any.	Δέν ὑπάρχει καθόλου/Δέν ὑπάρχουν καθόλου.	dhehn eepahrkhee kahtholoo/dhehn eepahrkhoon kahtholoo

A few common words

big/small	μεγάλος/μικρός	meh**gah**loss/mee**kross**
quick/slow	γρήγορος/ἀργός	**gree**goross/ahr**goss**
early/late	νωρίς/ἀργά	no**reess**/ahr**gah**
cheap/expensive	φτηνός/ἀκριβός	ftee**noss**/ahkree**voss**
near/far	κοντά/μακρυά	kon**dah**/mahkree**ah**
hot/cold	ζεστός/κρύος	zeh**stoss**/**kree**oss
full/empty	γεμᾶτος/ἄδειος	yeh**mah**toss/**ah**dheeoss
easy/difficult	εὔκολος/δύσκολος	**ehv**koloss/**dhee**skoloss
heavy/light	βαρύς/ἐλαφρός	vah**reess**/ehlah**fross**
open/shut	ἀνοικτός/κλειστός	ahnee**ktoss**/klee**stoss**
right/wrong	σωστός/λάθος	so**stos**/**lah**thoss
old/new	παληός/καινούργιος	pahlee**oss**/kehn**noor**yeeoss
old/young	γέρος/νέος	**yeh**ross/**neh**oss
beautiful/ugly	ὡραῖος/ἄσχημος	o**reh**oss/**ahss**kheemoss
good/bad	καλός/κακός	kah**loss**/kah**koss**
better/worse	καλύτερος/χειρότερος	kah**lee**tehross/khee**ro**tehross

Some prepositions and a few more useful words

at	στό	sto
on	ἐπάνω	eh**pah**no
in	μέσα	**meh**ssah
to	πρός	pross
from	ἀπό	ah**po**
inside	μέσα	**meh**ssah
outside	ἔξω	**ehk**so
up	ἐπάνω	eh**pah**no
down	κάτω	**kah**to
before	πρίν	preen
after	μετά	meh**tah**
with	μέ	meh
without	χωρίς	kho**reess**
through	ἀνάμεσα	ah**nah**mehssah
towards	πρός	pross
until	μέχρι	**meh**khree
during	κατά τή διάρκεια	katah tee dhee**ahr**keeah
and	καί	keh

or	ἤ	ee
not	δέν	dhehn
nothing	τίποτε	teepoteh
none	κανένα	kahnehnah
very	πολύ	polee
also	ἐπίσης	ehpeesseess
soon	σύντομα	seendomah
perhaps	ἴσως	eessoss
here	ἐδῶ	ehdho
there	ἐκεῖ	ehkee
now	τώρα	torah
then	τότε	toteh

Arrival

Your passport, please.	Τό διαβατήριό σας, παρακαλῶ.	to dheeahvahteereeo sahss pahrahkahlo
Here it is.	Ὁρίστε.	oreesteh
Have you anything to declare?	Ἔχετε κάτι νά δηλώσετε;	ehkhehteh kahtee nah dheelosehteh
No, nothing at all.	Ὄχι, τίποτε.	okhee teepoteh
Porter!	Ἀχθοφόρε.	ahkhthoforeh
Can you help me with my luggage, please?	Μπορεῖτε νά μέ βοηθήσετε μέ τίς ἀποσκευές μου, παρακαλῶ.	boreeteh nah meh voeetheessehteh meh teess ahposkehvehss moo pahrahkahlo
That's my suitcase.	Αὐτή εἶναι ἡ βαλίτσα μου.	ahftee eeneh ee vahleetsah moo
Where's the bus to the centre of town, please?	Ποῦ εἶναι τό λεωφορεῖο γιά τό κέντρο τῆς πόλεως, παρακαλῶ;	poo eeneh to lehoforeeo yeeah to kehndro teess polehoss pahrahkahlo
This way, please.	Ἀπό ἐδῶ, παρακαλῶ.	ahpo ehdho pahrahkahlo

Changing money

Can you change a traveller's cheque, please?	Μπορεῖτε νά ἀλλάξετε ἕνα τράβελερ τσέκ, παρακαλῶ;	boreeteh nah ahlahksehteh ehnah trahvehlehr tsehk pahrahkahlo
Where's the nearest bank, please?	Ποῦ εἶναι ἡ πλησιέστερη τράπεζα, παρακαλῶ;	poo eeneh ee pleesseeehstehree trahpehzah pahrahkahlo

Car rental

I'd like a car.	Θά ἤθελα ἕνα αὐτοκίνητο.	thah **ee**thehlah **eh**nah ahftoke**ee**neeto
For how long?	Γιά πόσο καιρό;	**yee**ah **pos**so keh**ro**
A day/Four days/ A week/Two weeks.	Μία ἡμέρα/ Τέσσερεις ἡμέρες/ Μία ἑβδομάδα/ Δύο ἑβδομάδες.	**mee**ah ee**meh**rah/ **teh**ssehreess eemeh**rehss**/ **mee**ah ehvdhomah**dhah**/ **dhee**o ehvdhomah**dhehss**

Taxi

Where can I get a taxi?	Ποῦ μπορῶ νά βρῶ ἕνα ταξί;	poo bo**ro** nah vro **eh**nah tah**ksee**
What's the fare to ...?	Ποιά εἶναι ἡ τιμή γιά...;	pee**ah ee**neh ee tee**mee** **yee**ah
Take me to this address, please.	Πηγαίνετέ με σ'αὐτή τή διεύθυνσι, παρακαλῶ.	peeyeh**neh**teh meh sahf**tee** tee dhee**ehf**theensee pahrahkah**lo**
I'm in a hurry.	Εἶμαι βιαστικός.	**ee**meh veeahstee**koss**
Could you drive more slowly, please?	Μπορεῖτε νά ὁδηγῆτε πιό ἀργά, παρακαλῶ;	bo**ree**teh nah odhee**yee**teh pee**o**o ahr**gah** pahrahkah**lo**

Hotel and other accommodation

My name is ...	Τό ὄνομά μου εἶναι...	to **on**omah moo **ee**neh
Have you a reservation?	Ἔχετε κρατήσει δωμάτιο;	eh**kheh**teh krah**tee**ssee dhomah**tee**o
Yes, here's the confirmation.	Μάλιστα, ἰδού ἡ διαβεβαίωσηη.	**mah**leestah ee**dhoo** ee dheeahvehveh**veh**ossee
I'd like ...	Θά ἤθελα...	thah **ee**thehlah
I'd like a single room/a double room.	Θά ἤθελα ἕνα μονό δωμάτιο/ἕνα διπλό δωμάτιο.	thah **ee**thehlah **eh**nah mo**no** dhomah**tee**o/**eh**nah dhee**plo** dhomah**tee**o
a room with a bath/ with a shower	ἕνα δωμάτιο μέ μπάνιο/μέ ντούς	**eh**nah dhomah**tee**o meh **bah**neeo/meh dhooss

How much?

| What's the price per night/per week/per month? | Ποιά εἶναι ἡ τιμή γιά μία νύχτα/μία ἑβδομάδα/ἕνα μῆνα; | pee**ah ee**neh ee tee**mee** **yee**ah **mee**ah **neek**htah/ **mee**ah ehvdhomah**dhah**/ **eh**nah **mee**nah |
| May I see the room? | Μπορῶ νά δῶ τό δωμάτιο; | bo**ro** nah dho to dhomah**tee**o |

I'm sorry, I don't like it.	Μέ συγχωρεῖτε, δέν μοῦ ἀρέσει.	meh seenkhor**eeteh** dhehn moo ahr**ehs**see
Yes, that's fine. I'll take it.	Ναί, εἶναι καλό. Θά τό πάρω.	neh **ee**neh kah**lo**. thah to **pah**ro
What's my room number, please?	Ποιός εἶναι ὁ ἀριθμός τοῦ δωματίου μου, παρακαλῶ;	pee**oss ee**neh o ahreeth-**moss** too dhomah**tee**oo moo pahrah**kah**lo
Number 123.	Νούμερο 123.	**noo**mehro 123

Service, please

Who is it?	Ποιός εἶναι;	pee**oss ee**neh
Just a minute.	Ἕνα λεπτό.	**eh**nah leh**pto**
Come in! The door's open.	Ὁρίστε! Ἡ πόρτα εἶναι ἀνοικτή.	or**ee**steh. ee **por**tah **ee**neh ahne**ektee**
May we have breakfast in our room?	Μποροῦμε νά πάρουμε τό πρόγευμα στό δωμάτιό μας;	bor**oo**meh nah **pah**roomeh to **pro**yehvmah sto dhoma**htee**oo mahss

Breakfast

I'll have ...	Θά πάρω ...	thah **pah**ro
I'll have some fruit juice.	Θά πάρω ἕνα χυμό φρούτων.	thah **pah**ro **eh**nah **khee**mo **froo**ton
a boiled egg	ἕνα βραστό αὐγό	**eh**nah vrah**sto** ahv**go**
a fried egg	ἕνα τηγανιτό αὐγό	**eh**nah teeyahnee**to** ahv**go**
some bacon/some ham	χοιρομέρι/ζαμπόν	kheero**meh**ree zahm**bon**
some toast	μερικά τόστ	mehree**kah** tost
a pot of tea	τσάι	**tsah**ee
a cup of tea	ἕνα φλυτζάνι τσάι	**eh**nah fleen**tzah**nee **tsah**ee
some coffee	καφέ	kah**feh**
some chocolate	κακάο	kah**kah**ho
more butter	περισσότερο βούτυρο	pehre**ess**otehro **voo**teero
some hot water	ζεστό νερό	zeh**sto** neh**ro**

Difficulties

The central heating doesn't work.	Ἡ κεντρική θέρμανση δέν δουλεύει.	ee kehndhree**kee thehr**mahnsee dhehn dhoo**leh**vee
the light/the socket	τό φῶς/ἡ πρίζα	to foss/ee **pree**zah
the tap/the toilet	τό ρομπινέ/ἡ τουαλέττα	to rombee**neh**/ee tooah**leh**tah

| There's no hot water. | Δέν ἔχει ζεστό νερό. | dhenn **eh**khee zeh**sto** neh**ro** |
| May I see the manager, please? | Μπορῶ νά δῶ τόν διευθυντή, παρακαλῶ; | bo**ro** nah dho ton dheeeehf**theendee** pahrahkah**lo** |

Telephone—Mail

There's a call for you.	Σας ζητοῦν στό τηλέφωνο.	sahss zee**toon** sto tee**leh**fono
Hold the line, please.	Περιμένετε στό ἀκουστικό σας, παρακαλῶ.	pehree**meh**nehteh sto ahkoo**steek**o sahss pahrahkah**lo**
Operator, I've been cut off.	Δεσποινίς μέ διέκοψαν.	dhehspee**neess** meh dhee**eh**kopsahn
Did anyone telephone me?	Μοῦ τηλεφώνησε κανείς;	moo teeleh**foneesseh** kah**neess**
Is there any mail for me?	Ὑπάρχουν γράμματα γιά μένα;	ee**pahr**khoon **grah**mahtah yee**ah meh**nah
Are there any messages for me?	Ὑπάρχουν παραγγελίες γιά μένα;	ee**pahr**khoon pahrzhngge**hleeehss** yee**ah meh**nah

Checking out

May I have my bill, please?	Μπορῶ νά ἔχω τόν λογαριασμό, παρακαλῶ;	bo**ro** nah **eh**kho ton lo**ğ**ahreeahz**mo** pahrahkah**lo**
We're in a great hurry.	Εἴμαστε πολύ βιαστικοί.	**ee**mahsteh po**lee** veeah-**steek**ee
It's been a very enjoyable stay.	Ἡ διαμονή ἦταν πολύ εὐχάριστη.	eedheeahmo**nee ee**tahn po**lee** ehf**khah**reestee

Eating out

Good evening, sir/ Good evening, madam.	Καλησπέρα, κύριε/Καλησπέρα, κυρία.	kahlees**peh**rah keer**eeeh**/kahlees**peh**rah keer**eeah**
Good evening. I'd like a table for two, please.	Καλησπέρα. Θά ἤθελα ἕνα τραπέζι γιά δύο, παρακαλῶ.	kahlees**peh**rah. thah **ee**thehlah **eh**nah trah**peh**zee yee**ah dhee**o pahrahkah**lo**
Do you have a fixed-price menu?	Ἔχετε φαγητό μέ καθωρισμένη τιμή;	**eh**khehteh fahyee**to** meh kahthoreez**meh**nee tee**mee**

May I see the à la carte menu?	Μπορῶ νά δῶ τό μενοῦ ἀ-λά-κάρτ;	boro nah dho to mehnoo ahlahkahrt
May we have an ashtray, please?	Μπορούμε νά ἔχουμε ἕνα στακτοδοχεῖο, παρακαλῶ;	boroomeh nah ehkhoomeh ehnah stahktodhokheeo pahrahkahlo
some bread	ψωμί	psomee
a fork	ἕνα πειρούνι	ehnah peeroonee
a knife	ἕνα μαχαίρι	ehnah mahkhehree
a spoon	ἕνα κουτάλι	ehnan kootahlee
a plate	ἕνα πιάτο	ehnah peeahto
a glass	ἕνα ποτήρι	ehnah poteeree
a napkin	ἕνα τραπεζομάντηλο	ehnah trahpehzomahndeelo
another chair	μία καρέκλα ἀκόμη	meeah kahrehklah ahkomee
Where's the gentlemen's toilet (men's room)?	Ποῦ εἶναι οἱ τουαλέττες τῶν ἀνδρῶν;	poo eeneh ee tooahlehtehss ton ahndhron
Where's the ladies' toilet (ladies' room)?	Ποῦ εἶναι οἱ τουαλέττες τῶν γυναικῶν;	poo eeneh ee tooahlehtehss ton yeenehkon

Appetizers

I'd like some . . .	Θά ἤθελα . . .	thah eethehlah
I'd like some assorted appetizers.	Θά ἤθελα μία ποικιλία ὀρεκτικῶν.	thah eethehlah meeah peekeeleeah orehkteekon
orange juice	ἕ να χυμό πορτοκαλιοῦ	ehnah kheemo portokahleeoo
ham	ζαμπόν	zahmbon
melon	πεπόνι	pehponee
pâté	πατέ	pahteh
smoked salmon	καπνιστό σολωμό	kahpneesto solomo
shrimps (shrimp)	γαρίδες	ĝahreedhehss

Soup

Have you any . . . ?	Ἔχετε . . . ;	ehkhehteh
Have you any chicken soup?	Ἔχετε κοτόσουπα;	ehkhehteh kotossoopah
vegetable soup	χορτόσουπα	khortossoopah
onion soup	κρεμμυδόσουπα	krehmeedhossoopah

Fish

I'd like some . . .	Θά ἤθελα . . .	thah **ee**thehlah
I'd like some fish.	Θά ἤθελα ψάρι.	thah **ee**thehlah **psah**ree
sole	γλῶσσα	**glo**sah
trout	πέστροφα	**peh**strofah
lobster	ἀστακό	ahstah**ko**
crayfish	καραβίδες	kahrah**vee**dhehss
prawns	καβούρια	kah**voo**reeah
I'd like it . . .	Θά τό ἤθελα . . .	thah to **ee**thehlah
I'd like it steamed.	Θά τό ἤθελα στόν ἀτμό.	thah to **ee**thehlah ston aht**mo**
grilled	ψητό	psee**to**
boiled	βραστό	vrah**sto**
baked	μαγειρευμένο	mahyeerehv**meh**no
fried	τηγανιτό	teeğahnee**to**

Meat—Poultry—Game

I'd like some . . .	Θά ἤθελα . . .	thah **ee**thehlah
I'd like some beef.	Θά ἤθελα μοσχάρι.	thah **ee**thehlah moss**khah**ree
a beef steak	μία μπριζόλα	**mee**ah bree**zo**lah
some roast beef	ροζ-μπήφ	roz**beef**
a veal cutlet	μία μοσχαρίσια μπριζόλα	**mee**ah mosskhah**ree**-sseeah bree**zo**lah
mutton	ἀρνί	ahr**nee**
lamb	ἀρνάκι γάλακτος	ahr**nah**kee **ğah**lahktoss
a pork chop	μία χοιρινή μπριζόλα	**mee**ah kheeree**nee** bree**zo**lah
roast pork	ψητό χοιρινό	psee**to** kheeree**no**
hare	λαγό	lah**ğo**
chicken	κοτόπουλο	ko**to**poolo
roast chicken	κοτόπουλο ψητό	ko**to**poolo psee**to**
duck	πάπια	**pah**peeah
How do you like your meat?	Πῶς θέλετε τό κρέας σας;	poss **theh**lehteh to **kreh**ahss sahss
rare	λίγο ψημένο	**lee**ğo psee**meh**no
medium	μέτριο	**meh**treeo
well done	καλοψημένο	kahlopsee**meh**no

Vegetables

What vegetables have you got?	Τί λαχανικά ἔχετε;	tee lahkhahnee**kah** **eh**khehteh
I'd like some . . .	Θά ἤθελα . . .	thah **ee**thehlah

I'd like some asparagus.	Θὰ ἤθελα σπαράγγια.	thah **ee**thehlah spah**rahng**geeah
green beans	φασόλια φρέσκα	fah**ss**oleeah **freh**skah
mushrooms	μανιτάρια	mahnee**tah**reeah
carrots	καρόττα	kah**rot**ah
onions	κρεμμύδια	kreh**mee**dheeah
red cabbage	κόκκινο λάχανο	**ko**keeno **lah**khahno
spinach	σπανάκι	spah**nah**kee
rice	ρύζι	**ree**zee
peas	μπιζέλια	bee**zeh**leeah
tomatoes	τομάτες	toh**mah**tehss
green salad	πράσινη σαλάτα	**prah**sseenee sahlahtah
potatoes	πατάτες	pah**tah**tehss

Desserts

Nothing more, thanks.	Τίποτε ἄλλο, εὐχαριστῶ.	**tee**poteh **ah**lo ehfkhahree**sto**
Just a small portion, please.	Μία μικρή μερίδα, παρακαλῶ.	**mee**ah meek**ree** meh**ree**dhah pahrahkah**lo**
Have you any ice-cream?	Ἔχετε παγωτά;	**eh**khehteh pah**ġo**tah
fruit salad	φρουτοσαλάτα	frootossah**lah**tah
fresh fruit	φρέσκα φροῦτα	**freh**skah **froo**tah
cheese	τυρί	tee**ree**

Drink

What would you like to drink?	Τί θὰ θέλατε νά πιῆτε;	tee thah **thehl**ahteh nah pee**ee**eteh
I'll have a beer, please.	Θὰ πάρω μία μπύρα, παρακαλῶ.	thah **pah**ro **mee**ah **beer**ah pahrahkah**lo**
I'll have a whisky, please.	Θά πάρω ἕνα οὐΐσκυ, παρακαλῶ.	thah **pah**ro eh**nah** ooee**skee** pahrahkah**lo**

Wine

I'd like a bottle of wine.	Θὰ ἤθελα ἕνα μπουκάλι κρασί.	thah **ee**thehlah eh**nah** boo**kah**lee krah**ssee**
red wine	κόκκινο κρασί	**ko**keeno krah**ssee**
rosé wine	ρόζέ κρασί	**ro**zeh krah**ssee**
white wine	ἄσπρο κρασί	**ah**spro krah**ssee**
Cheers!	Στὴν ὑγειά σας!	steen eeyee**ah** sahss

The bill (check)

May I have the bill (check) please?	Μπορῶ νά ἔχω τό λογαριασμό, παρακαλῶ;	boro nah ehkho to loğahreeahzmo pahrahkahlo
Is service included?	Τό φιλοδώρημα περιλαμβάνεται;	to feelodhoreemah pehreelahmvahnehteh
Everything's included.	῞Ολα περιλαμβάνονται.	olah pehreelahmvahnondheh
Thank you, that was a very good meal.	Εὐχαριστῶ, τό γεῦμα ἦταν πολύ καλό.	ehfkhahreesto to yehvmah eetahn polee kahlo

Travelling

Where's the railway station, please?	Ποῦ εἶναι ὁ σιδηροδρομικός σταθμός, παρακαλῶ;	poo eeneh o seedheerodhromeekoss stahthmoss pahrahkahlo
Where's the ticket office, please?	Ποῦ εἶναι τό γραφεῖο ἐκδόσεως εἰσιτηρίων, παρακαλῶ;	poo eeneh to ğrahfeeo ehkdhossehoss eesseeteereeon pahrahkahlo
I'd like a ticket to ...	Θά ἤθελα ενα εἰσιτήριο γιά ...	thah eethehlah ehnah eesseeteereeoyeeah
First or second class?	Πρώτη ἢ δευτέρα θέση;	protee ee dhehftehrah thehssee
First class, please.	Πρώτη θέση, παρακαλῶ.	protee thehssee pahrahkahlo
Single or return (one way or round-trip)?	᾿Απλῆ διαδρομή ἢ μετ᾿ἐπιστροφῆς;	ahplee dheeahdhromee ee mehtehpeestrofeess
Do I have to change trains?	Πρέπει νά ἀλλάξω τραῖνο;	prehpee nah ahlahkso trehno
What platform does the train leave from?	᾿Από ποιά ἀποβάθρα φεύγει τό τραῖνο;	ahpo peeah ahpovahthrah fehvyee to trehno
Where's the nearest underground (sub-way) station?	Ποῦ εἶναι ὁ πλησιέστερος σταθμός τοῦ ᾿Ηλεκτρικοῦ;	poo eeneh o pleesseeeehstehross stathmoss too eelehktreekoo
Where's the bus station, please?	Ποῦ εἶναι ο σταθμός τῶν λεωφορείων παρακαλῶ;	poo eeneh o stathmoss ton lehoforeeon pahrahkahlo

When's the first bus to . . . ?	Πότε είναι τό πρῶτο λεωφορεῖο γιά . . . ;	poteh eeneh to proto lehoforeeo yeeah
the last bus	τό τελευταῖο λεωφορεῖο	to tehlehfteho lehoforeeo
the next bus	τό ἐπόμενο λεωφορεῖο	to ehpomehno lehoforeeo
Please let me off at the next stop.	Παρακαλῶ, θέλω νά κατεβῶ στήν ἐπομένη στάση.	pahrahkahlo thehlo nah kahtehvo steen ehpomehnee stahssee

Relaxing

What's on at the cinema (movies)?	Τί παίζουν στόν κινηματογράφο;	tee pehzoon ston keeneemahtoġrahfo
What's on at the theatre?	Τί παίζουν στό θέατρο;	tee pehzoon sto thehahtro
What time does the film begin? And the play?	Τί ὥρα ἀρχίζει τό φίλμ; Καί τό ἔργο;	tee orah ahrkheezee to feelm? keh to ehrġo
Are there any tickets for tonight?	Ὑπάρχουν εἰσητήρια γι'ἀπόψε;	eepahrkhoon eessee-teereeah yeeahpopseh
Where can we go dancing?	Ποῦ μποροῦμε νά πᾶμε νά χορέψουμε;	poo boroomeh nah pahmeh nah khorehpsoomeh
Would you like to dance?	Θά θέλατε νά χορέψετε;	thah thehlahteh nah khorehpsehteh

Introductions

How do you do?	Πῶς εἶσθε;	poss eestheh
How are you?	Τί κάνετε;	tee kahnehteh
Very well, thank you. And you?	Πολύ καλά, εὐχαριστῶ. Καί ἐσεῖς;	polee kahlah ehfkhahreesto. keh ehsseess
May I introduce Miss Philips?	Μπορῶ νά σᾶς συστήσω τή δεσποινίδα Φίλιπς;	boro nah sahss seesteesso tee dhehspeeneedhah Philips
My name is . . .	Ὀνομάζομαι . . .	onomahzomeh
I'm very pleased to meet you.	Χαίρω πολύ πού σᾶς γνωρίζω.	khehro polee poo sahss gnoreezo
How long have you been here?	Πόσο καιρό εἶσθε ἐδῶ;	poso kehro eestheh ehdho
It was nice meeting you.	Χάρηκα πού σᾶς γνώρισα.	khahreekah poo sahss gnoreessah

Dating

Would you like a cigarette?	Θά θέλατε ἕνα τσιγάρο;	thah **thehl**ahteh **eh**nah tsee**gah**ró
May I get you a drink?	Μπορῶ νά σᾶς φέρω ἕνα ποτό;	boro nah sahss **feh**ro **eh**nah poto
Do you have a light, please?	῎Εχετε φωτιά, παρακαλῶ;	**eh**khehteh foteeah pahrahkahlo
Are you waiting for someone?	Περιμένετε κάποιον;	pehree**meh**nehteh **kah**peeon
Are you free this evening?	Εἶσθε ἐλεύθερη ἀπόψε;	**ees**theh ehl**ehf**thehree ah**pop**seh
Where shall we meet?	Ποῦ θά συναντηθοῦμε;	poo thah seenahndee**thoo**meh
What time shall I meet you?	Τί ὥρα θά σᾶς συναντήσω;	tee **o**rah thah sahss seenahn**dees**so
May I take you home?	Μπορῶ νά σᾶς πάω στό σπίτι σας;	boro nah sahss **pah**o sto **spee**tee sahss
Thank you, it's been a wonderful evening.	Εὐχαριστῶ, ἦταν μία ὑπέροχη βραδυά.	ehfkhahr**ees**to **ee**tahn **mee**ah eepeh**ro**khee vrahdhee**ah**
What's your telephone number?	Ποιός εἶναι ὁ ἀριθμός τοῦ τηλεφώνου σας;	pee**oss** **ee**neh o ahreeth**moss** too teelehfo**no**o sahss
Do you live alone?	Μένετε μόνη σας;	**meh**nehteh **mo**nee sahss
What time is your last train?	Τί ὥρα εἶναι τό τελευταῖο τραῖνο σας;	tee **o**rah **ee**neh to tehl**ehf**teho **treh**no sahss
Good-night...	Καληνύκτα...	kahlee**neek**tah

Banks

Where's the nearest bank, please?	Ποῦ εἶναι ἡ πλησιέστερη τράπεζα, παρακαλῶ;	poo **ee**neh ee pleesee**eh**stehre **trah**pehzah pahrahkahlo
Where can I cash some traveller's cheques?	Ποῦ μπορῶ νά ἐξαργυρώσω μερικά τράβελερς τσέκ;	poo boro nah ehksahryee**ross**o mehree**kah** **trah**vehlehrs tsehk
What time does the bank open? What time does it close?	Τί ὥρα ἀνοίγει ἡ τράπεζα; Τί ὥρα κλείνει;	tee **o**rah ah**nee**yee ee **trah**pehzah? tee **o**rah **klee**nee

| I'm expecting some money from home. Has it arrived? | Περιμένω χρήματα ἀπό τό σπίτι. Μήπως ἦλθαν; | pehreemehno khreemahtah ahpo to speetee. meeposs eelthahn |
| Can you give me some small change, please? | Μπορεῖτε νά μοῦ δώσετε μερικά κέρματα, παρακαλῶ; | boreeteh nah moo dhossehteh mehreekah kehrmahtah pahrahkahlo |

Shops, stores and services

Where is the nearest chemist's (pharmacy)?	Ποῦ εἶναι τό πλησιέστερο φαρμακεῖο;	poo eeneh to pleesseeehstehro fahrmahkeeo
the nearest hairdresser's	τό πλησιέστερο κουρεῖο	to pleesseeehstehro kooreeo
the photo shop	τό φωτογραφεῖο	to fotograhfeeo
the jeweller's	τό κοσμηματοπωλεῖο	to kozmeemahtopoleeo
the department store	τό ἐμπορικό κατάστημα	to ehmboreeko kahtahsteemah
the police station	τό ἀστυνομικό τμῆμα	to ahsteenomeeko tmeemah
the garage	τό γκαράζ	to gahrahz
How do I get there?	Πῶς νά πάω ἐκεῖ;	poss nah paho ehkee
Is it within walking distance?	Μπορῶ νά πάω μέ τά πόδια;	boro nah paho meh tah podheeah

Service

Can you help me, please?	Μπορεῖτε νά μέ βοηθήσετε, παρακαλῶ;	boreeteh nah meh voeetheessehteh pahrahkahlo
Can you show me this? And that, too.	Μπορεῖτε νά μοῦ δείξετε αὐτό; Καί ἐκεῖνο ἐπίσης.	boreeteh nah moo dheeksehteh ahfto? keh ehkeeno ehpeesseess
It's too expensive/ too big/too small.	Εἶναι πολύ ἀκριβό/ πολύ μεγάλο/ πολύ μικρό.	eeneh poleeahkreevo/polee mehgahlo/ polee meekro
Can you show me some more?	Μπορεῖτε νά μοῦ δείξετε περισσότερα;	boreeteh nah moo dheeksehteh pehreessotehrah
something better	κάτι καλύτερο	kahtee kahleetehro
something cheaper	κάτι φθηνότερο	kahtee ftheenotehro

How much is this? And that?	Πόσο κοστίζει αὐτό; Καί ἐκεῖνο;	posso kosteezee ahfto? keh ehkeeno
It's not quite what I want.	Δέν εἶναι ἀκριβῶς αὐτό πού θέλω.	dhehn eeneh ahkreevoss ahfto poo thehlo
I like it.	Μοῦ ἀρέσει.	moo ahrehsee

Chemist's (Pharmacy)

| I'd like something for a cold/for a cough/for travel sickness. | Θά ἤθελα κάτι γιά τό κρύωμα/γιά τό βῆχα/γιά τή ναυτία. | thah eethehlah kahtee yeeah to kreeomah/yeeah to veekhah/yeeah tee nahfteeah |
| Can you recommend something for hay-fever/for sunburn? | Μπορεῖτε νά μοῦ συστήσετε κάτι γιά τόν ὑψηλό πυρετό/γιά τά ἐγκαύματα τοῦ ἡλίου; | boreeteh nah moo seesteessehteh kahtee yeeah ton eepseelo peerehto/ yeeah tah ehnggahvmahtah too eeleeoo |

Toiletry

May I have some razor blades?	Μπορῶ νά ἔχω μερικά ξυραφάκια ξυρίσματος;	boro nah ehkho mehreekah kseerahfahkeeah kseereezmahtoss
some shaving cream	κρέμα ξυρίσματος	krehmah kseereezmahtoss
some toothpaste	ὁδοντόπαστα	odhondopahstah
I'd like some soap.	Θά ἤθελα ἕνα σαπούνι.	thah eethehlah ehnah sahpoonee
some suntan oil	λάδι ἡλίου	lahdhee eeleeoo

At the barber's

I'd like a haircut, please.	Θά ἤθελα νά μοῦ κόψετε τά μαλλιά παρακαλῶ.	thah eethehlah nah moo kopsehteh tah mahleeah pahrahkahlo
Short/Leave it long.	Κοντά/'Αφῆστε τα μακρυά.	kondah/ahfeesteh tah mahkreeah
A razor cut, please.	Κόφιμο μέ ξυράφι, παρακαλῶ.	kopseemo meh kseerahfee pahrahkahlo

At the hairdresser's

| I'd like a shampoo and set, please. | Θά ἤθελα λούσιμο καί μίζ-αν-πλί, παρακαλῶ. | thaht eethehlah looseemo keh meezahnplee pahrahkahlo |

I'd like a bleach.	Θά ἤθελα μία ντεκολορασιόν.	thah eethehlah meeah dehkolorahseeon
a permanent	μία περμανάντ	meeah pehrmahnahnd
a colour rinse	ἕνα ντεκαπάζ	ehnah dehkahpahz
a manicure	μανικιούρ	mahneekeeoor

Photography

I'd like a film for this camera.	Θά ἤθελα ἕνα φίλμ γι'αὐτή τή μηχανή.	thah eethehlah ehnah feelm yeeahftee tee meekhahnee
This camera doesn't work.	Αὐτή ἡ μηχανή δέν δουλεύει.	ahftee ee meekhahnee dhehn dhoolehvee

At the post office

Where's the nearest post office, please?	Ποῦ εἶναι τό πλησιέστερο ταχυδρομεῖο, παρακαλῶ;	poo eeneh to pleesseeehstehro tahkhee-dhromeeo pahrahkahlo
I'd like to send this by express (special delivery)/by air mail.	Θά ἤθελα νά στείλω αὐτό ἐξπρές/ἀεροπορικῶς.	thah eethehlah nah steelo ahfto ehksprehss/ ahehroporeekoss

Service stations

Where is the nearest service station, please?	Ποῦ εἶναι τό πλησιέστερο πρατήριο βενζίνης, παρακαλῶ;	poo eeneh to pleesseeehstehro prahtee-reeo vehnzeeneess pahrahkahlo
Fill her up, please.	Νά τό γεμίσετε, παρακαλῶ.	nah to yehmeessehteh pahrahkahlo
Check the oil, please.	Ἐλέγξατε τό λάδι, παρακαλῶ.	ehlehnksahteh to lahdhee pahrahkahlo
Would you check the tyres?	Θά μπορούσατε νά ἐλέγξετε τά λάστιχα;	thah boroossahteh nah ehlehnksehteh tah lahsteekhah

Street directions

Can you show me on the map where I am?	Μπορεῖτε νά μοῦ δείξετε στό χάρτη ποῦ εἶμαι;	boreeteh nah moo dheeksehteh sto khahrtee poo eemeh
You're on the wrong road.	Ἔχετε πάρει λάθος δρόμο.	ehkhehteh pahree lahthoss dhromo

133

Go back to . . .	Γυρίστε πίσω στό . . .	yee**ree**steh **pee**sso sto
Go straight ahead.	Νά πᾶτε εὐθεία.	nah **pah**teh ehf**thee**ah
It's on the left/on the right.	Εἶναι ἀριστερά/ δεξιά.	**ee**neh ahreesteh**rah**/ dhehksee**ah**

Accidents

May I use your telephone?	Μπορῶ νά χρησιμοποιήσω τό τηλέφωνό σας;	boro nah khreesseemopee**ee**sso to teel**eh**fono sahss
Call a doctor quickly.	Καλέστε ἕνα γιατρό γρήγορα.	kah**leh**steh **eh**nah yeea**tro** gree**go**rah
Call an ambulance.	Καλέστε ἕνα ἀσθενοφόρο.	kah**leh**steh **eh**nah ahsthehno**fo**ro
Please call the police.	Παρακαλῶ καλέστε τήν ἀστυνομία.	pahrahkah**lo** kah**leh**steh teen ahsteeno**mee**ah

Numbers

one	ἕνα	**eh**nah
two	δύο	**dhee**o
three	τρία	**tree**ah
four	τέσσερα	**teh**sehrah
five	πέντε	**pehn**deh
six	ἕξη	**eh**ksee
seven	ἑπτά	ehp**tah**
eight	ὀκτώ	o**kto**
nine	ἐννέα	eh**neh**ah
ten	δέκα	**dheh**kah
eleven	ἕντεκα	**ehn**dehkah
twelve	δώδεκα	**dho**dhehkah
thirteen	δεκατρία	dhehkah**tree**ah
fourteen	δεκατέσσερα	dhehkah**teh**sehrah
fifteen	δεκαπέντε	dhehkah**pehn**deh
sixteen	δεκαέξη	dhehkah**eh**ksee
seventeen	δεκαεπτά	dhehkaehp**tah**
eighteen	δεκαοκτώ	dhehkaho**kto**
nineteen	δεκαεννέα	dhehkaeh**neh**ah
twenty	εἴκοσι	**ee**kossee
twenty-one	εἴκοσι ἕνα	**ee**kossee **eh**nah
thirty	τριάντα	tree**ahn**dah
forty	σαράντα	shah**rahn**dah
fifty	πενήντα	peh**neen**dah
sixty	ἑξῆντα	ee**kseen**dah
seventy	ἑβδομῆντα	ehvdho**meen**dah

eighty	ὀγδόντα	oĝdhondah
ninety	ἐνενήντα	ehnehneendah
one hundred	ἑκατό	ehkahto
one thousand	χίλια	kheeleeah
ten thousand	δέκα χιλιάδες	dhehkah kheeleeahdhehss

Days

It's Sunday.	Εἶναι Κυριακή.	eeneh keereeahkee
Monday	Δευτέρα	dhehftehrah
Tuesday	Τρίτη	treetee
Wednesday	Τετάρτη	tertahrtee
Thursday	Πέμπτη	pehmptee
Friday	Παρασκευή	pahrahskehvee
Saturday	Σάββατο	shavahto
yesterday	χθές	khthehss
today	σήμερα	seemehrah
tomorrow	αὔριο	ahvreeo
morning/afternoon	πρωΐ/ἀπόγευμα	proee/ahpoyehvmah
evening/night	βράδυ/νύκτα	vrahdhee/neektah

Months

January	Ἰανουάριος	eeahnooahreeoss
February	Φεβρουάριος	fehvrooahreeoss
March	Μάρτιος	mahrteeoss
April	Ἀπρίλιος	ahpreeleeoss
May	Μάϊος	maheeoss
June	Ἰούνιος	eeooneeoss
July	Ἰούλιος	eeooleeoss
August	Αὔγουστος	ahvgoostoss
September	Σεπτέμβριος	sehptehmvreeoss
October	Ὀκτώβριος	oktovreeoss
November	Νοέμβριος	noehmvreeoss
December	Δεκέμβριος	dhehkehmvreeoss
Merry Christmas!	Καλά Χριστούγεννα.	kahlah khreestooyehnah
Happy New Year!	Εὐτυχισμένος ὁ καινούργιος χρόνος.	ehfteekheezmehnoss o kehnooryeeoss khronoss

ITALIAN

Guide to Pronunciation

Letter	Approximate pronunciation	Symbol	Example	
Consonants				
b, d, f, k, l, m, n, p, q, t, v	are pronounced as in English			
c	1) before **e** and **i**, like **ch** in **ch**ip	ch	**cerco**	**chayr**koa
	2) elsewhere, like **c** in **c**at	k	**conto**	**koan**toa
ch	like **c** in **c**at	k	**che**	kay
g	1) before **e** and **i**, like **j** in **j**et	j	**leggero**	layd**jair**oa
	2) elsewhere, like **g** in **g**o	g	**grande**	**grahn**day
gh	like **g** in **g**o	g	**ghiaccio**	geeaht**chee**oa
gl	like **lli** in million	ly	**gli**	lyee
gn	like **ni** in onion	ñ	**bagno**	**bar**ñoa
h	always silent		**ha**	ah

r	trilled like a Scottish r	r	**caro**	**kar**roa
s	1) generally like **s** in s**i**t	s/ss	**casa**	**kar**ssah
			questo	koo**ay**stoa
	2) sometimes like **z** in z**oo**	z	**viso**	**vee**zoa
sc	1) before **e**, **i**, like **sh** in **sh**ut	sh	**uscita**	oo**shee**tah
	2) elsewhere, like **sk** in **sk**in	sk	**scarpa**	**skahr**pah
z or zz	1) generally like **ts** in hi**ts**	ts	**grazie**	**graht**seeay
	2) sometimes like **ds** in roa**ds**	dz	**romanzo**	roa**mahnd**zoa

Vowels

a	1) short, like **a** in c**a**r, but shorter	ah	**gatto**	**gaht**toa
	2) long, like **a** in c**a**r	ar	**casa**	**kar**ssah
e	1) can always be pronounced like **ay** in g**ay**	ay	**sera**	**say**rah
	2) in correct speech, it is sometimes pronounced like **e** in g**e**t or, when long, more like **ai** in h**ai**r	eh	**bello**	**beh**lloa
		ai	**bene**	**bai**nay
i	like the **ee** in m**ee**t	ee	**vini**	**vee**nee
o	1) can always be pronounced like **oa** in g**oa**t	oa	**sole**	**soa**lay
	2) in correct speech, it is sometimes pronounced like **o** in g**o**t, or when long, more like **aw** in l**aw**	o	**notte**	**not**tay
		aw	**rosa**	**raw**zah
u	like the **oo** in f**oo**t	oo	**fumo**	**foo**moa

Two or more vowels

In groups of vowels, **a**, **e**, and **o** are strong vowels, and **i** and **u** are weak vowels. When two strong vowels are next to each other, they are pronounced as two separate syllables, e.g., *beato* = bay**ah**toa. When a strong and weak vowel are next to each other, the weak one is pronounced more quickly and with less stress (less loudly) than the strong one, e.g., *piede* = pee**ay**day; such sounds are diphthongs and constitute only one syllable. If the weak vowel is stressed, then it is pronounced as a separate syllable, e.g., *due* = **doo**ay. Two weak vowels together are pronounced as a diphthong, and it is generally the second one that is more strongly stressed, e.g., *guida* = goo**ee**dah.

Stressing of words

Generally, the vowel of the next to the last syllable is stressed. When a final vowel is stressed, it has an accent written over it (´ or `). Normally an accent is used only when the stress falls on a final vowel, and not when it falls on syllables before the next to the last one.

ITALIAN

Some basic expressions

Yes.	**Si.**	see
No.	**No.**	no
Please.	**Per favore.**	pair fah**vo**aray
Thank you.	**Grazie.**	**grah**tseeay
Thank you very much.	**Mille grazie.**	**meel**lay **grah**tseeay
That's all right.	**Prego.**	**pray**goa

Greetings

Good morning.	**Bongiorno.**	boan**joar**noa
Good afternoon.	**Bongiorno.**	boan**joar**noa
Good evening.	**Buona sera.**	boo**awn**ah **say**rah
Good night.	**Buona notte.**	boo**awn**ah **not**tay
Good-bye.	**Arrivederci.**	ahreevay**dair**chee
See you later.	**A più tardi.**	a pyoo **tahr**dee
This is Mr....	**Questo è il signor ...**	koo**ayss**toa ay eel see**ñor**
This is Mrs....	**Questa è la signora ...**	koo**ayss**tah ay lah see**ñoar**ah
This is Miss ...	**Questa è la signorina ...**	koo**ayss**tah ay lah see**ñoaree**nah
I'm very pleased to meet you.	**Piacere.**	peeah**chay**ray
How are you?	**Come sta?**	**koa**may stah
Very well, thank you.	**Molto bene. Grazie.**	**moal**toa **bai**nay. **grah**tseeay
And you?	**E lei?**	ay **la**iee
Fine.	**Bene.**	**bai**nay
Excuse me.	**Mi scusi.**	mee **skoo**zee

Questions

Where?	**Dove?**	**doa**vay
Where is...?	**Dov'è...?**	**doa**vai
Where are...?	**Dove sono...?**	**doa**vay **soa**noa

ITALIAN

ITALIAN

When?	Quando?	kwahndoa
What?	Cosa?	kawssah
How?	Come?	koamay
How much?	Quanto?	kwahntoa
How many?	Quanti?	kwahntee
Who?	Chi?	kee
Why?	Perchè?	pehrkay
Which?	Quale?	kwarlay
What do you call this?	Come si chiama questo?	koamay see keearmah kooaysstoa
What do you call that?	Come si chiama quello?	koamay see keearmah kooaylloa
What does this mean?	Cosa significa questo?	kawssah seeñeefeekah kooaystoa
What does that mean?	Cosa significa quello?	kawssah seeñeefeekah kooaylloa

Do you speak ... ?

Do you speak English?	Parla inglese?	pahrlah eengglayssay
Do you speak German?	Parla tedesco?	pahrlah taydayskoa
Do you speak French?	Parla francese?	pahrlah frahnchayzay
Do you speak Spanish?	Parla spagnolo?	pahrlah spahñoaloa
Do you speak Italian?	Parla italiano?	pahrlah eetahlyarnoa
Could you speak more slowly, please?	Può parlare più adagio, per piacere?	pwo pahrlarray peeoo ahdarjoa pair peeah-chayray
Please point to the phrase in the book.	Per favore, mi indichi la frase nel libro.	pair fahvoaray mee eendeekee lah frarzay nehl leebroa
Just a minute. I'll see if I can find it in this book.	Un momento. Vedo se posso trovarla nel libro.	oon moamayntoa. vaydoa say posssoa troavarrlah nayl leebroa
I understand.	Capisco.	kahpeesskoa
I don't understand.	Non capisco.	noan kahpeesskao

Can...?

Can I have...?	**Posso avere...?**	poss soa ahvayray
Can we have...?	**Possiamo avere...?**	possseearmoa ahvayray
Can you show me...?	**Può indicarmi...?**	pwo eendeekarrmee
Can you tell me...?	**Può dirmi...?**	pwo deermee
Can you help me, please?	**Può aiutarmi, per piacere?**	pwo ighootarrmee pair peeahchayray

Wanting

I'd like...	**Vorrei...**	vorraiee
We'd like...	**Vorremmo...**	vorrehmmoa
Please give me...	**Per favore, mi dia...**	pair fahvoaray mee deeah
Give it to me, please.	**Me lo dia, per favore.**	may loa deeah pair fahvoaray
Please bring me...	**Per favore, mi porti...**	pair fahvoaray mee portee
Bring it to me, please.	**Me lo porti, per favore.**	may loa portee pair fahvoaray
I'm hungry.	**Ho fame.**	oa farmay
I'm thirsty.	**Ho sete.**	oa saytay
I'm tired.	**Sono stanco.**	soanoa stahngkoa
I'm lost.	**Mi sono perso.**	mee soanoa pehrsoa
It's important.	**È importante.**	ay eemportahntay
It's urgent.	**È urgente.**	ay oorjehntay
Hurry up!	**Si affretti!**	see ahffrayttee

It is/There is...

It is/It's...	**È...**	ai
Is it...?	**È...?**	ai
It isn't...	**Non è...**	noan ai
There is/There are...	**C'è/Ci sono...**	chai/chee soanoa
Is there/Are there...?	**C'è/Ci sono...?**	chai/chee soanoa

ITALIAN

| There isn't/There aren't... | **Non c'è/Non ci sono...** | noan chai/noan chee soanoa |
| There isn't any/There aren't any. | **Non ce n'è/Non ce ne sono.** | noan chay nai/noan chay nay soanoa |

A few common words

big/small	**grande/piccolo**	grahnday/peekkoaloa
quick/slow	**rapido/lento**	rarpeedoa/lehntoa
early/late	**presto/tardi**	prehsstoa/tahrdee
cheap/expensive	**economico/costoso**	aykoanomeekoa/kosstoasoa
near/far	**vicino/lontano**	veecheenoa/lontarnoa
hot/cold	**caldo/freddo**	kahldoa/frayddoa
full/empty	**pieno/vuoto**	peeaynoa/vooawtoa
easy/difficult	**facile/difficile**	farcheelay/deefeecheelay
heavy/light	**pesante/leggero**	paysahntay/laydjairoa
open/shut	**aperto/chiuso**	ahpehrtoa/keeoossoa
right/wrong	**giusto/sbagliato**	joosstoa/zbahlyartoa
old/new	**vecchio/nuovo**	vehkkeeoa/nooawvoa
old/young	**vecchio/giovane**	vehkkeeoa/joavahnay
beautiful/ugly	**bello/brutto**	behlloa/broottoa
good/bad	**buono/cattivo**	booawnoa/kahtteevoa
better/worse	**migliore/peggiore**	meelyoaray/paydjoaray

Some prepositions and a few more useful words

at	**a**	ah
on	**sopra**	soaprah
in	**in**	een
to	**a**	ah
from	**da**	dah
inside	**dentro**	dayntroa
outside	**fuori**	fooawree
up	**sù**	soo
down	**giù**	joo
before	**prima di**	preemah dee
after	**dopo di**	dawpoa dee
with	**con**	kon
without	**senza**	sayntsah
through	**attraverso**	ahttrahvehrsoa
towards	**verso**	vehrsoa
until	**fino a**	feenoa
during	**durante**	doorahntay
and	**e**	ay
or	**o**	oa
not	**non**	noan
nothing	**niente**	neeehntay
none	**nessuno**	naysssoonoa

ITALIAN

very	**molto**	**moal**toa
also	**anche**	**ahng**kay
soon	**presto**	**prehss**toa
perhaps	**forse**	**for**say
here	**qui**	koo**ee**
there	**là**	lah
now	**ora**	**oa**rah
then	**poi**	poy

Arrival

Your passport, please.	**Il passaporto, per favore.**	eel pahsssah**por**toa pair fah**voa**ray
Here it is.	**Eccolo.**	**ehk**koaloa
Have you anything to declare?	**Ha qualcosa da dichiarare?**	ah kwahl**kaw**ssah dah deekeeah**rar**ray
No, nothing at all.	**No. Non ho nulla.**	noa noan oa **noo**llah
Porter!	**Facchino!**	fahk**kee**noa
Can you help me with my luggage, please?	**Può prendere le mie valige, per favore?**	pwo **prehn**dayray lay **mee**ay vah**lee**jay pair fah**voa**ray
That's my suitcase.	**Quella è la mia valigia.**	koo**ay**llah ai lah **mee**ah vah**lee**jah
Where's the bus to the centre of town, please?	**Dov'è l'autobus per il centro della città, per favore?**	doa**vai** lowtoa**booss** pair eel **chehn**troa **day**llah cheet**tah** pair fah**voa**ray
This way, please.	**Da questa parte, per piacere.**	dah koo**ayss**tah **pahr**tay pair peeah**chay**ray

Changing money

Can you change a traveller's cheque, please?	**Può cambiarmi un traveller's cheque, per favore?**	pwo kahmbee
arrmee oon ''traveller's cheque'' pair fah**voa**ray
Where's the nearest bank, please?	**Dov'è la banca più vicina, per favore?**	doa**vai** lah **bahng**kah pee**oo** vee**chee**nah pair fah**voa**ray

Car rental

I'd like a car.	**Vorrei un'automobile.**	vor**rai**ee oon owtoa**maw**beelay
For how long?	**Per quanto tempo?**	pair koo**ahn**toa **tehm**poa
A day/Four days/ A week/Two weeks.	**Un giorno/Quattro giorni/Una settimana/Due settimane.**	oon **joar**noa/koo**ahtt**roa **joar**nee/**oo**nah sayteemar-nah/**doo**ay saytteemar**nay**

ITALIAN

Taxi

Where can I get a taxi?	Dove posso trovare un tassi?	doavay posssoa troavarray oon tahsssee
What's the fare to...?	Quanto costa la corsa per...?	kwahntoa kosstah lah korsah pair
Take me to this address, please.	Mi porti a questo indirizzo, per favore.	mee portee ah kooaysstoa eendeereettsoa pair fahvoaray
I'm in a hurry.	Ho fretta.	oa frayttah
Could you drive more slowly, please?	Può guidare più adagio, per favore?	pwo gooeedarray peeoo ahdarjoa pair fahvoaray

Hotel and other accommodation

My name is...	Mi chiamo...	mee keearmoa
Have you a reservation?	Ha fatto la prenotazione?	ah fahttoa lah praynoatahtseeoanay
Yes, here's the confirmation.	Sì; ecco la conferma.	see ehkkoa lah konfehrmah
I'd like...	Vorrei...	vorraiee
I'd like a single room/a double room.	Vorrei una camera singola/per due persone.	vorraiee oonah karmayrah seenggoalah/pair dooay payrsoanay
a room with a bath/ with a shower	una camera con bagno/con doccia	oonah karmayrah kon barñoa/kon dotchah

How much?

What's the price per night/per week/per month?	Qual è il prezzo per una notte/per una settimana/per un mese?	kwahlai eel prehttsoa pair oonah nottay/pair oonah saytteemarnah/pair oon mayssay
May I see the room?	Posso vedere la camera?	posssoa vaydayray lah karmayrah
I'm sorry, I don't like it.	Mi dispiace: non è di mio gradimento.	mee despeearchay noan ai dee meeoa grahdeemayntoa
Yes, that's fine. I'll take it.	Sì, va bene. La prendo.	see vah bainay lah prayndoa
What's my room number, please?	Qual è il numero della mia camera?	kwahlai eel noomayroa dayllah meeah karmayrah
Number 123.	Numero 123.	noomayroa 123

Service, please

Who is it?	**Chi è?**	kee ai
Just a minute.	**Un momento, per favore.**	oon moamayntoa pair fahvoaray
Come in! The door's open.	**Avanti! La porta è aperta.**	ahvahntee lah portah ai ahpehrtah
May we have breakfast in our room?	**Possiamo fare la prima colazione in camera?**	posssearmoa farray lah preemah koalahtseeoanay een karmayran

Breakfast

I'll have . . .	**Vorrei . . .**	vorraiee
I'll have some fruit juice.	**Vorrei un succo di frutta.**	vorraiee oon sookkoa dee froottah
a boiled egg	**un uovo alla "coque"**	oon ooawvoa ahllah kok
a fried egg	**un uovo al tegame**	oon ooawvoa ahl taygarmay
some bacon/some ham	**della pancetta affumicata/del prosciutto**	dayllah pahnchehttah ahffoomeekartah/dayl proashoottoa
some toast	**del pane tostato**	dayl parnay toasstartoa
a pot of tea	**del té**	dayl tay
a cup of tea	**una tazza di té**	oonah tahttsah dee tay
some coffee	**del caffé**	dayl kahffay
some chocolate	**della cioccolata**	dayllah choakkoalartah
more butter	**un altro po'di burro**	oon ahltroa po dee boorroa
some hot water	**dell'acqua calda**	daylahkkooah kahldah

Difficulties

The central heating doesn't work.	**Il riscaldamento centrale non funziona.**	eel reesskahldahmayntoa chayntrarlay noan foontseeoanah
the light/the socket the tap/the toilet	**la luce/la presa il rubinetto/il gabinetto**	lah loochay/lah praysah eel roobeenayttoa/eel gahbeenayttoa
There's no hot water.	**Non c'è acqua calda.**	noan chai ahkkooah kahldah
May I see the manager, please?	**Posso vedere il direttore, per piacere?**	posssoa vaydayray eel deerayttoaray pair peeahchayray

ITALIAN

Telephone—Mail

There's a call for you.	C'è una telefonata per lei.	chai oonah taylayfoanartah pair laiee
Hold the line, please.	Resti in linea, per piacere.	rehsstee een leenayah pair peeahchayray
Operator, I've been cut off.	Signorina, mi hanno interrotto.	seeñoareenah mee ahnnoa eentehrrottoa
Did anyone telephone me?	Mi ha telefonato qualcuno?	mee ah taylayfoanartoa kwahlkoonoa
Is there any mail for me?	C'è posta per me?	chai posstah pair may
Are there any messages for me?	Ci sono comunicazioni per me?	chee soanoa komoonee-kahtseeoanee pair may

Checking out

May I have my bill, please?	Posso avere il mio conto, per favore?	posssoa ahvayray eel meeoa koantoa pair fahvoaray
We're in a great hurry.	Abbiamo molta fretta.	ahbbeearmoa moaltah frayttah
It's been a very enjoyable stay.	È stato un soggiorno molto piacevole.	ai startoa oon soadjoarnoa moaltoa peeahchayvoalay

Eating out

Good evening, sir/ Good evening, madam.	Buona sera, signore/Buona sera, signora.	booawnah sayrah seeñoaray/booawnah sayrah seeñoarrah
Good evening. I'd like a table for two, please.	Buona sera. Vorrei una tavola per due, per favore.	booawnah sayrah. vorraiee oonah tarvoalah pair dooay pair fahvoaray
Do you have a fixed-price menu?	Avete un menu a prezzo fisso?	ahvaytay oon maynoo ah prehttsoa feesssoa
May I see the à la carte menu?	Posso vedere il menu a scelta?	posssoa vaydayray eel maynoo ah shayltah
May we have an ashtray, please?	Posso avere un portacenere, per favore?	posssoa ahvayray oon portahchaynayray pair fahvoaray
some bread	un po' di pane	oon po dee parnay
a fork	una forchetta	oonah forkehttah
a knife	un coltello	oon koalltehlloa

ITALIAN

a spoon	un cucchiaio	oon kookkeeighoa
a plate	un piatto	oon peeahttoa
a glass	un bicchiere	oon beekkeeairay
a napkin	un tovagliolo	oon toavahlyawloa
another chair	un'altra sedia	oonahltrah saideeah
Where's the gentle-men's toilet (men's room)?	Dove sono i gabinetti per uomini?	doavay soanoa ee gahbeenayttee pair ooomeenee
Where's the ladies' toilet (ladies' room)?	Dove sono i gabinetti per signore?	doavay soanoa ee gahbeenayttee pair seeñoaray

Appetizers

I'd like some . . .	Vorrei . . .	vorraiee
I'd like some assorted appetizers.	Vorrei degli antipasti assortiti.	vorraiee daylyee ahnteepahsstee ahssorteetee
orange juice	un succo d'arancia	oon sookkoa dahrahnchah
ham	del prosciutto	day proashoottoa
melon	del melone	dayl mayloanay
pâté	del pâté	dayl pahtay
smoked salmon	del salmone affu-micato	dayl sahlmoanay ahffoomeekartoa
shrimps (shrimp)	dei gamberetti	daiee gahmbayrayttee

Soup

Have you any . . . ?	Ha . . . ?	ah
Have you any chicken soup?	Ha un brodo di pollo?	ah oon brawdoa dee poalloa
vegetable soup	una minestra di verdure	oonah meenehsstrah dee vehrdooray
onion soup	una minestra di cipolle	oonah meenehsstrah dee cheepoallay

Fish

I'd like some . . .	Vorrei . . .	vorraiee
I'd like some fish.	Vorrei del pesce.	vorraiee dayl payshay
sole	della sogliola	dayllah sawlyoalah
trout	delle trote	dayllay trawtay
lobster	un'aragosta	oon ahrahgoasstah
crayfish	dei gamberi d'acqua dolce	daiee gahmbayree dahkkooah dolchay
prawns	dei gamberi	daiee gahmbayree

ITALIAN

ITALIAN

I'd like it ...	**Li vorrei ...**	lee vorraiee
I'd like it steamed.	**Li vorrei al vapore.**	lee vorraiee ahl vahpoaray
grilled	**alla griglia**	ahllah greelyah
boiled	**bolliti**	bolleetee
baked	**al forno**	ahl fornoa
fried	**fritti**	freettee

Meat—Poultry—Game

I'd like some ...	**Vorrei ...**	vorraiee
I'd like some beef.	**Vorrei del manzo.**	vorraiee dayl **mahn**dzoa
a beef steak	**una bistecca di manzo**	oonah bees**tayk**kah dee **mahn**dzoa
some roast beef	**un arrosto di manzo**	oon ahr**roas**stoa dee **mahn**dzoa
a veal cutlet	**una cotoletta di vitello**	oonah koatoa**layt**tah dee vee**teh**lloa
mutton	**del montone**	dayl moan**toa**nay
lamb	**dell'agnello**	dayl ah**ñeh**lloa
a pork chop	**una braciola di maiale**	oonah brah**choa**lah dee mi**ghar**lay
roast pork	**un arrosto di maiale**	oon ahr**ros**stoa dee mi**ghar**lay
hare	**della lepre**	**dayl**lah **lai**pray
chicken	**del pollo**	dayl **poal**loa
roast chicken	**del pollo arrosto**	dayl **poal**loa ahr**roas**stoa
duck	**dell'anatra**	dayl **ar**nahtrah
How do you like your meat?	**Come vuole la carne?**	**koa**may **voo**awlay lah **kahr**nay
rare	**al sangue**	ahl **sahn**gooay
medium	**non troppo cotta**	noan **trop**poa **kot**tah
well done	**ben cotta**	bain **kot**tah

Vegetables

What vegetables have you got?	**Quali legumi ha?**	**koo**arlee lay**goo**mee ah
I'd like some ...	**Vorrei ...**	vorraiee
I'd like some asparagus.	**Vorrei degli asparagi.**	vorraiee **dayl**yee ah**spar**rahjee
green beans	**dei fagiolini**	daiee fahjoa**lee**nee
mushrooms	**dei funghi**	daiee **foong**gee
carrots	**delle carote**	**dayl**lay kah**raw**tay
onions	**delle cipolle**	**dayl**lay chee**poal**lay
red cabbage	**dei cavoli rossi**	daiee **kah**voalee **ros**ssee

spinach	degli spinaci	daylyee speenarchee
rice	del riso	dayl reesoa
peas	dei piselli	daiee peesehllee
tomatoes	dei pomodori	daiee poamoadawree
green salad	dell'insalata	dayl eensahlartah
potatoes	delle patate	dayllay pahtartay

Desserts

Nothing more, thanks.	Nient'altro. Grazie.	neeehntahltroa grahtseeay
Just a small portion, please.	Solo una piccola porzione, per favore.	soaloa oonah peekkoalah portseeoanay pair fahvoaray
Have you any ice-cream?	Ha un gelato?	ah oon jaylartoa
fruit salad	una macedonia	oonah mahchaydawneeah
fresh fruit	della frutta fresca	dayllah froottah fraysskah
cheese	del formaggio	dayl formahdjoa

Drink

What would you like to drink?	Cosa desidera da bere?	kawssah dayzeedayrah dah bayray
I'll have a beer, please.	Mi dia una birra, per piacere.	mee deeah oonah beerrah pair peeahchayray
I'll have a whisky, please.	Mi dia un whisky, per favore.	mee deeah oon whisky (wisskee) pair fahvoaray

Wine

I'd like a bottle of wine.	Vorrei una bottiglia di vino.	vorraiee oonah botteelyah dee veenoa
red wine	di vino rosso	dee veenoa roasssoa
rosé wine	di rosé	dee roazay
white wine	di vino bianco	deeveenoa beeahngkoa
Cheers!	Salute!	sahlootay

The bill (check)

| May I have the bill (check) please? | Posso avere il mio conto, per piacere? | posssoa ahvayray eel meeoa koantoa pair peeahchayray |
| Is service included? | È compreso il servizio? | ai koampraygzoa eel sayrveetseeoa |

| Everything's included. | **Tutto compreso.** | toottoa koamprayzoa |
| Thank you, that was a very good meal. | **Grazie. Abbiamo mangiato molto bene.** | grahtseeay ahbbeearmoa mahnjartoa moaltoa bainay |

Travelling

Where's the railway station, please?	**Dove si trova la stazione, per favore?**	doavay see trawvah lah stahtseeoanay pair fahvoaray
Where's the ticket office, please?	**Dove si trova lo sportello dei biglietti, per favore?**	doavay see trawvah loa sportehlloa daiee beelyayttee pair fahvoaray
I'd like a ticket to ...	**Vorrei un biglietto per ...**	vorraiee oon beelyayttoa pair
First or second class?	**Di prima o di seconda classe?**	dee preemah oa dee saykoandah klahsssay
First class, please.	**Di prima classe, per piacere.**	dee preemah klahsssay pair peeahchayray
Single or return (one way or round-trip)?	**Andata o andata e ritorno?**	ahndartah oa ahndartah ay reetornoa
Do I have to change trains?	**Devo cambiare treno?**	dayvoa kahmbeearray traynoa
What platform does the train leave from?	**Da che binario parte il treno?**	dah kay beenarreeoa pahrtay eel traynoa
Where's the nearest underground (subway) station?	**Dov'è la più vicina stazione della metropolitana?**	doavai lah peeoo vee-cheenah stahtseeoanay dayllah maytroapoaleetarnah
Where's the bus station, please?	**Dov'è la stazione degli autobus, per piacere?**	doavai lah stahtseeoanay daylyee owtoabooss pair peeahchayray
When's the first bus to ...?	**Quando passa il primo autobus per ...?**	kwahndoa pahsssah eel preemoa owtoabooss pair
the last bus/the next bus	**l'ultimo autobus/il prossimo autobus**	loolteemoa owtoabooss/ eel prossseemoa owtoabooss
Please let me off at the next stop.	**Mi faccia scendere alla prossima fermata, per piacere.**	mee fahtchah shayn-dayray ahllah prossseemah fehrmartah pair peeahchayray

ITALIAN

Relaxing

What's on at the cinema (movies)?	**Cosa danno al cinema?**	**kaw**ssah **dahn**noa ahl **chee**naymah
What's on at the theatre?	**Cosa danno al teatro?**	**kaw**ssah **dahn**noa ahl tayartroa
What time does the film begin? And the play?	**A che ora incomincia il film? E la rappresentazione?**	ah kay **o**arah eengkoa-**meen**cheeah eel feelm? ay lah rahpprayssayntah-tsee**oa**nay
Are there any tickets for tonight?	**Ci sono ancora posti liberi per questa sera?**	chee **so**anoa ahng**koa**rah **poas**tee **lee**bayree pair koo**ayss**tah **say**rah
Where can we go dancing?	**Dove possiamo andare a ballare?**	**doa**vay posss**ee**armoa ahn**dar**ray ah bahl**lar**ray
Would you like to dance?	**Vuole ballare?**	voo**aw**lay bahl**lar**ray

Introductions

How do you do?	**Bongiorno.**	boan**joar**noa
How are you?	**Come sta?**	**koa**may stah
Very well, thank you. And you?	**Molto bene, grazie. E lei?**	**moal**toa **bai**nay **grah**tseeay. ay **la**iee
May I introduce Miss Philips?	**Posso presentarle la signorina Philips?**	**posss**oa prayzayn**tar**rlay lah seeñoa**ree**nah Philips
My name is...	**Mi chiamo...**	mee kee**ar**moa
I'm very pleased to meet you.	**Sono molto lieto di fare la sua conoscenza.**	**so**anoa **moal**toa lee**ay**toa dee **far**ray lah **soo**ah koanoa**shehn**tsah
How long have you been here?	**Da quanto tempo è qui?**	dah **kwahn**toa **tehm**poa ai **koo**ee
It was nice meeting you.	**Sono lieto di aver fatto la sua conoscenza.**	**so**anoa lee**ay**toa dee ah**vayr** **faht**toa lah **soo**ah koanoa**shehn**tsah

Dating

Would you like a cigarette?	**Accetta una sigaretta?**	aht**chayt**tah **oo**nah seegah**rayt**tah
May I get you a drink?	**Posso offrirle da bere?**	**posss**oa off**freer**lay dah **bay**ray

ITALIAN

Do you have a light, please?	**Mi fa accendere, per piacere?**	mee fah aht**chehn**dayray pair peeah**chay**ray
Are you waiting for someone?	**Attende qualcuno?**	aht**tehn**dayray kooahl-**koo**noa
Are you free this evening?	**È libera, stasera?**	ai lee**bay**rah stah**say**rah
Where shall we meet?	**Dove possiamo incontrarci?**	**doa**vay posssee**ar**moa eengkon**trarr**chee
What time shall I meet you?	**A che ora la vedrò?**	ah kay **oar**ah lah vay**droa**
May I take you home?	**Posso accompagnarla a casa?**	**poss**soa ahkkoampah-ñarrlah ah kar**ssah**
Thank you, it's been a wonderful evening.	**Grazie! È stata una magnifica serata.**	**grah**tseeay! ai **star**tah oonah man**ñee**feekah say-**rar**tah
What's your telephone number?	**Qual'è il suo numero di telefono?**	kwah**lai** eel **soo**oa **noo**mayroa dee tay**lai**foanoa
Do you live alone?	**Vive sola?**	**vee**vay **soa**lah
What time is your last train?	**A che ora parte il suo ultimo treno?**	ah kay **oar**ah **pahr**tay eel **soo**oa **ool**teemoa **tray**noa
Good-night . . .	**Buona notte . . .**	**bwo**nah **not**tay

Banks

Where's the nearest bank, please?	**Dov'è la banca più vicina, per favore?**	**doa**vai lah **bahng**kah peeoo vee**chee**nah pair fah**voa**ray
Where can I cash some traveller's cheques?	**Dove posso cambiare un traveller's cheque?**	**doa**vay **poss**soa kahm-beearray oon "traveller's cheque"
What time does the bank open/What time does it close?	**A che ora apre la banca/A che ora chiude?**	ah kay **oar**ah **ah**pray la **bahng**kah/ah kay **oar**ah kee**oo**day
I'm expecting some money from home. Has it arrived?	**Aspetto del denaro da casa. È arrivato?**	ahs**payt**toa dayl day**nar**roa dah **kar**ssah. ai ahr-ree**var**toa
Can you give me some small change, please?	**Potrebbe darmi della moneta spicciola, per favore?**	poa**trayb**bay **darr**mee **dayl**lah moa**nay**tah speet**choa**lah pair fah**voa**ray

Shops, stores and services

Where is the nearest chemist's (pharmacy)?	Dov'è la più vicina farmacia?	doavai lah peeoo vee-cheenah fahrmahcheeah
the nearest hair-dresser's	il parrucchiere più vicino	eel pahrrookkeeairay peeoo veecheenoa
the photo shop	il fotografo	eel foatawgrahfoa
the jeweller's	la gioielleria	lah joyayllayreeah
the department store	il grande magazzino	eel grahnday mahgahddzeenoa
the police station	la questura (il posto di pollzia)	lah kooaysstoorah (eel poasstoa dee poalee-tseeah)
the garage	l'autorimessa	lowtoareemaysssah
How do I get there?	Come ci si può arrivare?	koamay chee see pwo ahrreevarray
Is it within walking distance?	Ci si può andare anche a piedi?	chee see pwo ahndarray ahngkay ah peeaydee

Service

Can you help me, please?	Può aiutarmi, per piacere?	pwo ighootarrmee pair peeahchayray
Can you show me this? And that, too.	Può mostrarmi questo? E anche quello.	pwo moasstrarrmee kooaysstoa? ay ahngkay kooayloa
It's too expensive/too big/too small.	È troppo caro/troppo grande/troppo piccolo.	ay troppoa karroa/troppoa grahnday/troppoa peek-koaloa
Can you show me some more?	Mi può mostrare una scelta più ampia?	mee pwo moasstrarray oonah shayltah peeoo ahmpeeah
something better	qualcosa migliore	kwahlkawssah meelyoaray
something cheaper	qualcosa di più economico	kwahlkawssah dee peeoo aykoanawmeekoa
How much is this? And that?	Quanto costa questo? E quello?	kwahntoa kosstah kooaysstoa? ay kooaylloa
It's not quite what I want.	Non è proprio quello che volevo.	noan ay prawpreeoa kooaylloah kay voalayvoa
I like it.	Questo mi piace.	kooaysstoa mee peearchay

Chemist's (Pharmacy)

I'd like something for a cold/for a cough/for travel sickness.	Vorrei qualcosa per il raffreddore/per la tosse/per il mal di moto.	vorraiee kwahlkawssah pair eel rahffrayddoaray/ pair lah toasssay/pair eel mahl dee mawtoa
Can you recommend something for hay-fever/for sunburn?	Può consigliarmi qualcosa per la febbre del fieno/per una scottatura di sole?	pwo koanseelyarrmee kwahlkawssah pair lah faybbray dayl feealnoa/ pair oonah skottahtoorah dee soalay

Toiletry

May I have some razor blades?	Potrei avere delle lamette da barba?	poatraiee ahvayray dayllay lahmayttay dah bahrbah
some shaving cream	una crema da barba	oonah kraimah dah bahrbah
some toothpaste	un dentifricio	oon daynteefreechoa
I'd like some soap.	Vorrei una saponetta.	vorraiee oonah sahpoanayttah
some suntan oil	dell'olio per la tintarella	dayl awlyoa pair lah teentahrehllah

At the barber's

I'd like a haircut, please.	Vorrei farmi tagliare i capelli, per favore.	vorraiee farrmee tahlyarray ee kahpayllee pair fahvoaray
Short/Leave it long.	Corti/Li lasci lunghi.	koartee/lee lahshee loonggee
A razor cut, please.	Un taglio col rasoio, per piacere.	oon tarlyoa koal rahsaweeoa pair peeahchayray

At the hairdresser's

I'd like a shampoo and set, please.	Vorrei uno shampoo e una messa in piega, per piacere.	vorraiee oonoa ''shampoo'' ay oonah maysssah een peeaigah pair peeahchayray
I'd like a bleach.	Vorrei una decolo-razione.	vorraiee oona daykoaloarahtseeoanay
a permanent	una permanente	oonah paymahnehntay
a colour rinse	un ''cachet''	oon kahshay
a manicure	una manicure	oonah mahneekooray

ITALIAN

Photography

I'd like a film for this camera.
Vorrei un rullino per questa macchina fotografica.
vorraiee oon roolleenoa pair kooaysstah mahkkeenah foatoagrarfeekah

This camera doesn't work.
Questa macchina fotografica non funziona.
kooaysstah mahkkeenah foatoagrarfeekah noan foontseeoanah

At the post office

Where's the nearest post office, please?
Dove si trova l'ufficio postale più vicino, per favore?
doavay see trawvah looffeechoa poasstarlay peeoo veecheenoa pair fahvoaray

I'd like to send this by express (special delivery)/by air mail.
Vorrei spedire questo per espresso/per via aerea.
vorraiee spaydeeray kooaysstoa pair aysssprehsssoa/pair veeah ahairayah

Service stations

Where is the nearest service station, please?
Dove si trova la più vicina stazione di rifornimento, per favore?
doavay see trawvah lah peeoo veecheenah stahtseeoanay dee reefornee-mayntoa pair fahvoaray

Fill her up, please.
Faccia il pieno, per favore.
fahtchah eel peeainoa pair fahvoaray

Check the oil, please.
Controlli l'olio, per favore.
koantroallee lawlyoa pair fahvoaray

Would you check the tyres?
Vorrebbe controllare le gomme?
vorraybbay koantroallarray lay gommay

Street directions

Can you show me on the map where I am?
Può indicarmi sulla carta dove mi trovo?
pwo eendeekarrmee soollah kahrtah doavay mee trawvoa

You're on the wrong road.
È sulla strada sbagliata.
ay soollah strardah zbahlyartah

Go back to ...
Ritorni a ...
reetoarnee ah

Go straight ahead.
Continui diritto.
koanteenooee deereettoa

It's on the left/on the right.
È a sinistra/a destra.
ai ah seeneesstrah/ah dehstrah

ITALIAN

Accidents

May I use your telephone?	**Potrei usare il suo telefono?**	poatraiee oozarray eel soooa taylaifoanoa
Call a doctor quickly.	**Chiami subito un medico.**	keearmee soobeetoa oon maideekoa
Call an ambulance.	**Chiami un'auto-ambulanza.**	keearmee oon owtoaahm-boolahntsah
Please call the police.	**Per piacere, chiami la polizia.**	pair peeahchayray keearmee lah poaleetseeah

Numbers

one	**uno**	oonoa
two	**due**	dooay
three	**tre**	tray
four	**quattro**	kooahttroa
five	**cinque**	cheengkooay
six	**sei**	sehee
seven	**sette**	sehttay
eight	**otto**	ottoa
nine	**nove**	nawvay
ten	**dieci**	deeaichee
eleven	**undici**	oondeechee
twelve	**dodici**	doadeechee
thirteen	**tredici**	traydeechee
fourteen	**quattordici**	kooahttordeechee
fifteen	**quindici**	kooeendeechee
sixteen	**sedici**	saydeechee
seventeen	**diciassette**	deechahsssehttay
eighteen	**diciotto**	deechottoa
nineteen	**diciannove**	deechahnawvay
twenty	**venti**	vayntee
twenty-one	**ventuno**	vayntoonoa
thirty	**trenta**	trayntah
forty	**quaranta**	kooahrahntah
fifty	**cinquanta**	cheengkooahntah
sixty	**sessanta**	saysssahntah
seventy	**settanta**	sayttahntah
eighty	**ottanta**	oattahntah
ninety	**novanta**	noavahntah
one hundred	**cento**	chehntoa
one thousand	**mille**	meellay
ten thousand	**diecimila**	deeehcheemeelah

Days

It's Sunday.	È domenica.	ai doamayneekah
Monday	**lunedì**	loonaydee
Tuesday	**martedì**	mahrtaydee
Wednesday	**mercoledì**	mehrkoalaydee
Thursday	**giovedì**	joavaydee
Friday	**venerdì**	vaynayrdee
Saturday	**sabato**	sarbahtoa
yesterday	**ieri**	eeairee
today	**oggi**	odjee
tomorrow	**domani**	doamarnee
morning/afternoon	**mattino/pomeriggio**	mahtteenoa/poamay-reedjoa
evening/night	**sera/notte**	sayrah/nottay

Months

January	**gennaio**	jaynighoa
February	**febbraio**	fehbbrighoa
March	**marzo**	mahrtsoa
April	**aprile**	ahpreelay
May	**maggio**	mahdjoa
June	**giugno**	jooñoa
July	**luglio**	loolyoa
August	**agosto**	ahgoasstoa
September	**settembre**	sayttehmbray
October	**ottobre**	oattoabray
November	**novembre**	noavehmbray
December	**dicembre**	deechehmbray
Merry Christmas!	**Buon Natale!**	bwon nahtarlay!
Happy New Year!	**Buon Anno!**	bwon ahnnoa

ITALIAN

NORWEGIAN

Guide to Pronunciation

Letter	Approximate pronunciation	Symbol	Example	

Consonants

b, d, f, h, m, n, p, t, v	as in English			
g	1) before **i**, **y** or **ei**, like **y** in **y**et	y	**gi**	yee
	2) otherwise, like **g** in **g**o	g	**g**ate	**g**arter
j, gj, hj, lj	like **y** in **y**et	y	**j**a	yar
			hjem	yehm
k	1) before **i**, **y** or **j**, like **ch** in German i**ch**, or something like **ch** in Scottish lo**ch**; it is similar to the first sound of **h**uge	kh	**k**irke	**kh**eerker
			kyst	khewst
	2) otherwise like **k** in **k**it	k	**k**affe	**k**ahffer
l	always as in **l**ee, never as in bel**l**	l	ta**l**e	tar**l**er

| r | in southwestern Norway, it is pronounced in the back of the mouth (as in French), elsewhere it is slightly rolled in the front of the mouth | r | **rask** | rahsk |

N.B. In the groups **rd**, **rl**, **rn** and **rt**, the r tends not to be pronounced but influences the pronunciation of the following consonant, which is then pronounced with the tongue behind the upper teeth ridge (turned upwards at the front). We don't use a special symbol for this retroflex pronunciation of **d**, **l**, **n** or **t**.

rs	is generally pronounced like **sh** in **shut** in eastern Norway	sh	**norsk**	noshk
s	always as in **so**	s/ss	**rose**	**roo**sser
sj, skj, sk	when followed by **i**, **y** or **øy**, like **sh** in **shut**	sh	**sjø**	shur
			ski	shee

N.B. The letters **c**, **q**, **w**, **z** are only found in foreign words, and tend to be pronounced as in the language of origin.

Vowels

In Norwegian, vowels in stressed syllables are long when followed by, at most, one pronounced consonant. They are generally short when followed by two or more consonants.

a	1) when long, like **a** in car	ar	**dag**	darg
	2) when short, fairly like **u** in cut or **o** in American college	ah	**vaske**	**vah**sker
e	1) when long, like **ay**, in **say**, but a pure sound, *not* a diphthong	ay	**se**	say
	2) when short, like **e** in **get**	eh	**penn**	pehn
	3) when followed by **r**, like **a** in **bad**; long or short	æææ	**her**	hæær
		æ	**sterk**	stærk
	4) when unstressed, like **er** in other	er	**nese**	**nay**sser
i	1) when long, like **ee** in **see**, but with the tongue more raised, and the lips more drawn back at the sides	ee	**ti**	tee
	2) when short, like **ee** in **meet**	i	**drikke**	**drik**ker
o	1) when long, like **oo** in **soon**, but with the lips more rounded (when followed by **-rt**, **-st**, **-m** and **-nd**, it can be short	oo	**god**	goo
			ost	oost
	2) when short, generally like **o** in hot	o	**tolv**	tol

NORWEGIAN

u	a difficult sound; something like the **ew** in **few**, or Scottish **oo** in **good**; you will find it very hard to distinguish from Norwegian **y**, so we use the same symbol for both	ew	**mur**	mewr
y	put your tongue in the position for the **ee** in **bee**, and then round your lips as for the **oo** in **pool**: the vowel you pronounce like this should be more or less correct	ew	**by** **tynn**	bew tewn
æ	1) before **r** like **a** in **bad**; usually long but sometimes short	ææ	**lære**	læærer
		æ	**lærd**	læd
	2) otherwise, like **ay** in **say**	ay	**hæl**	hayl
å	1) when long, like **aw** in **saw**	aw	**på**	paw
	2) when short (rare), more like **o** in **hot**	o	**gått**	got
ø	like **u** in **fur**; either long or short	ur	**dør** **søtt**	durr surt

Diphthongs

au	this sounds like **ow** in **now**, but, in fact, the first part is a Norwegian **ø**-sound	ow	**sau**	sow
ei	like **ay** in **say** but often reminiscent of **igh** in **sigh**	ay	**vei**	vay
øy	fairly like **oy** in **boy**	oy	**høy**	hoy

Silent letters

1) The letter **g** is generally silent in the endings **-lig** and **-ig**.
2) The letter **d** is generally silent after **l** or **n** or after **r** at the end of a word (with lengthening of the vowel) or often after a long vowel, e.g. holde, land, gård.
3) The letter **v** is silent in a few words, e.g., selv, tolv, halv, sølv.

Some basic expressions

Yes.	**Ja.**	yar
No.	**Nei.**	nay
Please.	**Vennligst.**	**vehn**ligst
Thank you.	**Takk.**	tahk
Thank you very much.	**Mange takk.**	**mahng**er tahk
That's all right.	**Ingen årsak.**	**ing**ern **aws**hahk

Greetings

Good morning.	**God morgen.**	goo **maw**ern
Good afternoon.	**God dag.**	goo darg
Good evening.	**God kveld.**	goo kvehl
Good night.	**God natt.**	goo naht
Good-bye.	**Adjø.**	ah**dyur**
See you later.	**På gjensyn.**	paw **yehn**sewn
This is Mr....	**Dette er herr...**	**deht**ter ær haer
This is Mrs....	**Dette er fru...**	**deht**ter ær frew
This is Miss...	**Dette er frøken...**	**deht**ter ær **frur**kern
I'm very pleased to meet you.	**Det gleder meg å treffe Dem.**	day **glay**derr may aw **trehf**fer dehm
How are you?	**Hvordan går det?**	**voor**dahn gawr day
Very well, thank you. And you?	**Bare bra, takk.** **Og med Dem?**	**bar**rer brar tahk. awg may(d) dehm
Fine.	**Fint.**	fint
Excuse me.	**Unnskyld.**	**oon**shewl

Questions

Where?	**Hvor?**	**voor**
Where is...?	**Hvor er...?**	**voor** ær
Where are...?	**Hvor er...?**	**voor** ær
When?	**Når?**	nawr

What?	**Hva?**	var
How?	**Hvordan?**	**voor**dahn
How much?	**Hvor mye?**	**voor** mewer
How many?	**Hvor mange?**	**voor** mahnger
Who?	**Hvem?**	vehm
Why?	**Hvorfor?**	**voor**for
Which?	**Hvilken?**	**vil**kern
What do you call this?	**Hva heter dette?**	var **hay**terr **deht**ter
What do you call that?	**Hva heter det?**	var **hay**terr day
What does this mean?	**Hva betyr dette?**	var ber**tewr deht**ter
What does that mean?	**Hva betyr det?**	var ber**tewr** day

Do you speak ... ?

Do you speak English?	**Snakker De engelsk?**	**snahk**kerr dee **ehng**erlsk
Do you speak German?	**Snakker De tysk?**	**snahk**kerr dee tewsk
Do you speak French?	**Snakker De fransk?**	**snahk**kerr dee frahnsk
Do you speak Spanish?	**Snakker De spansk?**	**snahk**kerr dee spahnsk
Do you speak Italian?	**Snakker De italiensk?**	**snahk**kerr de itah**leeehn**sk
Could you speak more slowly, please?	**Kunne De snakke litt saktere?**	**kewn**ner dee **snahk**ker lit **sahk**terrer
Please point to the phrase in the book.	**Kunne De peke på setningen i boken.**	**kewn**ner dee **pay**ker paw **seht**ningern ee **book**ern
Just a minute. I'll see if I can find it in this book.	**Et øyeblikk. Jeg skal se om jeg kan finne det i denne boken.**	eht **oy**erblik yay skal say om yay karn **fin**ner day ee **dehn**ner **book**ern
I understand.	**Jeg forstår.**	yay for**shtawr**
I don't understand.	**Jeg forstår ikke.**	yay for**shtawr ik**ker

NORWEGIAN

NORWEGIAN

Can...?

Can I have...?	**Kan jeg få...?**	kahn yay faw
Can we have...?	**Kan vi få...?**	kahn vee faw
Can you show me...?	**Kan De vise meg...?**	kahn dee **vee**sser may
Can you tell me...?	**Kan De si meg...?**	kahn dee see may
Can you help me, please?	**Kan De være så vennlig å hjelpe meg?**	kahn dee **væær**er saw **vehn**lee aw **yehl**per may

Wanting

I'd like...	**Jeg vil gjerne ha...**	yay vil **yææ**ner har
We'd like...	**Vi ville gjerne ha...**	vee **vi**ler **yææ**ner har
Please give me...	**Vennligst, gi meg...**	**vehn**ligst yee may
Give it to me, please.	**Vennligst, gi det til meg.**	**vehn**ligst yee day til may
Please bring me...	**Vennligst, hent...til meg.**	**vehn**ligst hehnt...til may
Bring it to me, please.	**Vennligst, hent det til meg.**	**vehn**ligst hehnt day til may
I'm hungry.	**Jeg er sulten.**	yay ær **sewl**tern
I'm thirsty.	**Jeg er tørst.**	yay ær tursht
I'm tired.	**Jeg er trett.**	yay ær treht
I'm lost.	**Jeg har gått meg vill.**	yay har got may vil
It's important.	**Det er viktig.**	day ær **vik**tee
It's urgent.	**Det haster.**	day **hahss**terr
Hurry up!	**Skynd Dem!**	shewn dehm

It is/There is...

It is/It's...	**Det er...**	day ær
Is it...?	**Er det...?**	ær day
It isn't...	**Det er ikke...**	day ær **ik**ker
There is/There are...	**Det finnes...**	day **finn**erss
Is there/Are there...?	**Finnes det...?**	**finn**erss day

| There isn't/There aren't . . . | **Det finnes ikke . . .** | day finnerss ikker |
| There isn't any/ There aren't any. | **Det finnes ingen.** | day finnerss ingern |

A few common words

big/small	**stor/liten**	stoor/**lee**tern
quick/slow	**hurtig/langsom**	hewtee/**lahng**som
early/late	**tidlig/sen**	teedlee/sayn
cheap/expensive	**billig/dyr**	billee/dewr
near/far	**nær/langt borte**	næær/lahngt **boo**ter
hot/cold	**varm/kald**	vahrm/kahl
full/empty	**full/tom**	fewl/tom
easy/difficult	**lett/vanskelig**	leht/**vahn**skeriee
heavy/light	**tung/lett**	tewng/leht
open/shut	**åpen/lukket**	awpern/**lewk**kert
right/wrong	**riktig/gal**	riktee/garl
old/new	**gammel/ny**	gahmmerl/new
old/young	**gammel/ung**	gahmmerl/ewng
beautiful/ugly	**pen/stygg**	payn/stewg
good/bad	**god/dårlig**	goo/**dawr**lee
better/worse	**bedre/verre**	**bay**drer/**vær**rer

Some prepositions and a few more useful words

at	**ved**	vay(d)
on	**på**	paw
in	**i**	ee
to	**til**	til
from	**fra**	frar
inside	**innenfor**	innernfor
outside	**utenfor**	ewternfor
up	**opp**	op
down	**ned**	nay(d)
before	**før**	furr
after	**etter**	ehtterr
with	**med**	may(d)
without	**uten**	ewtern
through	**gjennom**	yehnnom
towards	**mot**	moot
until	**til**	til
during	**i løpet av**	ee lurpert ahv
and	**og**	awg
or	**eller**	ehllerr
not	**ikke**	ikker
nothing	**ingenting**	ingernting

NORWEGIAN

none	**ingen**	**ing**ern
very	**veldig**	**vehl**dee
also	**også**	**awg**saw
soon	**snart**	snahrt
perhaps	**kanskje**	**kahn**sher
here	**her**	hæær
there	**der**	dæær
now	**nå**	naw
then	**da**	dar

Arrival

Your passport, please.	**Passet Deres, takk.**	**pahss**sert **dayr**erss tahk
Here it is.	**Vær så god.**	væær shaw goo
Have you anything to declare?	**Har De noe å fortolle?**	harr dee **noo**er aw for**toll**er
No, nothing at all.	**Nei, ingen ting.**	nay **ing**ernting
Porter!	**Bærer!**	**bæær**err
Can you help me with my luggage, please?	**Kan De hjelpe meg med bagasjen?**	kahn dee **yehl**per may may(d) bah**gar**shern
That's my suitcase.	**Det er min kuffert.**	day ær meen **kewff**errt
Where's the bus to the centre of town, please?	**Hvor tar man bussen inn til centrum?**	voor tarr mahn **bewss**sern in til **sehn**trewm
This way, please.	**Denne vei.**	**dehn**ner vay

Changing money

Can you change a traveller's cheque, please?	**Kan De innløse en reisesjekk?**	kahn dee **in**lursser ayn **righ**ssershehk
Where's the nearest bank, please?	**Hvor ligger nærmeste bank?**	voor **ligg**err **næær**merster bahnk

Car rental

I'd like a car.	**Jeg vil gjerne leie en bil.**	yay vil **yææn**er **lay**er ayn beel
For how long?	**Hvor lenge?**	voor **lehng**er
A day/Four days/ A week/Two weeks.	**En dag/Fire dager/ En uke/To uker.**	ayn darg/**feer**er **darg**err/ ayn **ewk**er/too **ewk**err

Taxi

Where can I get a taxi?	Hvor kan jeg få tak i en drosje?	voor kahn yay faw tark ee ayn **dro**sher
What's the fare to...?	Hva koster det til...?	var **koss**terr day til
Take me to this address, please.	**Venn**ligst, kjør meg til denne adressen.	**vehn**ligst khurr may til **dehn**ner ah**drehss**sern
I'm in a hurry.	Jeg har det travelt.	yay harr day **trar**verlt
Could you drive more slowly, please?	Kunne De kjøre litt saktere?	**kew**nner dee **khur**rer lit **sahk**terrer

Hotel and other accommodation

My name is...	Mitt navn er...	mit nahvn ær
Have you a reservation?	Har De reservert?	harr dee raysehr**vayrt**
Yes, here's the confirmation.	Ja, her er bekreftelsen.	yar hæær ær ber**krehf**terl-ssern
I'd like...	Jeg vil gjerne ha...	yay vil **yææ**ner har
I'd like a single room/a double room.	Jeg vil gjerne ha et enkelt rom/et dobbelt rom.	yay vil **yææ**ner har eht **ehng**kerlt room/eht **dob**berlt room
a room with a bath/with a shower	et rom med bad/med dusj	eht room may(d) bard/may(d) dewsh

How much?

What's the price per night/per week/per month?	Hva koster det for en natt/for en uke/for en måned?	var **koss**terr day for ayn naht/for ayn **ew**ker/for ayn **maw**nerd
May I see the room?	Kan jeg få se rommet?	kahn yay faw say **room**mert
I'm sorry, I don't like it.	Jeg beklager, men jeg liker det ikke.	yay ber**klar**gerr mayn yay **lee**kerr day **ik**ker
Yes, that's fine. I'll take it.	Ja, det er bra. Jeg tar det.	yar day ær brar yay tarr day
What's my room number, please?	Hvilket værelsenummer har jeg?	**vil**kert **vææ**rerlsser**newm**merr harr yay
Number 123.	Nummer 123.	**newm**merr 123

NORWEGIAN

NORWEGIAN

| Where's the gentle-men's toilet (men's room)? | **Hvor er herre-toalettet?** | voor ær **hæ**rerr-twahlehtter(t) |
| Where's the ladies' toilet (ladies' room)? | **Hvor er dametoalettet?** | voor ær **da**rmer-twahlehtter(t) |

Appetizers

I'd like some . . .	**Jeg vil gjerne ha . . .**	yay vil **yææ**ner har
I'd like some assorted appetizers.	**Jeg vil gjerne ha noen assorterte hors-d'œuvres.**	yay vil **yææ**ner har **noo**ern ahssor**tair**ter or**durv**r
orange juice	**appelsinsaft**	**ahp**perlsseenssahft
ham	**skinke**	**shing**ker
melon	**melon**	may**loon**
pâté	**postei**	pooss**tay**
smoked salmon	**røkelaks**	**rur**kerlahks
shrimps (shrimp)	**reker**	**ray**kerr

Soup

Have you any . . . ?	**Har de . . . ?**	harr dee
Have you any chicken soup?	**Har De hønse-suppe?**	harr dee **hurn**ssersssewpper
vegetable soup	**grønnsaksuppe**	**grurn**ssahksewpper
onion soup	**løksuppe**	**lurk**sewpper

Fish

I'd like some . . .	**Jeg vil gjerne ha . . .**	yay vil **yææ**ner har
I'd like some fish.	**Jeg vil gjerne ha fisk.**	yay vil **yææ**ner har fisk
sole	**sjøtunge**	**shur**tewnger
trout	**ørret**	**urr**rert
lobster	**hummer**	**hew**mmerr
crayfish	**kreps**	krehps
prawns	**store reker**	**stoo**rer **ray**kerr
I'd like it . . .	**Jeg vil gjerne ha det . . .**	yay vil **yææ**ner har day
I'd like it steamed.	**Jeg vil gjerne ha det dampet.**	yay vil **yææ**ner har day **dahm**pert
grilled	**griljert**	gril**yairt**
boiled	**kokt**	kookt
baked	**ovnstekt**	**oovn**staykt
fried	**stekt**	staykt

Service, please

Who is it?	**Hvem er det?**	vehm ær day
Just a minute.	**Et øyeblikk.**	eht **oy**erblik
Come in! The door's open.	**Kom inn! Døren er åpen.**	kom in **dur**rern ær **aw**pern
May we have breakfast in our room?	**Kan vi få frokost på rommet?**	kahn vee faw **fro**koost paw **room**mert

Breakfast

I'll have ...	**Jeg vil ha ...**	yay vil har
I'll have some fruit juice.	**Jeg vil ha litt fruktsaft.**	yay vil har lit **frewkt**sahft
a boiled egg	**et kokt egg**	eht kookt ehg
a fried egg	**et speilegg**	eht **spay**lehg
some bacon/some ham	**litt bacon/litt skinke**	lit **bay**kern/lit **shing**ker
some toast	**litt ristet loff**	litt **ris**stert loof
a pot of tea	**en kanne te**	ayn **kahn**ner tay
a cup of tea	**en kopp te**	ayn kop tay
some coffee	**litt kaffe**	lit **kahf**fer
some chocolate	**litt sjokolade**	lit shookoo**lar**der
more butter	**mer smør**	mair smurr
some hot water	**litt varmt vann**	lit vahrmt vahn

Difficulties

The central heating doesn't work.	**Sentralvarmen virker ikke.**	sehn**trarl**vahrmern **veer**ker **ik**ker
the light/the socket	**lyset/støpslet**	**lew**sser(t)/**sturp**sler(t)
the tap/the toilet	**vannkranen/ toalettet**	**vahn**krarnern/twah**leht**ter(t)
There's no hot water.	**Det er ikke noe varmt vann.**	day ær **ik**ker **noo**er vahrmt vahn
May I see the manager, please?	**Kan jeg få snakke med direktøren?**	kahn yay faw **snahk**ker may(d) deerehk**tur**rern

Telephone—Mail

| There's a call for you. | **Det er telefon til Dem.** | day ær tayler**foon** til dehm |
| Hold the line, please. | **Ikke legg på røret.** | **ik**ker lehg paw **rur**rer(t) |

NORWEGIAN

Operator, I've been cut off.	**Frøken, jeg er blitt avbrutt.**	frur**kern** yay ær blit ahv**brewt**
Did anyone telephone me?	**Har noen ringt til meg?**	harr **noo**ern ringt til may
Is there any mail for me?	**Er det noe post til meg?**	ær day **noo**er post til may
Are there any messages for me?	**Er det noen beskjed til meg?**	ær day **noo**ern ber**shay(d)** til may

Checking out

May I have my bill, please?	**Kan jeg få regningen, takk.**	kahn yay faw **ray**ningern tahk
We're in a great hurry.	**Vi har det svært travelt.**	vee harr day svæt **trar**verlt
It's been a very enjoyable stay.	**Det har vært et meget hyggelig opphold.**	day harr væt eht **may**ert **hewg**gerlee **op**hol

Eating out

Good evening, sir/ Good evening, madam.	**God aften.**	goo **ahf**tern
Good evening. I'd like a table for two, please.	**God aften. Jeg vil gjerne ha et bord for to, takk.**	goo **ahf**tern. yay vil **yææ**ner har eht boor for too tahk
Do you have a fixed-price menu?	**Har De en fastsatt meny?**	harr dee ayn **fahst**saht may**new**
May I see the à la carte menu?	**Kan jeg få se menyen?**	kahn yay faw say may**new**ern
May we have an ashtray, please?	**Kan vi få et askebeger.**	kahn vee faw eht **ahs**ker-**bay**gerr
some bread	**litt brød**	lit brurd
a fork	**en gaffel**	ayn **gahff**erl
a knife	**en kniv**	ayn kneev
a spoon	**en skje**	ayn shay
a plate	**en tallerken**	ayn **tahl**lerrkern
a glass	**et glass**	eht glahss
a napkin	**en serviett**	ayn sær**vieht**
another chair	**en stol til**	ayn stool til

Meat—Poultry—Game

I'd like some . . .	**Jeg vil gjerne ha . . .**	yay vil **yææ**ner har
I'd like some beef.	**Jeg vil gjerne ha oksekjøtt.**	yay vil **yææ**ner har **ook**serkhurt
a beef steak	**en biff**	ayn bif
some roast beef	**roastbeef**	**roast**beef
a veal cutlet	**en kalve-kotelett**	ayn **kahl**verkotterleht
mutton	**fårekjøtt**	**faw**rerkhurt
lamb	**lammekjøtt**	**lahm**merkhurt
a pork chop	**en svinekotelett**	ayn **svee**nerkotterleht
roast pork	**svinestek**	**svee**nerstayk
hare	**hare**	**har**rer
chicken	**kylling**	**khew**lling
roast chicken	**stekt kylling**	staykt **kew**lling
duck	**and**	ahnd
How do you like your meat?	**Hvordan vil De ha kjøttet tilberedt?**	**voor**dahn vil dee har **khurt**tert tilber**reht**
rare	**blodig**	**bloo**dee
medium	**medium**	**may**diewm
well done	**godt stekt**	got staykt

Vegetables

What vegetables have you got?	**Hvilke grønnsaker har De?**	**vil**ker **grurns**sakerr harr dee
I'd like some . . .	**Jeg vil gjerne ha . . .**	yay vil **yææ**ner har
I'd like some asparagus.	**Jeg vil gjerne ha asparges.**	yay vil **yææ**ner har ah**spar**gerss
green beans	**grønne bønner**	**grur**nner **burn**nerr
mushrooms	**sopp**	sop
carrots	**gulrøtter**	**gewl**rurtterr
onions	**løk**	lurk
red cabbage	**rødkål**	**rurd**kawl
spinach	**spinat**	spi**nart**
rice	**ris**	rees
peas	**erter**	**æ**terr
tomatoes	**tomater**	too**mar**terr
green salad	**grønn salat**	grurn sah**lart**
potatoes	**poteter**	poo**tay**terr

Desserts

Nothing more, thanks.	**Takk, jeg er forsynt.**	tahk yay ær fo**shewnt**

NORWEGIAN

Just a small portion, please.	**Bare en liten porsjon.**	barrer ayn **lee**tern por**shoon**
Have you any ice-cream?	**Har De iskrem?**	harr dee **ees**krehm
fruit salad	**frukt-salat**	**frewkt**sahlart
fresh fruit	**frisk frukt**	frisk frewkt
cheese	**ost**	oost

Drink

What would you like to drink?	**Hva vil de ha å drikke?**	var vil dee har aw **drik**ker
I'll have a beer, please.	**Jeg vil gjerne ha en øl.**	yay vil **yææ**ner har ayn url
I'll have a whisky, please.	**Jeg vil gjerne ha en whisky.**	yay vil **yææ**ner har ayn **wiss**kee

Wine

I'd like a bottle of wine.	**Jeg vil gjerne ha en flaske vin.**	yay vil **yææ**ner har ayn **flah**sker veen
red wine	**rødvin**	rur(d)vin
rosé wine	**rosévin**	roa**say**vin
white wine	**hvitvin**	**veet**vin
Cheers!	**Skål!**	skawl

The bill (check)

May I have the bill (check) please?	**Kan jeg få regningen, takk!**	karn yay faw **ray**ningern tahk
Is service included?	**Er service inkludert?**	ær sær**vee**esser ingklew**dai(r)t**
Everything's included.	**Alt er inkludert.**	ahlt ær ingklew**dai(r)t**
Thank you, that was a very good meal.	**Takk, det var et utmerket måltid.**	tahk day varr eht ewt**mær**kert **mawl**tid

Travelling

Where's the railway station, please?	**Hvor ligger jernbanestasjonen?**	voor **lig**gerr **yææn**barnerstah**shoo**nern
Where's the ticket office, please?	**Hvor er billettkontoret?**	voor ær billeht**kontoo**rert
I'd like a ticket to ...	**Jeg vil gjerne ha en billett til ...**	yay vil **yææ**ner har ayn **bill**eht til

First or second class?	Første eller annen klasse?	furshter ehllerr ahnnern klahssser
First class, please.	Første, takk.	furshter tahk
Single or return (one way or round-trip)?	Enveis eller tur-retur?	aynvayss ehller tewr-rertewr
Do I have to change trains?	Må jeg bytte tog?	maw yay bewtter tawg
What platform does the train leave from?	Fra hvilken platform går toget?	frar vilkern plahtform gawr tawgert
Where's the nearest underground (subway) station?	Hvor ligger nærmeste under-grunnstasjon?	voor liggerr nærmersster ewnnergrewnstahshoon
Where's the bus station, please?	Hvor er buss-stasjonen?	voor ær bewss-stahshoonern
When's the first bus to . . . ?	Når går den første bussen til . . . ?	nawr gawr dayn furshter bewsssern til
the last bus	den siste bussen	dayn sisster bewsssern
the next bus	den neste bussen	dayn nehsster bewsssern
Please let me off at the next stop.	Vil De slippe meg av på neste stop-pested?	vil dee slipper may ahv paw nehsster stopper-stehd

Relaxing

What's on at the cinema (movies)?	Hva går på kino?	var gawr paw kheenoo
What's on at the theatre?	Hva går på teatret?	var gawr paw tayartrer(t)
What time does the film begin? And the play?	Når begynner filmen? Og stykket?	nawr beryewnnerr filmern? awg stewkkert
Are there any tickets for tonight?	Er det noen billetter igjen til i kveld?	ær day nooern billehtterr eeyern til ee kvehl
Where can we go dancing?	Hvor kan vi gå for å danse?	voor kahn vee gaw for aw dahnser
Would you like to dance?	Vil De danse?	vil dee dahnser

Introductions

How do you do?	God dag.	goo darg
How are you?	Hvordan står det til?	voordahn stawr day til

NORWEGIAN

Very well, thank you. And you?	**Bare bra, takk. Og med Dem?**	barrer brar tahk. awg may(d) dehm
May I introduce Miss Philips?	**Kan jeg få presentere frøken Philips?**	kahn yay faw praysahng-tayrert frurkern Philips
My name is...	**Mitt navn er...**	mit nahvn ær
I'm very pleased to meet you.	**Det gleder meg å treffe Dem.**	day glayderr may aw trehffert dehm
How long have you been here?	**Hvor lenge har De vært her?**	voor lehnger harr dee væt hær
It was nice meeting you.	**Det var hyggelig å treffe Dem.**	day varr hewggerlee aw trehffer dehm

Dating

Would you like a cigarette?	**Vil De ha en sigarett?**	vil dee har ayn sigahreht
May I get you a drink?	**Kan jeg by Dem på en drink?**	kahn yay bew dehm paw ayn drink
Do you have a light, please?	**Unnskyld, har De en fyrstikk?**	ewnshewl harr dee ayn fewshtik
Are you waiting for someone?	**Venter De på noen?**	vehnterr dee paw nooern
Are you free this evening?	**Er De ledig i kveld?**	ær dee laydee ee kvehl
Where shall we meet?	**Hvor skal vi møtes?**	voor skahl ve murterss
What time shall I meet you?	**Når skal jeg møte Dem?**	nawr skahl ,yay murter dehm
May I take you home?	**Kan jeg få følge Dem hjem?**	kahn yay faw furler dehm yehm
Thank you, it's been a wonderful evening.	**Mange takk, det har vært en hyggelig kveld.**	mahnger tahk day harr væt ayn hewggerlee kvehl
What's your telephone number?	**Hva er telefon-nummeret Deres?**	var ær taylerfoon-newmmerrer(t) dayrerss
Do you live alone?	**Bor De alene?**	boor dee ahlayner
What time is your last train?	**Når går det siste toget Deres?**	nawr gawr day sisster tawger(t) dayrerss
Good-night...	**God natt...**	goo naht

Banks

Where's the nearest bank, please?	**Unnskyld, hvor ligger nærmeste bank?**	ewnshewl voor **lig**gerr **nær**merster bahnk
Where can I cash some traveller's cheques?	**Hvor kan jeg innløse noen reisesjekker?**	voor kahn yay **in**lursser **noo**ern **righ**ssershehkkerr
What time does the bank open/What time does it close?	**Når åpner banken/ Når stenger den?**	nawr **awp**nerr **bahng**kern/nawr **stehng**err dehn
I'm expecting some money from home. Has it arrived?	**Jeg venter penger hjemmefra. Har de kommet?**	yay **vehn**terr **pehng**err **yehm**merfrar. harr dee **kom**mert
Can you give me some small change, please?	**Kan De gi meg litt vekslepenger?**	kahn dee yee may lit **vehk**slerpehngerr

Shops, stores and services

Where is the nearest chemist's (pharmacy)?	**Hvor er nærmeste apotek?**	voor ær **nær**merster ahpo**tayk**
the nearest hairdresser's	**den nærmeste frisør**	dehn **nær**merster fri**surr**
the photo shop	**fotoforretningen**	**foo**tooforrehtningern
the jeweller's	**gullsmeden**	**gewl**ssmaydern
the department store	**varemagasinet**	**var**rermahgahsseener(t)
the police station	**politistasjonen**	pooli**tee**stahshoonern
the garage	**parkeringshuset**	pahr**kay**ringsshewsser(t)
How do I get there?	**Hvordan kommer jeg dit?**	**voor**dahn **kom**merr yay deet
Is it within walking distance?	**Er det for langt å gå dit?**	ær day for lahngt aw gaw deet

Service

Can you help me, please?	**Kan De være så vennlig å hjelpe meg?**	kahn dee **væ**ærer saw **vehn**lee aw **yehl**per may
Can you show me this? And that, too.	**Kan De vise meg den? Og den også.**	kahn dee **vee**ser may dehn awg dehn **awg**saw
It's too expensive/ too big/too small.	**Det er for dyrt/for stort/for lite.**	day ær for dewrt/for stoot/for **lee**ter

NORWEGIAN

Can you show me some more?	Kan De vise meg flere?	kahn dee **vee**sser may flayrer
something better	noe bedre	**noo**er baydrer
something cheaper	noe billigere	**noo**er billigerrer
How much is this? And that?	Hvor mye koster dette? Og det?	voor **mewer koss**terr dehtter? awg day
It's not quite what I want.	Det er ikke akkurat hva jeg vil ha.	day ær **ikker** ahkhewrart var yay vil har
I like it.	Jeg liker det.	yay **lee**kerr day

Chemist's (Pharmacy)

| I'd like something for a cold/for a cough/for travel sickness. | Jeg vil gjerne ha noe for en for-kjølelse/mot hoste/ mot reisesyke. | yay vil **yææ**ner har **noo**er for ayn for**khur**lerlser/ moot **hooss**ter/moot **righ**ssersssewker |
| Can you recommend something for hay-fever/for sunburn? | Kan De anbefale noe mot høysnue/ mot sol brenthet? | kahn dee ahn**ber**farler **noo**er moot **hoy**ssnewer/ moot **sool**brehnthayt |

Toiletry

May I have some razor blades?	Kan jeg få noen barberblader?	kahn yay faw **noo**ern bahr**bayr**blarderr
some shaving cream	en barberkrem	ayn bahr**bayr**krehm
some toothpaste	en tannpasta	ayn **tahn**pahsstah
I'd like some soap.	Jeg vil gjerne ha en såpe.	yay vil **yææ**ner har ayn **saw**per
some suntan oil	en solbadolje	ayn **sool**bardolyer

At the barber's

I'd like a haircut, please.	Jeg vil gjerne ha håret klippet.	yay vil **yææ**ner har **haw**rer(t) **klip**pert
Short/Leave it long.	Kort/La det være langt.	kot/lar day **væ**ærer lahngt
A razor cut, please.	Skåret med barber kniv.	**skaw**rert may(d) bahr-**bayr**kneev

At the hairdresser's

| I'd like a shampoo and set, please. | Jeg vil gjerne ha vask og legg. | yay vil **yææ**ner har vahsk awg lehg |

I'd like a bleach.	**Jeg vil gjerne ha det bleket.**	yay vil **yææ**ner har day **blay**kert
a permanent	**en permanent**	ayn pehrmah**nehnt**
a colour rinse	**en farge-skylling**	ayn **fahr**yer shewlling
a manicure	**en manikyr**	ayn mahnee**kewr**

Photography

I'd like a film for this camera.	**Jeg ville gjerne ha en film til dette apparatet.**	yay vil **yææ**ner har ayn film til **deh**tter ahppah**rar**ter(t)
This camera doesn't work.	**Dette apparatet virker ikke.**	**deh**tter ahppah**rar**tert **veer**ker ikker

At the post office

Where s the nearest post office, please?	**Hvor ligger det nærmeste post-kontoret?**	voor **ligg**err day **nær**merster **post**kontoorert
I'd like to send this by express (special delivery)/by air mail.	**Jeg vil gjerne sende dette som ilpost/med luftpost.**	yay vil **yææ**ner **sehn**ner **deh**tter som **eel**post/may(d) **lewft**post

Service stations

Where is the nearest service station, please?	**Kan De si meg hvor den nærmeste ben-sinstasjonen ligger?**	kahn dee see may voor dehn **nær**merster behn-**seen**stahshoonern **ligg**err
Fill her up, please.	**Full tank, takk.**	fewl tahnk tahk
Check the oil, please.	**Vil de kontrollere oljen!**	vil dee kontrol**lay**rer **ol**yern
Would you check the tyres?	**Vil De kontrollere dekkene!**	vil dee kontrol**lay**rer **dehk**kerner

Street directions

Can you show me on the map where I am?	**Kan De vise meg hvor jeg er på dette kartet?**	kahn dee **vee**sser may voor yay ær paw **deh**tter **kah**ter(t)
You're on the wrong road.	**De er på feil vei.**	dee ær paw fayl vay
Go back to . . .	**Kjør tilbake til . . .**	khurr til**bar**ker til
Go straight ahead.	**Kjør rett frem.**	khurr reht frehm
It's on the left/on the right.	**Det er på venstre/på høyre side.**	day ær paw **vehn**strer/paw **hoy**rer **see**der

NORWEGIAN

Accidents

May I use your telephone?	**Kan jeg få låne telefonen Deres?**	kahn yay faw **lawner** taylerfoonern dayrerss
Call a doctor quickly.	**Tilkall en lege øyeblikkelig.**	tilkahl ayn **layger** oyerblikkerlee
Call an ambulance.	**Ring etter en sykebil.**	ring ehtterr ayn **sewk**erbeel
Please call the police.	**Vennligst ring til politiet.**	**vehn**ligst ring til pooli**teeer**(t)

Numbers

one	**en**	ayn
two	**to**	too
three	**tre**	tray
four	**fire**	feerer
five	**fem**	fehm
six	**seks**	sehks
seven	**sju**	shew
eight	**åtte**	otter
nine	**ni**	nee
ten	**ti**	tee
eleven	**elleve**	ehlver
twelve	**tolv**	tol
thirteen	**tretten**	trehttern
fourteen	**fjorten**	fyootern
fifteen	**femten**	fehmtern
sixteen	**seksten**	sighstern
seventeen	**sytten**	sewttern
eighteen	**atten**	ahttern
nineteen	**nitten**	nittern
twenty	**tjue**	tyewer
twenty-one	**tjueen**	tyewerayn
thirty	**tretti**	trehttee
forty	**førti**	furtee
fifty	**femti**	fehmtee
sixty	**seksti**	sehkstee
seventy	**sytti**	sewttee
eighty	**åtti**	ottee
ninety	**nitti**	nittee
one hundred	**hundre**	hewnrer
one thousand	**tusen**	tewssern
ten thousand	**titusen**	teetewssern

Days

It's Sunday.	Det er søndag.	day ær surndarg
Monday	mandag	mahndarg
Tuesday	tirsdag	teerssdarg
Wednesday	onsdag	onssdarg
Thursday	torsdag	torshdarg
Friday	fredag	fraydarg
Saturday	lørdag	lurdarg
yesterday	i går	ee gawr
today	i dag	ee darg
tomorrow	i morgen	ee mawern
morning/afternoon	morgen/ettermiddag	mawern/ehtterrmiddarg
evening/night	aften/natt	ahftern/naht

Months

January	januar	yahnewarr
February	februar	faybrewarr
March	mars	mahsh
April	april	ahpreel
May	mai	migh
June	juni	yewnee
July	juli	yewlee
August	august	owgewst
September	september	sehptehmberr
October	oktober	oktawberr
November	november	novehmberr
December	desember	dayssehmberr
Merry Christmas!	God Jul! Godt	goo yewl! got newttawr
Happy New Year!	Nyttår!	

NORWEGIAN

POLISH

Guide to Pronunciation

Note that Polish has some diacritical letters—letters with accent marks—which we do not know in English.

Letter	Approximate pronunciation	Symbol	Example	
Consonants				
b, f, k, l, m, p, z	are pronounced as in English			
cz	like **ch** in **ch**urch	ch	**cz**y	**ch**i
dż	like **j** in **j**am	j	**dż**em	**j**ehm
g	as in **g**irl	g	**g**uma	**g**umah
j	like **y** in **y**et	y	**j**ak	**y**ahk
ł	like **w** in **w**in	w	**ł**adny	**wah**dni
n	as in English but put your tongue against the front teeth and not the teeth ridge	n	**n**a	nah
s	as in **s**it	s/ss	**s**am	sahm
sz	like **sh** in **sh**ine	sh	**sz**al	shahl
t, d	as in English but put your tongue against the front teeth and not against the teeth ridge	t d	**t**ak **d**om	tahk dom
w	like **v** in **v**an	v	**w**oda	**v**odah
ż or rz	like **s** in plea**s**ure	zh	**ż**lazo **rz**eka	**zh**ehlahzo **zh**ehkah

Sounds distinctly different

An often recurring phenomenon in the Slavic languages is "softening", or the "softened" pronunciation of consonants. Examples of this in Polish are ć, dź, ń, ś and ż. A similar effect can be produced by pronouncing y as in yet— but very, very short—after the consonant.

c	like the English sequence ts in tsetse pronounced quickly	ts	co	tso
ć	pronounced like the Polish c but softer	tsh	ciało	tshahwo
dz	like the English sequence ds in beds pronounced quickly	dz	dzwonek	dzvonehk
dź or dzi	pronounced like the Polish dz but softer	dzh	dziať	dzhahw
h or ch	similar to English h but with much more friction	h	herbata chudy	hehrbahtah hoodi
ń or ni	pronounced like the English n but softer	ñ	nie	ñeh
r	like the Scottish r (vibration of the tip of the tongue); note that it is also pronounced at the end of words	r	rak	rahk
ś or si	pronounced like the English s but softer	s'	się ktoś	s'eh ktos'
ż or zi	pronounced like the English z but softer	z'	zielony	z'ehloni

Notice that voiced sounds become completely devoiced at the end of a word or in the context of other voiceless sounds, i.e., they are pronounced like their voiceless counterparts (e.g., b of chleb is pronounced like p; w of rów is pronounced like f; rz and z in przez like sz and s, etc.).

Vowels

a	like English **u** in cult or American **o** in college	ah	**tak**	tahk
e	like **e** in ten	eh	**lek**	lehk
i	like **ee** in feet	ee	**ile**	eeleh
y	like **i** in fit	i	**ty**	ti
o	like **o** in cot	o	**kot**	kot
u or **ó**	a sound between the English **u** in put and **oo** in boots	oo	**drut**	droot
ą	is pronounced **on** before a consonant; when it's the final letter, it is pronounced like French **an** in fiancé	on	**prąd**	pront
		awng	**są**	sawng
ę	is pronounced **en** before a consonant or like **e** in bed when it is the final letter	ehn	**pęd**	pehnt
		eh	**tę**	teh

Some diphthongs

ej	like **a** in take	ay	**dobrej**	**dob**ray
aj	like **i** in like	igh	**daj**	digh

The stress falls in Polish on the next to the last syllable, e.g., **głodny** (**gwod**ni), **drogeria** (dro**geh**ryah).

Some basic expressions

Yes.	**Tak.**	tahk
No.	**Nie.**	ñeh
Please.	**Proszę.**	**pro**sheh
Thank you.	**Dziękuję.**	dzhehn**koo**yeh
Thank you very much.	**Dziękuję bardzo.**	dzhehn**koo**yeh **bahr**dzo
That's all right.	**Proszę bardzo.**	**pro**sheh **bahr**dzo

Greetings

Good morning.	**Dzień dobry.**	dzhehñ **do**bri
Good afternoon.	**Dzień dobry.**	dzhehñ **do**bri
Good evening.	**Dobry wieczór.**	**do**bri **vyeh**choor
Good night.	**Dobranoc.**	do**brah**nots
Good-bye.	**Do widzenia.**	do veed**zeh**ñah
See you later.	**Do zobaczenia.**	do zobah**cheh**ñah
This is Mr....	**To jest pan ...**	to yehst pahn
This is Mrs....	**To jest pani ...**	to yehst **pah**ñee
This is Miss ...	**To jest pani ...**	to yehst **pah**ñee
I'm very pleased to meet you.	**Miło mi pana/panią poznać.**	**mee**wo mee **pah**na/**pah**ñawng **poz**nahtsh
How are you?	**Jak się pan/pani miewa?**	yahk s'eh pahn/**pah**ñee **myeh**vah
Very well, thank you.	**Bardzo dobrze, dziękuję.**	**bahr**dzo **do**bzheh dzhehn**koo**yeh
And you?	**A pan/pani?**	ah pahn/**pah**ñee
Fine.	**Dobrze.**	**do**bzheh
Excuse me.	**Przepraszam.**	psheh**prah**shahm

Questions

Where?	**Gdzie?**	**gdzheh**
Where is ...?	**Gdzie jest ...?**	**gdzheh** yehst
Where are ...?	**Gdzie są ...?**	**gdzheh** sawng
When?	**Kiedy?**	**kyeh**di

What?	Co?	tso
How?	Jak?	yahk
How much?	Ile?	eeleh
How many?	Ile?	eeleh
Who?	Kto?	kto
Why?	Dlaczego?	dlahchehgo
Which?	Który?	ktoori
What do you call this?	Jak się to nazywa?	yahk s'eh to nahzivah
What do you call that?	Jak się tamto nazywa?	yahk s'eh tahmto nahzivah
What does this mean?	Co to znaczy?	tso to znahchi
What does that mean?	Co tamto znaczy?	tso tahmto znahchi

Do you speak ... ?

Do you speak English?	Czy pan/pani mówi po angielsku?	chi pahn/pahñee moovee po ahngyehlskoo
Do you speak German?	Czy pan/pani mówi po niemiecku?	chi pahn/pahñee moovee po nyehmyehtskoo
Do you speak French?	Czy pan/pani mówi po francusku?	chi pahn/pahñee moovee po frahntsooskoo
Do you speak Spanish?	Czy pan/pani mówi po hiszpańsku?	chi pahn/pahñee moovee po heeshpahñskoo
Do you speak Italian?	Czy pan/pani mówi po włosku?	chi pahn/pahñee moovee po vwoskoo
Could you speak more slowly, please?	Proszę mówić trochę wolniej.	prosheh mooveetsh troheh volñay
Please point to the phrase in the book.	Proszę wskazać odpowiednie zdanie w moich rozmówkach.	prosheh fskahzahtsh odpovyehdñeh zdahñeh fmoeeh rozmoofkahh
Just a minute. I'll see if I can find it in this book.	Chwlleczkę. Zobaczę czy to jest w moich rozmówkach.	hfeelehchkeh. zobahcheh chi to yehst fmoeeh rozmoofkahh
I understand.	Rozumiem.	rozoomyehm
I don't understand.	Nie rozumiem.	ñeh rozoomyehm

POLISH

Can...?

Can I have...?	**Czy mogę dostać...?**	chi **mo**geh **doss**tahtsh
Can we have...?	**Czy możemy dostać...?**	chi mo**zheh**my **doss**tahtsh
Can you show me...?	**Czy może mi pan/pani pokazać...?**	chi **mo**zheh mee pahn/**pah**ñee po**kah**zahtsh
Can you tell me...?	**Czy może mi pan/pani powiedzieć...?**	chi **mo**zheh mee pahn/**pah**ñee po**vyeh**dzhehtsh
Can you help me, please?	**Czy może mi pan/pani pomóc?**	chi **mo**zheh mee pahn/**pah**ñee po**moots**

Wanting

I'd like...	**Chciałbym...**	**htshahw**bim
We'd like...	**Chcielibyśmy...**	**htsheh**leebis'mi
Please give me...	**Proszę mi dać...**	**pro**sheh mee dahs
Give it to me, please.	**Proszę mi to dać.**	**pro**sheh mee to dahtsh
Please bring me...	**Proszę przynieść mi...**	**pro**sheh **pshi**ñehs'tsh mee
Bring it to me, please.	**Proszę mi to przynieść.**	**pro**sheh mee to **pshi**ñehs'tsh
I'm hungry.	**Jestem głodny.**	**yehss**tehm **gwod**ni
I'm thirsty.	**Chce mi się pić.**	htseh mee s'eh peetsh
I'm tired.	**Jestem zmęczony.**	**yehss**tehm zmehn**cho**ni
I'm lost.	**Zgubiłem się.**	zgoo**bee**wehm s'eh
It's important.	**To ważne.**	to **vahzh**neh
It's urgent.	**To pilne.**	to **peel**neh
Hurry up!	**Niech się pan/pani pospieszy!**	ñehh s'eh pahn/**pah**ñee po**spyeh**shi

It is/There is...

It is/It's...	**To jest...**	to yehst
Is it...?	**Czy to jest...?**	chi to yehst
It isn't...	**To nie jest...**	to ñeh yehst

There is/There are . . .	**Jest/Są . . .**	yehst/sawng
Is there/Are there . . . ?	**Czy jest/Czy są . . . ?**	chi yehst/chi sawng
There isn't/There aren't . . .	**Nie ma . . .**	ñeh mah
There isn't any/ There aren't any.	**Nie ma.**	ñeh mah

A few common words

big/small	**duży/mały**	doozhi/**mahwi**
quick/slow	**szybki/wolny**	shipkee/**volni**
early/late	**wczesny/późny**	fchehssni/**pooz'ni**
cheap/expensive	**tani/drogi**	tahñee/**drogee**
near/far	**bliski/daleki**	bleesskee/dahlehkee
hot/cold	**gorący/zimny**	gorontsi/**z'eemni**
full/empty	**pełny/pusty**	pehwni/**poossti**
easy/difficult	**łatwy/trudny**	wahtfi/**troodni**
heavy/light	**ciężki/lekki**	tshehnshkee/**lehkkee**
open/shut	**otwarty/zamknięty**	otfahrti/zahmkñehnti
right/wrong	**słuszny/niesluszny**	swooshni/**ñeh**swooshni
old/new	**stary/nowy**	stahri/**novi**
old/young	**stary/młody**	stahri/**mwodi**
beautiful/ugly	**piękny/brzydki**	pyehnkni/**bzhitkee**
good/bad	**dobry/zły**	dobri/**zwi**
better/worse	**lepiej/gorzej**	lehpyay/**gozhay**

A few prepositions and some more useful words

at	**w**	v
on	**na**	nah
in	**w**	v
to	**do**	do
from	**z**	z
inside	**wewnątrz**	vehvnontsh
outside	**na zewnątrz**	nah zehvnontsh
up	**do góry**	do goori
down	**na dół**	nah doow
before	**przed**	psheht
after	**po**	po
with	**z**	z
without	**bez**	behss
through	**przez**	pshehss
towards	**w kierunku**	fkyehroonkoo
until	**aż do**	ahzh do

during	podczas	potchahss
and	i	ee
or	lub	loop
not	nie	ñeh
nothing	nic	ñeets
none	żaden	zhahdehn
very	bardzo	bahrdzo
also	także	tahgzheh
soon	wkrótce	fkroottseh
perhaps	może	mozheh
here	tutaj	tootigh
there	tam	tahm
now	teraz	tehrahss
then	potem	potehm

Arrival

Your passport, please.	Paszport proszę.	pahshport prosheh
Here it is.	Proszę.	prosheh
Have you anything to declare?	Czy ma pan/pani coś do zadeklarowania?	chi mah pahn/pahñee tsos' do zahdehklahrovahñah
No, nothing at all.	Nie, nic nie mam.	ñeh ñeets ñeh mahm
Porter!	Bagażowy!	bahgahzhovi
Can you help me with my luggage, please?	Proszę pomóc mi nieść te walizki.	prosheh pomoots mee ñehs'tsh teh vahleeskee
That's my suitcase.	To moja walizka.	to moyah vahleeskah
Where's the bus for the centre of town, please?	Gdzie jest autobus do centrum?	gdzheh yehst ahwtobooss do tsehntroom
This way, please.	Proszę tędy.	prosheh tehndi

Changing money

| Can you change a traveller's cheque, please? | Czy może pan/pani wymienić mi czek podróżny? | chi mozheh pahn/pahñee vimyehñeetsh mee chehk podroozhni |
| Where's the nearest bank, please? | Gdzie jest najbliższy bank? | gdzheh yehst nighbleeshshi bahnk |

POLISH

Car rental

I'd like a car.	**Chcę wynająć samochód.**	htseh vi**nam**yontsh sah**mo**hoot
For how long?	**Na jak długo?**	nah yahk **dwoo**go
A day/Four days/ A week/Two weeks.	**Jeden dzień/Cztery dni/Tydzień/Dwa tygodnie.**	**yeh**dehn dzhehñ/**chtehr**i dñee/**ti**dzhehñ/dvah ti**god**ñeh

Taxi

Where can I get a taxi?	**Gdzie są taksówki?**	gdzheh sawng tahk**soof**kee
What's the fare to ... ?	**Ile kosztuje przejazd do ... ?**	**ee**leh kosh**too**yeh **pshe**hyahst do
Take me to this address, please.	**Proszę mnie zawieźć na ten adres.**	**pros**h'eh mñeh **zah**vyehs'tsh nah tehn **ah**drehss
I'm in a hurry.	**Spieszy mi się.**	**spyeh**shi mee s'eh
Could you drive more slowly, please?	**Proszę jechać wolniej.**	**pro**sheh **veh**hahtsh **vol**ñay

Hotel and other accommodation

My name is ...	**Nazywam się ...**	nah**zi**vahm s'eh
Have you a reservation?	**Czy ma pan/pani rezerwację?**	chi mah pahn/**pah**ñee rehzehr**vahts**yeh
Yes, here's the confirmation.	**Tak, oto kwit.**	tahk **o**to kfeet
I'd like ...	**Proszę ...**	**pro**sheh
I'd like a single room/a double room.	**Proszę pojedyńczy pokój/podwójny pokój.**	**pro**sheh poyeh**diñ**chi **po**kooy/pod**vooy**ni po**kooy**
a room with a bath/ with a shower	**pokól z łazienką/ z prysznicem**	po**kooy** zwahz'**ehn**kawng/ sprish**ñeet**sehm

How much?

What's the price per night/per week/per month?	**Ile kostuje za noc/za tydzień/za miesiąc?**	**ee**leh kosh**too**yeh zah nots/zah **ti**dzhehñ/zah **myehs**'onts
May I see the room?	**Czy mogę zobaczyć pokój?**	chi **mo**geh zo**bah**chitsh po**kooy**

I'm sorry, I don't like it.	**Niestety nie podoba mi się.**	ñehsstehti ñeh podobah mee s'eh
Yes, that's fine. I'll take it.	**Dobrze. Biorę go.**	dobzheh. byoreh go
What's my room number, please?	**Jaki jest numer mojego pokoju?**	yahkee yehst noomehr moyehgo pokoyoo
Number 123.	**Numer 123.**	noomehr 123

Service, please

Who is it?	**Kto tam?**	kto tahm
Just a minute.	**Chwileczkę.**	hfeelehchkeh
Come in! The door's open.	**Proszę! Drzwi otwarte.**	prosheh!, jvee otfahrteh
May we have breakfast in our room?	**Czy możemy zjeść śniadanie w pokoju?**	chi mozhehmi zyehs'tsh s'ñahdahñeh fpokoyoo

Breakfast

I'll have ...	**Proszę ...**	prosheh
I'll have some fruit juice.	**Proszę sok.**	prosheh sok
a boiled egg	**jajko gotowane**	yighko gotovahneh
a fried egg	**jajko smażone**	yighko smahzhoneh
some bacon/some ham	**bekon/szynkę**	behkon/shinkeh
some toast	**grzanki**	gzhahnkee
a pot of tea	**dzbanek herbaty**	dzbahnehk hehrbahti
a cup of tea	**filiżankę herbaty**	feeleezhahnkeh hehrbahti
some coffee	**kawę**	kahveh
some chocolate	**gorącą czekoladę**	gorontsawng chehkolahdeh
more butter	**trochę więcej masła**	troheh vyehntsay mahsswah
some hot water	**trochę gorącej wody**	troheh gorontsay vodi

Difficulties

The central heating doesn't work.	**Centralne ogrzewanie nie działa.**	tsehntrahlneh ogzhehvahñeh ñeh dzhahwah
the light/the socket	**światło/gniazdko**	s'fyahtwo/gñahsstko
the tap/the toilet	**kurek/ubikacja**	koorehk/oobeekahtsyah

| There's no hot water. | **Nie ma ciepłej wody.** | ñeh mah **tsheh**pway **vo**di |
| May I see the manager, please? | **Chciałbym poroz-mawiać z kierow-nikiem.** | **htshahw**bim poroz**mah**vyahtsh skehrov**nee**kehm |

Telephone—Mail

There's a call for you.	**Telefon do pana/pani.**	teh**leh**fon do **pah**nah/**pah**ñee
Hold the line, please.	**Proszę się nie roz-łanczać.**	**pro**sheh s'eh ñeh rozwon**chah**tsh
Operator, I've been cut off.	**Proszę pana, przer-wano mi.**	**pro**sheh **pah**nah pshehr**vah**no mee
Did anyone telephone me?	**Czy ktoś do mnie dzwonił?**	chi ktos' do mñeh **dzvo**ñeew
Is there any mail for me?	**Czy jest dla mnie poczta?**	chi yehst dlah mñeh **poch**tah
Are there any messages for me?	**Czy jest jakaś wiadomość dla mnie?**	chi yehst **yah**kahs' vyah**do**mos'tsh dlah mñeh

Checking out

May I have my bill, please?	**Proszę rachunek.**	**pro**sheh rah**hoo**nehk
We're in a great hurry.	**Bardzo się spie-szymy.**	**bahr**dzo s'eh spyeh**shi**mi
It's been a very en-joyable stay.	**Bardzo miło spę-dziliśmy tutaj czas.**	**bahr**dzo **mee**wo spehndzhee**lees'**mi **too**tigh chahss

Eating out

Good evening, sir/ Good evening, madam.	**Dobry wieczór panu/Dobry wieczór pani.**	**do**bri vyeh**choor pah**noo/**do**bri vyeh**choor pah**ñee
Good evening. I'd like a table for two, please.	**Dobry wieczór. Proszę o stolik dla dwóch osób.**	**do**bri vyeh**choor**. **pro**sheh o **sto**leek dlah dyooh **o**soop
Do you have a fixed-price menu?	**Czy są obiady firmowe?**	chi sawng o**byah**di feer**mo**veh
May I see the à la carte menu?	**Proszę kartę.**	**pro**sheh **kahr**teh

May we have an ashtray, please?	**Proszę popielniczkę.**	**pro**sheh popyehl**ñ**eechkeh
some bread	**pieczywo**	pyeh**chi**vo
a fork	**widelec**	vee**deh**lehts
a knife	**nóż**	noosh
a spoon	**łyżkę**	**wish**keh
a plate	**talerz**	**tah**lehsh
a glass	**szklankę**	**shklahn**keh
a napkin	**serwetkę**	sehr**veh**tkeh
another chair	**jeszcze jedno krzesło**	**yehsh**cheh **yehd**no **kshehss**wo
Where's the gentlemen's toilet (men's room)?	**Gdzie jest toaleta dla panów?**	gdzheh yehst twah**leh**tah dlah **pah**noof
Where's the ladies' toilet (ladies' room)?	**Gdzie jest toaleta dla pań?**	gdzheh yehst twah**leh**tah dlah pahñ

Appetizers

I'd like some ...	**Proszę ...**	**pro**sheh
I'd like some assorted appetizers.	**Proszę zestaw zakąsek.**	**pro**sheh **zehss**tahf zah**kon**sehk
orange juice	**sok pomarańczowy**	sok pomah**rahñ**chovi
ham	**szynkę**	**shin**keh
melon	**melona**	meh**lo**nah
pâté	**pasztet**	**pah**shteht
smoked salmon	**wędzonego łososia**	vehndzo**neh**go wossos'ah
shrimps (shrimp)	**krewetki**	kreh**veh**tkee

Soup

Have you any ...?	**Czy jest ...?**	chi yehst
Have you any chicken soup?	**Czy jest rosół?**	chi yehst **ross**oow
vegetable soup	**zupa jarzynowa**	**zoo**pah yahzhi**no**vah
onion soup	**zupa cebulowa**	**zoo**pah tsehboo**lo**vah

Fish

I'd like some ...	**Proszę ...**	**pro**sheh
I'd like some fish.	**Proszę rybę.**	**pro**sheh **ri**beh
sole	**solę**	**so**leh
trout	**pstrąga**	**pstron**gah
lobster	**homara**	ho**mah**rah
crayfish	**langustę**	lahn**gooss**teh
prawns	**krewetki**	kreh**veh**tkee

I'd like it...	**Proszę rybę...**	**pro**sheh **ri**beh
I'd like it steamed.	**Proszę rybę duszoną.**	**pro**sheh **ri**beh **doo**shonawng
grilled	**z rusztu**	**zroosh**too
boiled	**gotowaną**	**goto**vahnawng
baked	**zapiekaną**	**zah**pyeh**kah**nawng
fried	**smażoną**	**smah**zhonawng

Meat—Poultry—Game

I'd like some...	**Proszę...**	**pro**sheh
I'd like some beef.	**Proszę wołowinę.**	**pro**sheh **vo**wo**vee**neh
a beef steak	**befsztyk**	**behf**shtik
some roast beef	**pieczeń wołową**	**pyeh**chehñ **vo**wo**vawng**
a veal cutlet	**sznycel cielęcy**	**shnit**sehl tsheh**lehn**tsi
mutton	**baraninę**	**ba**rah**ñee**neh
lamb	**młodą baraninę**	**mwo**dawng **ba**rah**ñee**neh
a pork chop	**kotlet schabowy**	**kot**leht **shah**bovi
roast pork	**pieczeń wieprzową**	**pyeh**chehñ **vyehp**sho**vawng**
hare	**zająca**	**za**yontsah
chicken	**kurczę**	**koor**cheh
roast chicken	**kurczę pieczone**	**koor**cheh **pyeh**choneh
duck	**kaczkę**	**kah**chkeh
How do you like your meat?	**Jak ma być podane?**	yahk mah bitsh **po**dahneh
rare	**po angielsku**	po ahn**gehl**skoo
medium	**średnio wysmażone**	**s'rehd**ño viss**mah**zhoneh
well done	**mocno wysmażone**	**mots**no viss**mah**zhoneh

Vegetables

What vegetables have you got?	**Jakie są jarzyny?**	**yah**keh sawng yam**hzhi**ni
I'd like some...	**Proszę...**	**pro**sheh
I'd like some asparagus.	**Proszę szparagi.**	**pro**sheh **shpa**rah**gee**
green beans	**zieloną fasolkę**	**z'eh**lonawng fah**ssol**keh
mushrooms	**pieczarki**	**pyeh**chah**r**kee
carrots	**marchewkę**	**mah**r**hehf**keh
onions	**cebulę**	**tseh**booleh
red cabbage	**czerwoną kapustę**	**cheh**rvonawng **kah**pooss**teh**
spinach	**szpinak**	**shpee**nahk
rice	**ryż**	rish

peas	**groszek**	groshehk
tomatoes	**pomidory**	pomeedori
green salad	**sałatkę**	sahwahtkeh
potatoes	**ziemniaki**	z'ehmñahkee

Desserts

Nothing more, thanks.	**To wszystko, dziękuję.**	to fshisstko dzhehnkooyeh
Just a small portion, please.	**Małą porcję proszę.**	mahwawng portsyeh prosheh
Have you any ice-cream?	**Czy są lody?**	chi sawng lodi
fruit salad	**kompot**	kompot
fresh fruit	**świeże owoce**	s'fyehzheh ovotseh
cheese	**ser**	sehr

Drink

What would you like to drink?	**Czego pan/pani się napije?**	chehgo pahn/pahñee s'eh nahpeeyeh
I'll have a beer, please.	**Proszę piwo.**	prosheh peevo
I'll have a whisky, please.	**Proszę whisky.**	prosheh wisskee

Wine

I'd like a bottle of wine.	**Proszę butelkę wina.**	prosheh bootehlkeh veenah
red wine	**czerwonego wina**	chehrvonehgo veenah
rosé wine	**słodkiego wina**	swotkehgo veenah
white wine	**białego wina**	byahwehgo veenah
Cheers!	**Na zdrowie!**	nah zdrovyeh

The bill (check)

May I have the bill (check) please?	**Proszę o rachunek.**	prosheh o rahhoonehk
Is service included?	**Włącznie z obsługa?**	vwonchñeh zopswoogawng
Everything's included.	**Rachunek obejmuje wszystko.**	rahhoonehk obaymooyeh fshisstko
Thank you, that was a very good meal.	**Dziękuję, jedzenie było bardzo dobre.**	dzhehnkooyeh yehdzehñeh biwo bahrdzo dobreh

Travelling

Where's the railway station, please?	Przepraszam, gdzie jest stacja kolejowa?	pshehprahshahm gdzheh yehst stahtsyah kolehyovah
Where's the ticket office, please?	Przepraszam, gdzie jest kasa biletowa?	pshehprahshahm gdzheh yehst kahssah beelehtovah
I'd like a ticket to...	Proszę bilet do...	prosheh beeleht do
First or second class?	Pierwszej czy drugiej klasy?	pyehrshay chi droogay klahssi
First class, please.	Proszę pierwszą klasę.	prosheh pyehrshawng klahsseh
Single or return (one way or round-trip)?	Zwykły bilet czy powrotny?	zvikwi beeleht chi povrotni
Do I have to change trains?	Czy muszę się przesiadać?	chi moosheh s'eh pshehs'aydahtsh
What platform does the train leave from?	Z którego peronu odchodzi pociąg?	sktoorehgo pehronoo othodzhee potshonk
Where's the nearest underground station?	Gdzie jest najbliższa stacja metro?	gdzheh yehst nighbleeshshah stahtsyah mehtro
Where's the bus station, please?	Gdzie jest dworzec autobusowy?	gdzheh yehst dvozhehts ahwtoboossovi
When's the first bus to...?	Kiedy odchodzi pierwszy autobus do...?	kehdi othodzhee pyehrshi ahwtobooss do
the last bus	ostatni autobus	osstahtñee ahwtobooss
the next bus	następny autobus	nahsstehmpni ahwtobooss
Please let me off at the next stop.	Proszę mnie wypuścić na następnym przystanku.	prosheh mñeh vipoos'tsheetsh nah nahsstehmpnim pshisstahnkoo

Relaxing

What's on at the cinema (movies)?	Co grają w kinie?	tso grahyawng fkeeñeh
What's on at the theatre?	Co grają w teatrze?	tso grahyawng ftehahchsheh
What time does the film begin? And the play?	O której zaczyna się film? A sztuka?	o ktooray zahchinah s'eh feelm? ah shtookah
Are there any tickets for tonight?	Czy są bilety na dzisiaj wieczór?	chi sawng beelehti nah dzheess'igh vyehchoor

| Where can we go dancing? | **Gdzie można pójść potańczyć?** | gdzheh mozhnah pooys'tsh potahñchitsh |
| Would you like to dance? | **Czy mogę prosić?** | chi mogeh pross'eetsh |

Introductions

How do you do?	**Dzień dobry.**	dzhehñ dobri
How are you?	**Jak się pan/pani ma?**	yahk s'eh pahn/pahñee mah
Very well, thank you. And you?	**Dobrze, dziękuję. A pan/pani?**	dobzheh dzhehnkooyeh. ah pahn/pahñee
May I introduce Miss Philips?	**To jest pani Philips.**	to yehst pahñee Philips
My name is ...	**Nazywam się ...**	nahzivahm s'eh
I'm very pleased to meet you.	**Miło mi pana/panią poznać.**	meewo mee pahnah/pahñawng poznahtsh
How long have you been here?	**Od jak dawna pan/pani jest tutaj?**	od yahk dahvnah pahn/pahñee yehst tootigh
It was nice meeting you.	**Miło mi było pana/panią poznać.**	meewo mee biwo pahnah/pahñawng poznahtsh

Dating

Would you like a cigarette?	**Czy zapali pani?**	chi zahpahlee pahñee
May I get you a drink?	**Czy nie zechciałaby pani napić się czegoś?**	chi ñeh zehhtshahwahbi pahñee nahpeetsh s'eh chehgos'
Do you have a light, please?	**Czy mogę prosić o ogień?**	chi mogeh pross'eetsh o ogehñ
Are you waiting for someone?	**Czy pan/pani na kogoś czeka?**	chi pahn/pahñee nah kogos' chehkah
Are you free this evening?	**Czy pan/pani ma dzisiaj wolny wieczór?**	chi pahn/pahñee mah dzheess'igh volni vyehchoor
Where shall we meet?	**Gdzie się spotkamy?**	gdzheh s'eh spotkahmi
What time shall I meet you?	**O której się spotkamy?**	o ktooray s'eh spotkahmi
May I take you home?	**Czy mogę panią odwieźć do domu?**	chi mogeh pahñawng odvyehs'tsh do domoo

Thank you, it's been a wonderful evening.	Dziękuję za cudowny wieczór.	dzhehnkooyeh zah tsoodovni vyehchoor
What's your telephone number?	Jaki jest pana/pani numer telefonu?	yahkee yehst pahnah/pahñee noomehr tehlehfonoo
Do you live alone?	Czy pani mieszka sama?	chi pahñee myehshkah sahmah
What time is your last train?	O której ma pan/pani ostatni pociąg?	o ktotray mah pahn/pahñee ostahtnee potshonk
Good-night...	Dobranoc...	dobrahnots

Banks

Where's the nearest bank, please?	Przepraszam, gdzie jest najbliższy bank?	pshehprahshahm gdzheh yehst nighbleeshshi bahnk
Where can I cash some traveller's cheques?	Gdzie mogę wymienić czeki podróżne?	gdzheh mogeh vimyehñeetsh chehkee podroozhneh
What time does the bank open? What time does it close?	O której otwiera się bank? O której się zamyka?	o ktooray otfyehrah s'eh bahnk o ktooray s'eh zahmikah
I'm expecting some money from home. Has it arrived?	Oczekuję na przekaz pieniężny z domu. Czy już nadszedł?	ochehkooyeh nah pshehkahss pyehñehnzhni zdomoo. chi yoosh nahtsheht
Can you give me some small change, please?	Proszę mi dać drobne.	prosheh mee dahtsh drobneh

Shops, stores and services

Where is the nearest chemist's (pharmacy)?	Gdzie jest najbliższa apteka?	gdzheh yehst nighbleeshshah ahptehkah
the nearest hair-dresser's	zakład fryzjerski	zahkwaht friz yehrskee
the photo shop	fotooptyka	fotooptikah
the jeweller's	jubiler	yoobeelehr
the department store	dom towarowy	dom tovahrovi
the police station	posterunek milicji	postehroonehk meeleetsyee
the garage	warsztat samochodowy	vahrshtaht sahmohodovi

| How do I get there? | **Jak tam się mogę, dostać?** | yahk tahm s'eh mogeh dosstahtsh |
| Is it within walking distance? | **Czy dojdę tam pieszo?** | chi doydeh tahm pyehsho |

Service

Can you help me, please?	**Proszę pana/panią!**	prosheh pahnah/pahñawng
Can you show me this? And that, too.	**Proszę mi to pokazać! A także tamto!**	prosheh mee to pokahzahtsh! ah tahgzheh tahmto
It's too expensive/ too big/too small.	**Jest za drogi/za duży/za mały.**	yehst zah drogee/zah doozhi/zah mahwi
Can you show me some more?	**Czy może mi pan/pani pokazać trochę więcej?**	chi mozheh mee pahn/ pahñee pokahzahtsh troheh vyehntsay
something better something cheaper	**coś lepszego coś tańszego**	tsos'lehpshehgo tsos' tahñshehgo
How much is this? And that?	**Ile to kosztuje? A tamto?**	eeleh to koshtooyeh? ah tahmto
It's not quite what I want.	**Nie to chciałem.**	ñeh to htshahwehm
I like it.	**Podoba mi się to.**	podobah mee s'eh to

Chemist's (Pharmacy)

| I'd like something for a cold/for a cough/for travel sickness. | **Proszę coś na przeziębienie/na kaszel/na mdłości.** | prosheh tsos' nah pshehz'ehmbyehñeh/nah kahshehl/nah mdwos'tshee |
| Can you recommend something for hay-fever/for sunburn? | **Czy może mi pan/pani polecić coś na katar sienny/na oparzenie słoneczne?** | chi mozheh mee pahn/ pahñee polehtsheetsh tsos' nah kahtahr s'ehnni/ nah opahzhehñeh swonehchneh |

Toiletry

May I have some razor blades?	**Poproszę żyletki.**	poprosheh zhilehtkee
some shaving cream some toothpaste	**krem do golenia pastę do zębów**	krehm do golehñah pahssteh do zehmboof
I'd like some soap.	**Proszę mydło.**	prosheh midwo
some suntan oil	**olejek do opalania**	olehyehk do opahlahñah

At the barber's

I'd like a haircut, please.	**Proszę mnie ostrzyc.**	prosheh mñeh **oss**tshits
Short/Leave it long.	**Krótko/Długo.**	**kroo**tko/**dwoo**go
A razor cut, please.	**Strzyżenie brzytwą, proszę.**	stshi**zheh**ñeh **bzhit**fawng **pro**sheh

At the hairdresser's

I'd like a shampoo and set, please.	**Proszę mycie i trwałe ufarbowanie.**	prosheh **mit**sheh ee **trfah**weh oofahrbo**vah**ñeh
I'd like a bleach.	**Proszę rozjaśnić.**	prosheh rozyahs'**ñeetsh**
a permanent	**trwała**	**trfah**wawng
a colour rinse	**płukankę koloryzu- jącą**	pwoo**kahn**keh kolorizoo**yon**tsawng
a manicure	**manicure**	mahñee**kyoor**

Photography

I'd like a film for this camera.	**Proszę film do tego aparatu.**	prosheh feelm do **teh**go ahpah**rah**too
This camera doesn't work.	**Popsuł mi się aparat.**	**pop**soow mee s'eh ah**pah**raht

At the post office

Where's the nearest post office, please?	**Przepraszam, gdzie jest najbliższa poczta?**	psheh**prah**shahm gdzheh yehst nigh**blee**shshah **poch**tah
I'd like to send this by express (special delivery)/by air mail.	**Chcę to nadać ekspresem/pocztą lotniczą.**	htseh to **nah**dahtsh ehk**spreh**ssehm/**poch**tawng lot**ñee**chawng

Service stations

Where is the nearest service station, please?	**Przepraszam, gdzie jest najbliższa stacja benzynowa?**	psheh**prah**shahm gdzheh yehst nigh**blee**shshah **stah**tsyah behnzi**no**vah
Fill her up, please.	**Proszę napełnić zbiornik.**	prosheh nah**pehw**ñeetsh **zbyor**ñeek
Check the oil, please.	**Proszę sprawdzić olej.**	prosheh **sprah**vdzheetsh **o**lay
Would you check the tyres?	**Proszę sprawdzić opony.**	prosheh **sprah**vdzheetsh **o**poni

Street directions

Can you show me on the map where I am?	**Czy może pan/pani pokazać mi na mapie gdzie teraz jestem?**	chi **mo**zheh pahn/**pah**ñee po**kah**zahtsh mee nah **mah**pyeh gdzheh **teh**rahss **yehss**stehm
You're on the wrong road.	**Pan/pani jedzie nie tą szosą.**	pahn/**pah**ñee **yeh**dzheh ñeh tawng **sho**ssawng
Go back to . . .	**Proszę zawrócić do . . .**	**pro**sheh zah**vroot**sheetsh do
Go straight ahead.	**Proszę jechać prosto.**	**pro**sheh **yeh**hahtsh **pros**sto
It's on the left/on the right.	**To jest na lewo/na prawo.**	to yehst nah **leh**vo/nah **prah**vo

Accidents

May I use your telephone?	**Czy mogę skorzystać z telefonu?**	chi **mo**geh sko**zhiss**tahtsh steh**leh**fonoo
Call a doctor quickly.	**Proszę wezwać lekarza, szybko.**	**pro**sheh **vehz**vahtsh leh**kah**zhah **ship**ko
Call an ambulance.	**Proszę wezwać pogotowie.**	**pro**sheh **vehz**vahtsh pogo**tov**yeh
Please call the police.	**Proszę wezwać milicję.**	**pro**sheh **vehz**vahtsh meelee**ets**yeh

Numbers

one	**jeden**	**yeh**dehn
two	**dwa**	dvah
three	**trzy**	chshi
four	**cztery**	**chteh**ri
five	**pięć**	pyehñtsh
six	**sześć**	shehs'tsh
seven	**siedem**	**s'eh**dehm
eight	**osiem**	**os'**ehm
nine	**dziewięć**	**dzheh**vyehñtsh
ten	**dziesięć**	**dzhehs**'ehñtsh
eleven	**jedenaście**	yehdeh**nahs'**tsheh
twelve	**dwanaście**	dvah**nahs'**tsheh
thirteen	**trzynaście**	chshi**nahs'**tsheh
fourteen	**czternaście**	chtehr**nahs'**tsheh
fifteen	**piętnaście**	pyehtnah**s'**tsheh
sixteen	**szesnaście**	shehss**nahs'**tsheh
seventeen	**siedemnaście**	s'ehdehm**nahs'**tsheh
eighteen	**osiemnaście**	os'ehm**nahs'**tsheh
nineteen	**dziewiętnaście**	dzhehvyeht**nahs'**tsheh

twenty	**dwadzieścia**	dvah**dzhehs**'tshah
twenty-one	**dwadzieścia jeden**	dvah**dzhehs**'tshah **yeh**dehn
thirty	**trzydzieści**	chshid**zhehs**'tshee
forty	**czterdzieści**	chtehr**dzhehs**'tshee
fifty	**pięćdziesiąt**	pyehñ**dzhehs**'ont
sixty	**sześćdziesiąt**	shehs'**dzhehs**'ont
seventy	**siedemdziesiąt**	s'ehdehm**dzhehs**'ont
eighty	**osiemdziesiąt**	os'ehm**dzhehs**'ont
ninety	**dziewięćdziesiąt**	dzhehvyehñ**dzhehs**'ont
one hundred	**sto**	sto
one thousand	**tysiąc**	tis'onts
ten thousand	**dziesięć tysięcy**	**dzhehs**'ehñtsh tis'**ehn**tsi

Days

It's Sunday.	**Jest niedziela.**	yehst ñeh**dzhehl**ah
Monday	**poniedziałek**	poñeh**dzhah**wehk
Tuesday	**wtorek**	ftorehk
Wednesday	**środa**	s'rodah
Thursday	**czwartek**	chfahrtehk
Friday	**piątek**	pyontehk
Saturday	**sobota**	sobotah
yesterday	**wczoraj**	fchorigh
today	**dzisiaj**	dzhees'igh
tomorrow	**jutro**	yootro
morning/afternoon	**rano/popołudnie**	rahno/popowoodñeh
evening/night	**wieczór/noc**	vyehchoor/nots

Months

January	**styczeń**	stichehñ
February	**luty**	looti
March	**marzec**	mahzhehts
April	**kwiecień**	kfyehtshehñ
May	**maj**	migh
June	**czerwiec**	chehrvyehts
July	**lipiec**	leepyehts
August	**sierpień**	s'ehrpyehñ
September	**wrzesień**	vzhehss'ehñ
October	**październik**	pahz'**dzhehr**ñeek
November	**listopad**	leesstopaht
December	**grudzień**	groodzhehñ
Merry Christmas!	**Wesołych Świąt!**	vehsowih s'fyont!
Happy New Year!	**Szczęśliwego Nowego Roku!**	schehehns'leevehgo novehgo rokoo

PORTUGUESE

Guide to Pronunciation

Letter	Approximate pronunciation	Symbol	Example	
Consonants				
f, k, l, p, t, v	as in English			
b	as in English, but often less decisive (more like **v**)	b	**boca**	**b**oaker
		bh	**abrir**	er**bh**reer
c	1) before **e** and **i**, like **s** in s**i**t	s	**cedo**	**s**aydhoo
	2) elsewhere, like **k** in **k**ill	k	**casa**	**k**ahzer
ç	like **s** in s**i**t	s	**comecar**	koomer**sahr**
ch	like **sh** in **sh**ut	sh	**chamar**	**sh**ermahr
d	as in English, but often less decisive (more like **th** in **th**is)	d	**dia**	**d**eeer
		dh	**nada**	nah**dh**er
g	1) before **a**, **o** and **u** or a consonant, or after **l**, **n** and **r**, like **g** in **g**o	g	**garfo**	**g**ahrfoo
	2) between vowels, like a soft version of the **ch** in Scottish lo**ch**	ġ	**rogar**	rooġahr
	3) before **e** and **i**, like **s** in plea**s**ure	zh	**gelo**	**zh**ayloo

h	always silent		**homem**	omahng^y
j	like **s** in pleasure	zh	**já**	zhah
lh	like **lli** in million	ly	**olho**	olyoo
m	1) between a vowel and a consonant, or at the end of a word ("finally"), it indicates that the vowel is nasalized (see "Nasal vowels")		**embalar** **bom**	ahng^ybah**lahr** bawng
	2) elsewhere like **m** in met	m	**mais**	mighsh
n	1) when initial or between vowels, like **n** in no	n	**novo**	noavoo
	2) in a consonant group and in plural endings it nasalizes the preceding vowel, but is generally silent		**branco** **homens**	brahngkoo omahng^ysh
nh	like **ni** in onion	ny	**vinho**	veenyoo
q	like **k** in kill	k	**quadro**	kwahdhroo
r	strongly trilled as in Scottish speech	r	**rua**	rooer
s	1) when initial, after a consonant or written **ss**, like **s** in sit	s	**saber**	serbhayr
	2) between vowels (not necessarily in the same word), like **z** in razor	z	**casa** **as aves**	kahzer erz ahversh
	3) when final, or before **c, f, p, q, t**, like **sh** in shut	sh	**país**	pereesh
	4) elsewhere, like **s** in pleasure	zh	**cisne**	seezhner
x	1) generally like **sh** in shut	sh	**baixo**	bighshoo
	2) in **ex-** before a vowel, like **z** in razor	z	**exacto**	izahtoo
z	1) when initial or between vowels like **z** in razor	z	**zero**	zehroo
	2) when final or before **c, f, p, q, s** or **t**, like **sh** in shut	sh	**feliz**	ferleesh
	3) elsewhere like **s** in pleasure	zh	**luz da**	loozh der

PORTUGUESE

Vowels

a	1) when stressed (see under "Stressing") it is like a mixture of the **u** in cut and the **a** in party	ah	**nado**	**nah**dhoo
	2) when unstressed or before **m**, **n** or **nh** but not in the same syllable like **a** in about	er	**porta**	**por**ter
e	1) when stressed generally like **e** in get	eh	**pertu**	**pehr**too
	2) when stressed sometimes like **a** in late	ay	**cabelo**	ker**bhay**loo
	3) when unstressed, like **er** in other	er	**pesado**	per**zah**dhoo
	4) at the beginning of a word, and in certain other cases, like **i** in hit	i	**antes** **exacto**	**er**ntish i**zah**too
é	like **e** in get	eh	**café**	ker**feh**
ê	like **a** in late	ay	**mês**	maysh
i	1) when stressed like **ee** in seed	ee	**riso**	**ree**zoo
	2) when unstressed, like **i** in coming	i	**final**	fi**nahl**
o	1) when stressed, like **o** in rod	o	**fora**	**for**er
	2) when unstressed, usually like **oo** in foot	oo	**caso**	**kah**zoo
	3) sometimes when stressed or unstressed, like **o** in note (most common o-sound)	oa	**voltar** **Lisboa**	voal**tahr** lizh**voaer**
ô, ou	like **o** in note	oa	**pôs**	poash
u	1) generally like **oo** in soon	oo	**número**	**noo**merroo
	2) silent in **gu** and **qu** before **e** or **i**		**querer**	ker**rayr**

Diphthongs

A diphthong is two vowels pronounced as a single vowel sound, e.g., in English **boy** there is a diphthong consisting of **o** plus a weak **i** sound. In Portuguese diphthongs, **a**, **e** and **o** are strong vowels and **i** and **u** are weak vowels. In diphthongs the strong vowels are pronounced with more stress (louder) than the weak ones, e.g., **ai** is pronounced like **igh** in s**igh**, and **au** like **ow** in h**ow**. Sometimes the weak vowels can combine to make a diphthong. Apart from these generalizations the exact pronunciation of Portuguese diphthongs is not easy to predict.

PORTUGUESE

Nasal vowels

These are pronounced through the mouth and through the nose at the same time, just as in the French nasal vowels (e.g., in the French **bon**) and quite similar to the nasal twang heard in some areas of America and Britain.

ã, am, an	something like **ung** in l**ung**, or like **an** in French d**ans**	ahng **maçã**	mer**sahng**
em, en	something like **ing** in s**ing**, but recalling also the **a** in l**a**te	ayng **cento**	**sayng**too
im, in	a nasalized version of the **ea** in l**ea**rn	eeng **cinco**	**seeng**koo
õ, om, on	like **orn** in c**orn**cob or like **on** in French b**on**	awng **bom**	bawng
um, un	something like a North of England pronunciation of **ung** in l**ung** (a nasalized version of **u** in p**u**t)	oong **um**	oong

Semi-nasalized diphthongs

In these, the first element is nasalized and combined with a weak **i** (pronounced like **y** in **y**et) or **u** pronounced like **w** in **w**as).

ãe, ãi, êm, final en, usually final em			
	pronounced as **ã** followed by **y** in **y**et	ahng^y **mãe** sêm	mahng^y sahng^y
ão, final unstressed am			
	pronounced as **ã** followed by **w** in **w**as	ahng^w **mão**	mahng^w
õe, oi	pronounced as **õ** followed by **y** in **y**et	awng^y **põe**	pawng^y
ui	like nasal vowel **u** followed by **y** in **y**et	oong^y **muito**	**moong**^{y}too

Stressing

1) If a word ends with **a**, **e** or **o**, the stress falls on the next to the last syllable, e.g., **rosa** (pronounced **roa**zer). Plural endings **m** and **s** are generally disregarded.

2) All other words are stressed on the last syllable, e.g., **animal** (pronounced ernee**mahl**).

Words not stressed in accordance with these rules have an accent (´ or `) over the vowel of the stressed syllable.

Some basic expressions

Yes.	**Sim.**	seeng
No.	**Não.**	nahng[w]
Please.	**Por favor.**	poor fer**voar**
Thank you.	**Obrigado.**	obree**gah**dhoo
Thank you very much.	**Muito obrigado.**	**moong**[y]too obree**gah**dhoo
That's all right.	**Não tem de quê.**	nahng[w] tayng der kay

Greetings

Good morning.	**Bom dia.**	bawng **dee**er
Good afternoon.	**Boa tarde.**	boaer **tah**rder
Good evening.	**Boa noite.**	boaer **noy**ter
Good night.	**Boa noite.**	boaer **noy**ter
Good-bye.	**Adeus.**	er**dheh**oosh
See you later.	**Até logo.**	er**tay** loa**goo**
This is Mr....	**Apresento-lhe o Senhor ...**	erprer**zayn**toolyer oo say**ñoar**
This is Mrs....	**Apresento-lhe a Senhora ...**	erprer**zayn**toolyer er say**ñoa**er
This is Miss ...	**Apresento-lhe a Menina ...**	erprer**zayn**toolyer er mer**nee**ner
I'm very pleased to meet you.	**Muito prazer em conhecê-lo.**	**moong**[y]too prer**thehr** ayng koo**ñer**thayloo
How are you?	**Como está?**	**koa**moo ish**tah**
Very well, thank you.	**Muito bem, obrigado.**	**moong**[y]too bayng obree**gah**dhoo
And you?	**E você?**	ee vo**say**
Fine.	**Bem.**	bayng
Excuse me.	**Desculpe.**	dehsh**kool**per

Questions

Where?	**Onde?**	**on**der
Where is...?	**Onde está...?**	**on**der ish**tah**
Where are...?	**Onde estão...?**	**on**der ish**tahng**[w]

PORTUGUESE

When?	**Quando?**	kwahndoo
What?	**O quê?**	oo kay
How?	**Como?**	koamoo
How much?	**Quanto?**	kwahntoo
How many?	**Quantos?**	kwahntoosh
Who?	**Quem?**	kayng
Why?	**Porquê?**	poorkay
Which?	**Qual?**	kwahl
What do you call this?	**Como se chama isto?**	koamoo ser shermer eeshtoo
What do you call that?	**Como se chama aquilo?**	koamoo ser shermer erkeeloo
What does this mean?	**Que significa isto?**	kay seegneefeeker eeshtoo
What does that mean?	**Que significa aquilo?**	kay seegneefeeker erkeeloo

Do you speak . . . ?

Do you speak English?	**Fala inglês?**	fahler eengglaysh
Do you speak German?	**Fala alemão?**	fahler erlermahng^w
Do you speak French?	**Fala francês?**	fahler frahngsaysh
Do you speak Spanish?	**Fala espanhol?**	fahler ishperñol
Do you speak Italian?	**Fala italiano?**	fahler eeterlyahnoo
Could you speak more slowly, please?	**Pode falar mais devagar, por favor?**	poahdher ferlahr mighsh dervergahr poor fervoar
Please point to the phrase in the book.	**Por favor, indique-me a frase no livro.**	poor fervoar eendeeker-mer er frahzer noo leevroo
Just a minute. I'll see if I can find it in this book.	**Um momento por favor, vou ver se posso encontrá-la neste livro.**	oong moomayngtoo poor fervoar voa vayr ser posssoo ingkontrahrler nehster leevroo
I understand.	**Compreendo.**	kawngpriayngdoo
I don't understand.	**Não compreendo.**	nahng^w kawngpriayngdoo

Can...?

Can I have...?	**Pode dar-me?**	poadher **dahr**mer
Can we have...?	**Pode dar-nos...?**	poadher **dahr**noosh
Can you show me...?	**Pode mostrar-me...?**	poadher moosh**trahr**mer
Can you tell me...?	**Pode dizer-me...?**	poadher dee**zehr**mer
Can you help me, please?	**Pode ajudar-me, por favor?**	poadher erzhoo**dahr**mer poor fer**voar**

Wanting

I'd like...	**Queria...**	ker**reeer**
We'd like...	**Queríamos...**	ker**reeer**moosh
Please give me...	**Por favor, dê-me...**	poor fer**voar day**mer
Give it to me, please.	**Dê-mo, por favor.**	**day**moo poor fer**voar**
Please bring me...	**Por favor, traga-me...**	poor fer**voar** trah̊**ger**mer
Bring it to me, please.	**Traga-mo, por favor.**	trah̊**ger** moo poor fer**voar**
I'm hungry.	**Tenho fome.**	**teh**ñoo **fo**mer
I'm thirsty.	**Tenho sede.**	**teh**ñoo **sehd**her
I'm tired.	**Estou cansado.**	ish**toa** kern**sahd**hoo
I'm lost.	**Estou perdido.**	ish**toa** perr**dheed**hoo
It's important.	**É importante.**	eh impoor**tahn**ter
It's urgent.	**É urgente.**	eh oor**zhehn**ter
Hurry up!	**Depressa!**	der**preh**ser

It is/There is...

It is/It's...	**É...**	eh
Is it...?	**É...?**	eh
It isn't...	**Não é...**	nahng^w eh
There is/There are...	**Há...**	ah
Is there/Are there...?	**Há...?**	ah

PORTUGUESE

	Portuguese	Pronunciation
There isn't/There aren't . . .	**Não há . . .**	nawng w ah
There isn't any/There aren't any.	**Não há nenhum/** **Não há nenhuns** (**Não há nenhuma/** **Não há nenhumas**).	nawng w ah niñoong/ nawng w ah niñoongsh (nawng w ah niñoongmer/ nawng w ah niñoong-mersh)

A few common words

big/small	**grande/pequeno**	**grahn**der/per**keh**noo
quick/slow	**rápido/lento**	**rah**peedhoo/**lehn**too
early/late	**cedo/tarde**	**seh**dhoo/**tahr**der
cheap/expensive	**barato/caro**	ber**rah**too/**kah**roo
near/far	**perto/longe**	**pehr**too/**lawng**zher
hot/cold	**quente/frio**	**kehn**ter/**free**oo
full/empty	**cheio/vazio**	**shay**oo/ver**zee**oo
easy/difficult	**fácil/difícil**	**fah**seel/der**fee**seel
heavy/light	**pesado/leve**	per**zah**dhoo/**leh**ver
open/shut	**aberto/fechado**	er**behr**too/fer**shah**dhoo
right/wrong	**certo/errado**	**sehr**too/eh**rrah**dhoo
old/new	**velho/novo**	**veh**lyoo/**noa**voo
old/young	**idoso/jovem**	ee**dhoa**zoo/**zho**vayng
beautiful/ugly	**belo/feio**	**beh**loo/**fay**oo
good/bad	**bom/mau**	bawng/mow
better/worse	**melhor/pior**	mil**yor**/pee**or**

Some prepositions and a few more useful words

at	**a**	ah
on	**sobre**	**soa**brer
in	**em**	ayng
to	**para**	**per**rer
from	**de**	der
inside	**dentro**	**dehn**troo
outside	**fora**	**fo**rer
up	**em cima**	ayng **see**mer
down	**em baixo**	ayng **bigh**shoo
before	**antes**	**ern**tish
after	**depois**	der**poysh**
with	**com**	kawng
without	**sem**	sayng
through	**através**	ertrer**vehsh**
towards	**para**	**per**rer
until	**até**	er**teh**
during	**durante**	doo**rahn**ter

and	e	ee
or	ou	oa
not	não	nawng^w
nothing	nada	nahdher
none	nenhum	ningñoong
very	muito	moong^ytoo
also	também	tahngbayng
soon	em breve	ayng brehver
perhaps	talvez	tahlvaysh
here	aqui	erkee
there	ali	erlee
now	agora	ergorer
then	depois	derpoysh

Arrival

Your passport, please.	O passaporte, por favor.	oo pahserporter poor fervoar
Here it is.	Aqui está.	erkee ishtah
Have you anything to declare?	Tem alguma coisa declarar?	tayng ahlgoomer koyzer er dherklerrahr
No, nothing at all.	Não, nada.	nawng^w nahdher
Porter!	Bagageiro!	bergerzhayroo
Can you help me with my luggage, please?	Pode levar-me a bagagem, por favor?	poadher lervahrmer er bergahzhayng poor fervoar
That's my suitcase.	Esta é a minha mala.	ehshter eh er meeñer mahler
Where's the bus to the centre of town, please?	Onde posso apanhar o autocarro para o centro da cidade, por favor?	onder posssoo erperñahr oo owtookahrroo perrer oo sehntroo der seedhahdher poor fervoar
This way, please.	Por aqui, por favor.	poor erkee poor fervoar

Changing money

| Can you change a traveller's cheque, please? | Pode cambiar-me um cheque de viagem, por favor? | poadher kermbyahrmer oong shehk der vyahzhayng poor fervoar |
| Where's the nearest bank, please? | Onde fica o banco mais próximo, por favor? | onder feeker oo bahngkoo mighsh proseemoo poor fervoar |

PORTUGUESE

PORTUGUESE

Car rental

I'd like a car.	**Queria alugar um carro.**	kerreeer erlooĝahr oong kahrroo
For how long?	**Por quanto tempo?**	poor kwahntoo tayngpoo
A day/Four days/ A week/Two weeks	**Um dia/Quatro dias/Uma semana/ Duas semanas.**	oong deeer/kwahtroo deeersh/oomer sermahner/dooersh sermahnersh

Taxi

Where can I get a taxi?	**Onde posso encontrar um táxi?**	onder posssoo ingkontrahr oong tahksee
What's the fare to . . . ?	**Qual é o preço do percurso para . . . ?**	kwahl ay oo prehsoo doo perrkoorsoo perrer
Take me to this address, please.	**Leve-me a esta morada, por favor.**	lehvermer er ehshter moorahdher poor fervoar
I'm in a hurry.	**Estou com pressa.**	ishtoa kawng prehser
Could you drive more slowly, please?	**Pode ir mais devagar, por favor?**	poadher eer mighsh derverĝahr poor fervoar

Hotel and other accommodation

My name is . . .	**O meu nome é . . .**	oo mehoo noamer eh
Have you a reservation?	**Reservou?**	rerzerrvoa
Yes, here's the confirmation.	**Sim, aqui está a confirmação.**	seeng erkee ishtah er kawngfeermersahng^w
I'd like . . .	**Quero . . .**	kehroo
I'd like a single room/a double room.	**Quero um quarto de uma cama/um quarto de casal.**	kehroo oong kwahrtoo der oomer kermer/oong kwahrtoo der kerzahl
a room with a bath/with a shower	**um quarto com banho/com chuveiro**	oong kwahrtoo kawng bahñoo/kawng shoovayroo

How much?

What's the price per night/per week/per month?	**Qual é o preço por noite/por semana/ por mês?**	kwahl eh oo prehsoo poor noyter/poor sermahner/poor maysh
May I see the room?	**Posso ver o quarto?**	posssoo vehr oo kwahrtoo

I'm sorry, I don't like it.	Lamento, mas não gosto.	lermehntoo mersh nahng^wgoshtoo
Yes, that's fine. I'll take it.	Sim, está bem. Fico com ele.	seeng ishtah bayng. feekoo kawng ehler
What's my room number, please?	Qual é o número do meu quarto, por favor?	kwahl eh oo noomerroo doo mehoo kwahrtoo poor fervoar
Number 123.	Número 123.	noomerroo 123.

Service, please

Who is it?	Quem é?	kayng eh
Just a minute.	Um momento.	oong moomehntoo
Come in! The door's open.	Entre! A porta está aberta.	ehntrer er porter ishtah erbehrter
May we have breakfast in our room?	Podemos ter o pequeno almoço no quarto?	poodhehmoosh tehr oo perkehnoo ahlmosoo nookwahrtoo

Breakfast

I'll have . . .	Tomo . . .	tomoo
I'll have some fruit juice.	Tomo sumo de fruta.	tomoo soomoo der frooter
a boiled egg	um ovo kozido	oong ovoo koozeedhoo
a fried egg	um ovo estrelado	oong ovoo ishtrerlahdhoo
some bacon/some ham	toucinho/presunto	toaseeñoo/prerzoontoo
some toast	torradas	toorrahdhersh
a pot of tea	um bule de chá	oong booler der shah
a cup of tea	uma chávena de chá	oomer shahverner der shah
some coffee	café	kerfeh
some chocolate	chocolate	shookoolahter
more butter	mais manteiga	mighsh merntayğer
some hot water	água quente	ahgwer kaynter

Difficulties

The central heating doesn't work.	O aquecimento central não funciona.	oo erkehseemehntoo sehntrahl nahng^w foonsyoaner
the light/the socket	a luz/a tomada	er loosh/er toomahdher
the tap/the toilet	a torneira/a casa de banho	er toornayrer/er kahzer der bahñoo

There's no hot water.	**Não há água quente.**	nahng[w] ah ah g̊wer kaynter
May I see the manager, please?	**Posso falar com o director, por favor?**	posssoo ferlahr kawng oo deerehtoar poor fervoar

Telephone—Mail

There's a call for you.	**Há uma chamada para si.**	ah oomer shermahdher perrer see
Hold the line, please.	**Aguarde um momento, por favor.**	ergwahrder oong moomehntoo poor fervoar
Operator, I've been cut off.	**Telefonista, cortaram-me a ligação.**	terlerfooneeshter koortahrermmer er leegersahng[w]
Did anyone telephone me?	**Alguém me chamou?**	ahlgayng mer shermoa
Is there any mail for me?	**Há correio para mim?**	ah koorrayoo perrer meeng
Are there any messages for me?	**Há alguma mensagem para mim.**	ah ahlgoomer mayngsahzhayng perrer meeng

Checking out

May I have my bill, please?	**Pode dar-me a conta, por favor?**	poadher dahrmer er konter poor fervoar
We're in a great hurry.	**Temos muita pressa.**	taymoosh moong[y]ter prehser
It's been a very enjoyable stay.	**Tivemos uma óptima estadia.**	teevehmoosh oomer oteemer ishterdheeer

Eating out

Good evening, sir/ Good evening, madam.	**Boa noite, Senhor/Boa noite, Senhora.**	boaer noyter sayñoar/boaer noyter sayñoarer
Good evening. I'd like a table for two, please.	**Boa noite. Desejo uma mesa para dois, por favor.**	boaer noyter. derzehzhoo oomer mayzer perrer doysh poor fervoar
Do you have a fixed-price menu?	**Tem um menu de preço fixo?**	tayng oong mehnoo der prehsoo feeksoo
May I see the à la carte menu?	**Pode dar-me o menu?**	poadher dahrmer oo mehnoo

May we have an ashtray, please?	Pode-nos dar um cinzeiro, por favor?	poadhernoosh dahr oong seenzayroo poor fervoar
some bread	pão	pahng^w
a fork	um garfo	oong **gahr**foo
a knife	uma faca	**oo**mer **fah**ker
a spoon	uma colher	**oo**mer koo**lyehr**
a plate	um prato	oong **prah**too
a glass	um copo	oong **ko**poo
a napkin	um guardanapo	oong gwerrder**nah**poo
another chair	outra cadeira	**oa**trer kerd**hay**rer
Where's the gentle-men's toilet (men's room)?	Onde é a casa de banho dos cavalheiros?	**on**der eh er **kah**zer der **bah**ñoo doosh kerver-**lyay**roosh
Where's the ladies' toilet (ladies' room)?	Onde é a casa de banho das senhoras?	**on**der eh er **kah**zer der **bah**ñoo dersh say **ñoa**rersh

Appetizers

I'd like some ...	Queria ...	kerr**eeer**
I'd like some assorted appetizers.	Queria uns acepipes variados.	kerr**eeer** oongsh erser-**pee**persh verr**yah**doosh
orange juice	um sumo de laranja	oong **soo**moo der ler-**rahng**zher
ham	fiambre	**fyahng**brer
melon	melão	mer**lahng**^{w}
pâté	pâté	pah**tay**
smoked salmon	salmão fumado	sahl**mahng**^{w} foo**mah**dhoo
shrimps (shrimp)	camarões	kermer**rawng**^{y}sh

Soup

Have you any ... ?	Tem ... ?	tayng
Have you any chicken soup?	Tem caldo de galinha?	tayng **kah**ldoo der ger**lee**-ñer
vegetable soup	sopa de legumes	**soa**per der ler**goo**mersh
onion soup	sopa de cebola	**soa**per der cer**boa**ler

Fish

I'd like some ...	Queria ...	kerr**eeer**
I'd like some fish.	Queria peixe.	kerr**eeer** **pay**sher
sole	linguado	ling**gwah**dhoo
trout	truta	**troo**ter
lobster	lagosta	ler**goash**ter
crayfish	caranguejo	kerrerng**gay**zhoo
prawns	lagostins	lergoosh**teengsh**

I'd like it ...	Quero-o ...	kehroooo
I'd like it steamed.	Quero-o cozido a vapor.	kehroooo koozeedhoo er verpoar
grilled	grelhado	grilyahdhoo
boiled	cozido	koozeedhoo
baked	no forno	noo foarnoo
fried	frito	freetoo

Meat—Poultry—Game

I'd like some ...	Queria ...	kerreeer
I'd like some beef.	Queria carne de vaca.	kerreeer kahrner der vahker
a beef steak	um bife	oong beefer
some roast beef	rósbife	rozbeefer
a veal cutlet	uma costeleta de vitela	oomer kooshterlayter der veetehler
mutton	carneiro	kerrnayroo
lamb	borrego	boorayǵoo
a pork chop	uma costeleta de porco	oomer kooshterlayter der poarkoo
roast pork	porco assado	poarkoo ersahdhoo
hare	lebre	lehbrer
chicken	frango	frahnggoo
roast chicken	frango assado	frahnggoo ersahdhoo
duck	pato	pahtoo
How do you like your meat?	Como deseja a carne?	koamoo derzayzher er kahrner
rare	mal passada	mahl persahdher
medium	médio	mehdyoo
well done	bem passada	bayng persahdher

Vegetables

What vegetables have you got?	Que legumes tem?	ker lerǵoomersh tayng
I'd like some ...	Queria ...	kerreeer
I'd like some asparagus.	Queria espargos.	kerreeer ishpahrgoosh
green beans	feijão verde	fayzhahng^w vehrder
mushrooms	cogumelos	kooǵoomehloosh
carrots	cenouras	sinoarersh
onions	cebolas	serboalersh
red cabbage	repolho	rerpoalyoo
spinach	espinafres	ishpeenahfrersh

rice	arroz	erroash
peas	ervilhas	errveelyersh
tomatoes	tomates	toomahtersh
green salad	salada de alface	serlahdher der ahlfahser
potatoes	batatas	bertahtersh

Desserts

Nothing more, thanks.	Mais nada, obrigado.	mighsh nahdher obreeġahdhoo
Just a small portion, please.	Muito pouco, por favor.	moongᵞtoo poakoo poor fervoar
Have you any ice-cream?	Tem gelados?	tayng zherlahdoosh
fruit salad	salada de frutas	serlahder dher frootersh
fresh fruit	fruta fresca	frooter frayshker
cheese	queijo	kayzhoo

Drink

What would you like to drink?	Que deseja tomar?	ker derzayzher toomahr
I'll have a beer, please.	Queria uma cerveja, por favor.	kerreeer oomer serrvayzher poor fervoar
I'll have a whisky, please.	Queria um whisky, por favor.	kerreeer oong weeshkee poor fervoar

Wine

I'd like a bottle of wine.	Queria uma garrafa de vinho.	kerreeer oomer gerrahfer der veeñoo
red wine	vinho tinto	veeñoo teentoo
rosé wine	vinho rosé	veeñoo rozay
white wine	vinho branco	veeñoo brahngkoo
Cheers!	Saúde!	seroodher

The bill (check)

| May I have the bill (check) please? | Pode dar-me a conta, por favor? | poadher dahrmer er konter poor fervoar |
| Is service included? | O serviço está incluído? | oo serrveesoo ishtah eengklooeedhoo |

| Everything's included. | Tudo incluído. | toodhoo eengklooeedhoo |
| Thank you, that was a very good meal. | Obrigado, foi uma boa refeição. | obreegahdhoo foy oomer boaer rerfaysahng^w |

Travelling

Where's the railway station, please?	Onde é a estação de caminho de ferro, por favor?	onder eh er ishtersahng^w der kermeeñoo der feh-roo poor fervoar
Where's the ticket office, please?	Onde é a bilheteira, por favor?	onder eh er beelyertayrer poor fervoar
I'd like a ticket to ...	Queria um bilhete para ...	kerreeer oong beelyayter perrer
First or second class?	De primeira ou segunda classe?	der preemayrer oa ser-goonder klahser
First class, please.	De primeira, por favor.	der preemayrer poor fervoar
Single or return (one way or round-trip)?	Uma ida ou ida e volta?	oomer eeder oa eeder ee volter
Do I have to change trains?	Devo mudar de comboio?	dayvoo moodahr der koamboyoo
What platform does the train leave from?	De que cais parte o comboio?	der ker kighsh pahrter oo koamboyoo
Where's the nearest underground (subway) station?	Onde é a estação de metro mais próxima?	onder eh er ishtersahng^w der mehtroo mighsh pro-seemer
Where's the bus station, please?	Onde é a estação dos autocarros?	onder eh er ishtersahng^w doosh owtookahroosh
When's the first bus to ...?	A que horas parte o primeiro autocarro para ...?	er ker orersh pahrter oo preemayroo owtookahroo perrer
the last bus the next bus	o último autocarro o próximo autocarro	oo ooltimoo owtookahroo oo proseemoo owtookah-roo
Please let me off at the next stop.	Por favor, deixe-me sair na próxima paragem.	poor fervoar dayshermer sereer ner proseemer per-rahzhayng

Relaxing

| What's on at the cinema (movies)? | O que há no cinema? | oo ker ah noo seenaymer |

What's on at the theatre?	**O que há no teatro?**	oo ker ah noo tiahtroo
What time does the film begin? And the play?	**A que horas começa o filme? E a peça?**	ah ker orersh koomehser oo **feel**mer. ee er **peh**ser
Are there any tickets for tonight?	**Há bilhetes para esta noite?**	ah beel**yay**tersh perrer **ehsh**ter **noy**ter
Where can we go dancing?	**Onde podemos ir dançar?**	**onder poodheh**moosh eer dahn**sahr**
Would you like to dance?	**Quer dançar?**	kehr dahn**sahr**

Introductions

How do you do?	**Bom dia.**	bawng **dee**er
How are you?	**Como está?**	**koa**moo ish**tah**
Very well, thank you. And you?	**Muito bem, obrigado. E você?**	moong^ytoo bayng obree**gah**dhoo. ee vo**say**
May I introduce Miss Philips?	**Apresento-lhe a Menina Philips.**	erprer**zayn**toolyer er mer**nee**ner Philips
My name is . . .	**O meu nome é . . .**	oo **meh**oo **noa**mer eh
I'm very pleased to meet you.	**Tenho muito prazer em conhecê-lo.**	tayⁿoo moong^ytoo prer**zehr** ayng koo**ñer**sayloo
How long have you been here?	**Há quanto tempo está cá?**	ah **kwahn**too **tayng**poo ish**tah** kah
It was nice meeting you.	**Tive muito prazer em conhecê-lo.**	tee**ver** moong^ytoo prer**zehr** ayng koo**ñer**sayloo

Dating

Would you like a cigarette?	**Quer um cigarro?**	kehr oong see**gah**roo
May I get you a drink?	**Posso oferecer-lhe uma bebida?**	**poss**soo oferrer**sehr**lyer **oo**mer ber**bee**dher
Do you have a light, please?	**Tem lume, por favor?**	tayng **loo**mer poor fer**voar**
Are you waiting for someone?	**Espera alguém?**	ish**pay**rer ahl**gayng**
Are you free this evening?	**Está livre esta noite?**	ish**tah** **leev**rer **ehsh**ter **noy**ter
Where shall we meet?	**Onde nos podemos encontrar?**	**onder** noosh poo**dheh**moosh ingkoan**trahr**

PORTUGUESE

What time shall I meet you?	**A que horas posso encontra-la?**	er ker orersh **posss**oo ingkoan**trah**ler
May I take you home?	**Posso leva-la a casa?**	**posss**oo ler**vah**ler er **kah**zer
Thank you, it's been a wonderful evening.	**Obrigado por esta noite tão agradável.**	obreegah**dhoo** poor **ehsh**ter **noy**ter tahng^w ergrer-**dhah**vehl
What's your telephone number?	**Qual é o seu número de telefone?**	kwahl eh oo **seh**oo **noom**erroo de terler**fo**ner
Do you live alone?	**Vive só?**	**vee**ver so
What time is your last train?	**A que horas é o seu último comboio?**	er ker **or**ersh eh oo **seh**oo **ool**timoo koam**boy**oo
Good-night...	**Boa noite...**	**boa**er **noy**ter

Banks

Where's the nearest bank, please?	**Onde é o Banco mais próximo, por favor?**	onder eh oo **bahng**koo mighsh **proos**eemoo poor fer**voar**
Where can I cash some traveller's cheques?	**Onde posso trocar alguns cheques de viagem?**	onder **poss**oo troo**kahr** ahl**goong**sh shehks der vyah**zhayng**
What time does the bank open? What time does it close?	**A que horas abre o Banco? A que horas fecha?**	er ker orersh **ah**brer oo **bahng**koo? er ker orersh **feh**sher
I'm expecting some money from home. Has it arrived?	**Aguardo dinheiro da familia. Já chegou?**	ergwahrdhoo diñayroo der fermeelyer. zhah shergoa
Can you give me some small change, please?	**Pode dar-me alguns trocos, por favor?**	**poa**dher **dahr**mer ahl**goong**sh tro**koosh** poor fer**voar**

Shops, stores and services

Where is the nearest chemist's (pharmacy)?	**Onde é a farmácia mais próxima?**	onder eh er ferr**mah**seeer mighsh **proos**eemer
the nearest hairdresser's	**o cabeleireiro mais próximo**	o kerberlee**ray**roo mighsh **proos**eemoo
the photo shop	**a loja de artigos fotográficos**	er **lo**zher der errtee**goosh** footoograh**fee**koosh
the jeweller's	**a ourivesaria**	er oareevserr**ee**er
the department store	**o armazém**	oo ahrmer**zayng**

the police station	**o posto de policia**	oo **posh**too der **poolee**-seeer
the garage	**a garagem**	er ger**rah**zhayng
How do I get there?	**Como vou lá ter?**	**koa**moo voa lah tehr
Is it within walking distance?	**Pode-se ir a pé?**	**poad**herser eer ah peh

Service

Can you help me, please?	**Pode ajudar-me, por favor?**	**poad**her erzhood**hah**rmer poor fer**voar**
Can you show me this? And that, too.	**Pode mostrar-me isto? e aquilo também.**	**poad**her moosh**trah**rmer **eesh**too ee er**kee**loo tahm**bayng**
It's too expensive/ too big/too small.	**É muito caro/muito grande/muito pequeno.**	eh **moong**ʸtoo **kah**roo/ **moong**ʸtoo **grahn**der/ **moong**ʸtoo per**keh**noo

Can you show me some more?	**Pode mostrar-me mais alguns?**	**poad**her moosh**trah**rmer mighsh ahl**goong**sh
something better	**algo melhor**	**ahl**goo mil**yoar**
something cheaper	**algo mais barato**	**ahl**goo mighsh ber**rah**too
How much is this? And that?	**Quanto custa isto? E aquilo?**	**kwahn**too **koosh**ter **eesh**too? ee er**kee**loo
It's not quite what I want.	**Não é exatamente o que quero.**	nahngʷ eh izahter**mehn**ter oo ker **keh**roo
I like it.	**Gosto disto.**	**gosh**too **deesh**too

Chemist's (Pharmacy)

I'd like something for a cold/for a cough/for travel sickness.	**Queria qualquer coisa para a constipação/para a tosse/para o enjôo de viagem.**	ker**reeer** kwahl**kehr koy**zer **perr**er er kawngshtipersahngʷ/**perr**er er **tos**er/**perr**er oo ayng-**zhoa**oo der vyah**zhayng**
Can you recommend something for hay-fever/for sunburn?	**Pode indicar-me algo para a alergia do polen/para queimaduras do sol?**	**poad**her eendee**kah**rmer **ahl**goo **perr**er er erler-**zheeer** doo **po**layn/**perr**er kaymer**dhoo**rersh doo sol

PORTUGUESE

Toiletry

May I have some razor blades?	Pode dar-me lâminas de barbear?	poadher dahrmer lahmeenersh der berrbyahr
some shaving cream	creme para a barba	kreaymer perrer er bahrber
some toothpaste	uma pasta de dentes	oomer pahshter der dehntish
I'd like some soap.	Queria um sabonete.	kerreeer oom serboonehter
some suntan oil	um óleo para bronzear	oong olyoo perrer bronzeeahr

At the barber's

I'd like a haircut, please.	Quero cortar o cabelo, por favor.	kehroo koortahr oo kerbayloo poor fervoar
Short/Leave it long.	Curto/Deixe-o comprido.	koortoo/daysheroo kompreedoo
A razor cut, please.	A navalha, por favor.	er nervahlyer poor fervoar

At the hairdresser's

I'd like a shampoo and set, please.	Queria um champô e mise, por favor.	kerreeer oong shahmpoa ee meezer poor fervoar
I'd like a bleach.	Queria aloirar o cabelo.	kerreeer erloyrahr oo kerbayloo
a permanent	fazer uma permanente	ferzehr oomer pehrmernehnter
a colour rinse	pintar o cabelo	peentahr oo kerbayloo
a manicure	uma manicura	oomer merneekoorer

Photography

I'd like a film for this camera.	Queria um rolo para esta máquina fotográfica.	kerreeer oong roaloo perrer ehshter mahkeener footoagrahfeeker
This camera doesn't work.	Esta máquina não funciona bem.	ehshter mahkeener nahng^w foonsyoaner bayng

At the post office

Where's the nearest post office, please?
Qual é o correio mais próximo, por favor?
kwahl eh oo koorayoo mighsh proseemoo poor fervoar

I'd like to send this by express (special delivery)/by air mail.
Queria enviar isto por expresso/por avião.
kerreeer ayngveeahr eeshtoo poor ishprehsoo/ poor erveeaahng^w

Service stations

Where is the nearest service station, please?
Qual é a estação de serviço mais próxima, por favor?
kwahl eh er ishtersahng^w der serrveesoo mighsh proseemer poor fervoar

Fill her up, please.
Encha o depósito, por favor.
ayngsher oo derpozeetoo poor fervoar

Check the oil, please.
Verifique o óleo, por favor.
verreefeeker oo olyoo poor fervoar

Would you check the tyres?
Pode verificar os pneus?
poadher verreefeekahr oosh pnehoosh

Street directions

Can you show me on the map where I am?
Pode mostrar-me no mapa onde me encontro?
poadher mooshtrahrmer noo mahper onder mer ayngkontroo

You're on the wrong road.
Está na estrada errada.
ishtah ner ishtrahdher errahdher

Go back to...
Volte atrás até...
volter ertrahsh erteh

Go straight ahead.
Sempre em frente.
saymprer ayng fraynter

It's on the left/on the right.
É à esquerda/à direita.
eh ah ishkehrder/ah dirayter

Accidents

May I use your telephone?
Posso telefonar?
posssoo terlerfoonahr

Call a doctor quickly.
Chame um médico depressa.
shermer oong maydeekoo derprehser

Call an ambulance.
Chame uma ambulância.
shermer oomer ermboolahngseeer

Please call the police.
Chame a polícia, por favor.
shermer er pooleeseeer poor fervoar

PORTUGUESE

Numbers

one	**um**	oong
two	**dois**	doysh
three	**três**	traysh
four	**quatro**	**kwah**tro
five	**cinco**	**seeng**koo
six	**seis**	saysh
seven	**sete**	**seh**ter
eight	**oito**	**oy**too
nine	**nove**	**nov**er
ten	**dez**	dehsh
eleven	**onze**	**awng**zer
twelve	**doze**	**doa**zer
thirteen	**treze**	**tray**zer
fourteen	**catorze**	ker**toar**zer
fifteen	**quinze**	**keen**zer
sixteen	**dezasseis**	derzer**saysh**
seventeen	**dezassete**	derzer**seh**ter
eighteen	**dezoito**	der**zoy**too
nineteen	**dezanove**	derzer**nov**er
twenty	**vinte**	**veen**ter
twenty-one	**vinte e um**	**veen**ter ee oong
thirty	**trinta**	**treen**ter
forty	**quarenta**	kwer**reh**nter
fifty	**cinquenta**	seeng**kweh**nter
sixty	**sessenta**	ser**seh**nter
seventy	**setenta**	ser**teh**nter
eighty	**oitenta**	oy**teh**nter
ninety	**noventa**	noo**veh**nter
one hundred	**cem**	sayng
one thousand	**mil**	meel
ten thousand	**dez mil**	dehsh meel

Days

It's Sunday.	**É domingo.**	eh doo**meeng**goo
Monday	**segunda-feira**	ser**goon**der fayrer
Tuesday	**terça-feira**	**tehr**ser fayrer
Wednesday	**quarta-feira**	**kwah**rter fayrer
Thursday	**quinta-feira**	**keen**ter fayrer
Friday	**sexta-feira**	**saysh**ter fayrer
Saturday	**sábado**	**sah**berdhoo
yesterday	**ontem**	**awng**tayng
today	**hoje**	**oa**zher
tomorrow	**amanhã**	ahmer**ñahng**
morning/afternoon	**manhã/tarde**	mer**ñahng**/**tahr**der
evening/night	**noite/noite**	**noy**ter/**noy**ter

Months

January	**Janeiro**	zhernayroo
February	**Fevereiro**	ferverrayroo
March	**Março**	mahrsoo
April	**Abril**	erbreel
May	**Maio**	mighoo
June	**Junho**	zhooñoo
July	**Julho**	zhoolyoo
August	**Agosto**	ergoashtoo
September	**Setembro**	sertayngbroo
October	**Outubro**	oatoobroo
November	**Novembro**	noovayngbroo
December	**Dezembro**	derzayngbroo
Merry Christmas!	**Feliz Natal/Feliz**	ferleesh nertahl/ferleesh
Happy New Year!	**Ano Novo!**	ahnoo novoo

RUSSIAN

Guide to Pronunciation

Letter	Approximate pronunciation	Symbol	Example	
Vowels				
а	between the **a** in c**a**t and the **ar** in c**ar**t	ah	как	kahk
е	like **ye** in **ye**t	yeh	где	gdyeh
ё	like **yo** in **yo**nder	yo	мёд	myod
и	like **ee** in s**ee**	ee	синий	**see**nyee
й	like **y** in ga**y** or bo**y**	y	бой	boy
о	like **o** in h**o**t	o	стол	stol
у	like **oo** in b**oo**t	oo	улица	**oo**leetsah
ы	similar to **i** in h**i**t	i	вы	vi
э	like **e** in m**e**t	eh	эта	**eh**tah
ю	like **u** in d**u**ke	yoo	юг	yoog
я	like **ya** in **ya**rd	yah	мясо	**myah**sah

RUSSIAN

Consonants

б	like **b** in **b**it	b	был	bil
в	like **v** in **v**ine	v	ваш	vahsh
г	like **g** in **g**o	g	город	**g**orahd
д	like **d** in **d**o	d	да	dah
ж	like **s** in plea**s**ure	zh	жаркий	**zh**ahrkee
з	like **z** in **z**oo	z	за	zah
к	like **k** in **k**itten	k	карта	**k**ahrtah
л	like **l** in **l**ose	l	лампа	**l**ahmpah
м	like **m** in **m**y	m	масло	**m**ahsslah
н	like **n** in **n**ot	n	нет	**n**yeht
п	like **p** in **p**ot	p	парк	**p**ahrk
р	like **r** in **r**un	r	русский	**r**oosskee
с	like **s** in **s**ee	s/ss	слово	**s**lovah
т	like **t** in **t**ip	t	там	**t**ahm
ф	like **f** in **f**ace	f	ферма	**f**yehrmah
х	like **ch** in Scottish lo**ch**	kh	хлеб	**kh** lyehb
ц	like **ts** in si**ts**	ts	цена	**ts**eenah
ч	like **ch** in **ch**ip	ch	час	**ch**ahss
ш	like **sh** in **sh**ut	sh	ваша	vah**sh**ah
щ	like **sh** followed by **ch**	shch	щётка	**shch**yotkah

Other letters

ь   gives a ''soft'' pronunciation to the preceding consonant. A similar effect can be produced by pronouncing **y** as in yet—but very, very short—after the consonant. In our transcription we shall show this with an apostrophe (') after the soft consonant.

ъ   is sometimes used between two parts of a compound word, when the second part begins with я, ю, or е, to show that the pronunciation of the word should incorporate a clear separation of the two parts.

Diphthongs

ай	like **igh** in s**igh**	igh	чай	ch**igh**
яй	like the previous sound, but preceded by the **y** in yes	yigh	негодяй	nyehgo**dyigh**
ой	like **oy** in b**oy**	oy	вой	v**oy**
ей	like **ya** in **Ya**tes	yay	соловей	solov**yay**
ый	like **i** in b**i**t followed by the **y** in yes	iy	красивый	krahsee**viy**
уй	like **oo** in g**oo**d followed by the **y** in yes	ooy	луй	d**ooy**
	like the previous sound, but preceded by the **y** in yes	yooy	плюй	pl**yooy**

The effects of non-stress

If a vowel or diphthong is not stressed, it often changes its pronunciation. This could be called a weakening of the sound.

| о | unstressed, is pronounced like Russian **a** | ah | отец | ah**tyehts** |
| е, я, и, он, ей, ий | unstressed, are pronounced like a short **yee** sound | yee or ee | теперь английский | tyee**pyehr**' ahn**glee**skee |

The alphabet

The column at the left shows printed capital and small letters while the centre column shows handwritten capital and small letters. The right-hand column will help you to pronounce the names of these letters in Russian.

А а	*А а*	ah	Р р	*Р р*	ehr
Б б	*Б б*	beh	С с	*С с*	ehs
В в	*В в*	veh	Т т	*Т т*	teh
Г г	*Г г*	geh	У у	*У у*	oo
Д д	*Д д*	deh	Ф ф	*Ф ф*	ehf
Е е	*Е е*	yeh	Х х	*Х х*	khah
Ё ё	*Ё ё*	yoh	Ц ц	*Ц ц*	tseh
Ж ж	*Ж ж*	zheh	Ч ч	*Ч ч*	chah
З з	*З з*	zheh	Ш ш	*Ш ш*	shah
И и	*И и*	ee	Щ щ	*Щ щ*	shchah
Й й	*Й й*	ee **kraht**koyeh	Ъ ъ	*ъ*	**tvyor**diy znahk
К к	*К к*	kah	Ы ы	*ы*	yeh**ree**
Л л	*Л л*	ehl	Ь ь	*ь*	**myah**kee znahk
М м	*М м*	ehm	Э э	*Э э*	eh obo**rot**noyeh
Н н	*Н н*	ehn	Ю ю	*Ю ю*	yoo
О о	*О о*	o	Я я	*Я я*	yah
П п	*П п*	peh			

RUSSIAN

RUSSIAN

Some basic expressions

Yes.	Да.	dah
No.	Нет.	nyeht
Please.	Пожалуйста.	pah**zhah**loostah
Thank you.	Спаснбо.	spah**see**bah
Thank you very much.	Большое спасибо.	bahl'**shoy**ee spah**see**bah
That's all right.	Не за что.	nyee zah **shto**

Greetings

Good morning.	Доброе утро.	**dobrah**yee **oo**tro
Good afternoon.	Добрый день.	dobri **dyehn'**
Good evening.	Добрый вечер.	dobri **vyeh**chyeer
Good night.	Спокойной ночи.	spah**koy**nigh **no**chee
Good-bye.	До свидания.	dah sveed**dah**neeyah
See you later.	До встречи.	dah **vstryeh**chee
This is Mr....	Это господин ...	ehtah gahs**pah**deen
This is Mrs....	Это госпожа ...	ehtah gahspah**zhah**
This is Miss...	Это госпожа ...	ehtah gahspah**zhah**
I'm very pleased to meet you.	Очень приятно.	**ochyeen'** pree**yaht**nah
How are you?	Как дела?	kahk dyeh**lah**
Very well, thank you. And you?	Спасибо, хорошо. Как у Вас?	spah**see**bah khahrah**sho** kahk oo **vahs**
Fine.	Прекрасно.	pryee**krahs**nah
Excuse me.	Простите.	prah**stee**tyee

Questions

Where?	Где?	gdyeh
Where is ...?	Где ...?	gdyeh
Where are ...?	Где ...?	gdyeh
When?	Когда?	kahg**dah**
What?	Что?	shto
How?	Как?	kahk
How much?	Сколько?	**skol'**kah
How many?	Сколько?	**skol'**kah

Who?	Кто?	kto
Why?	Почему?	pahchyee**moo**
Which?	Какой?	kah**koy**
What do you call this?	Как это называется?	kahk **eh**tah nahzi**vah**yeetsah
What do you call that?	Как это называется?	kahk **eh**tah nahzi**vah**yeetsah
What does this mean?	Что это значит?	shto **eh**tah **znah**cheet
What does that mean?	Что это значит?	shto **eh**tah **znah**cheet

Do you speak ... ?

Do you speak English?	Вы говорите по-английски?	vi gahvah**ree**tyee pah ahn**glee**skee
Do you speak German?	Вы говорите по-немецки?	vi gahvah**ree**tyee pah nyee**myeht**skee
Do you speak French?	Вы говорите по-французски?	vi gahvah**ree**tyee pah frahn**tsoo**skee
Do you speak Spanish?	Вы говорите по-испански?	vi gahvah**ree**tyee pah ees**pahn**skee
Do you speak Italian?	Вы говорите по-итальянски?	vi gahvah**ree**tyee pah eetahl'**yahn**skee
Could you speak more slowly, please?	Могли-бы вы говорить медленнее?	mah**glee**bi **vi** gahvah**reet' myeh**dlyeenyehyee
Please point to the phrase in the book.	Покажите мне, пожалуйста, фразу в книге.	pahkah**zhee**tyee mnyeh pah**zhah**loostah **frah**zoo v **knee**gyee
Just a minute. I'll see if I can find it in this book.	Минуточку. Я посмотрю, смогу ли я её найти в книжке.	mee**noo**tahchkoo **yah** pahsmaht**ryoo** smah**goo**lee yah yee**yo nigh**tee v **knee**zhkyee
I understand.	Я понимаю.	**yah** pahnyee**mah**yoo
I don't understand.	Я не понимаю.	**yah** nyee pahnyee**mah**yoo

Can ... ?

Can I have ... ?	Можно ... ?	**mo**zhnah
Can we have ... ?	Можно ... ?	**mo**zhnah
Can you show me ... ?	Вы мне можете показать ... ?	vi mnyeh **mo**zhyeetyee pahkah**zaht'**

RUSSIAN

| Can you tell me . . . ? | Вы мне можете сказать . . . ? | vi mnyeh **mo**zhyeetyee skah**zaht'** |
| Can you help me, please? | Пожалуйста помогите мне. | pah**zhah**loostah pahmah**ghee**tyee mnyeh |

Wanting

I'd like . . .	Я хотел бы . . .	yah khah**tyehl** bi
We'd like . . .	Мы хотели бы . . .	mi khah**tyehl**ee bi
Please give me . . .	Дайте мне, пожалуйста, . . .	**dight**yee **mnyeh** pah**zhah**loostah
Give it to me, please.	Дайте мне зто, пожалуйста.	**dight**yee mnyeh **eh**tah pah**zhah**loostah
Please bring me . . .	Принесите мне, пожалуйста . . .	preenyee**see**tyee **mnyeh** pah**zhah**loostah
Bring it to me, please.	Принесите мне зто, пожалуйста.	preenyee**see**tyee **mnyeh eh**tah pah**zhah**loostah
I'm hungry.	Я голодный.	**yah** gahlodni
I'm thirsty.	Мне хочется пить.	mnyeh khochyeetsah **peet'**
I'm tired.	Я устал.	**yah** oostahl
I'm lost.	Я заблудился.	**yah** zahbloodeelsah
It's important.	Это важно.	**eh**tah **vah**zhnah
It's urgent.	Это срочно.	**eh**tah **sroch**nah
Hurry up!	Скорее!	skah**ryeh**hyee

It is/There is . . .

The words "it is/there is" are often dropped in Russian. For example, the word холодно (**kho**lahdnah) alone conveys the idea "It is cold".

It is/It's . . .	Это . . .	**eh**tah
Is it . . . ?	Это . . . ?	**eh**tah
It isn't . . .	Это не . . .	**eh**tah **nyeh**
There is/There are . . .	Есть . . .	yehst'
Is there/Are there . . . ?	Есть-ли . . . ?	**yehst'** lee
There isn't/There aren't . . .	Нет ли . . .	nyeht lee
There isn't any/ There aren't any.	Нет ли.	nyeht lee

RUSSIAN

A few common words

big/small	большой/ маленький	bahl**shoy**/**mah**lyeen'kee
quick/slow	быстро/медленно	bistrah/**myeh**dlyeenah
early/late	рано/поздно	**rah**nah/**poz**nah
cheap/expensive	дёшево/дорого	dyoshyeevah/**do**rahgah
near/far	близко/далеко	**blees**kah/dahlyee**ko**
hot/cold	горячо/холодно	gahryahchyo/**kho**lahdnah
full/empty	полный/пустой	**pol**ni/poo**stoy**
easy/difficult	легко/трудно	lyeekhko/**trood**nah
heavy/light	тяжёлый/легкий	tyee**zho**li/**lyokh**kee
open/shut	открыто/закрыто	ah**tkri**tah/zah**kri**tah
right/wrong	верно/неверно	**vyehr**nah/nyee**vyehr**nah
old/new	старый/новый	**stah**riy/**no**vi
old/young	старый/молодой	**stah**ri/mahlah**doy**
beautiful/ugly	красиво/уродливо	krah**see**vah/oo**rod**leevah
good/bad	хорошо/плохо	khahrah**sho**/**plo**khah
better/worse	лучше/хуже	**loo**chyee/**khoo**zhyee

Some prepositions and a few more useful words

at	в	v
on	на	nah
in	в	v
to	к	k
from	от	ot
inside	внутри	vnoo**tree**
outside	снаружи	snah**roo**zhee
up	вверх	vvyeh**rkh**
down	вниз	vnees
before	до	do
after	после	pos**lyee**
with	с	s
without	без	byeh**ss**
through	через	**chyeh**ryeess
towards	к	k
until	до	do
during	во время	vah **vryeh**myee
and	и	ee
or	или	**ee**lee
not	не	nyeh
nothing	ничего	neechyee**vo**
none	ни один	nyeh ah**deen**

very	очень	**o**chyeen'
also	тоже	**to**zhyee
soon	скоро	**sko**rah
perhaps	может быть	**mo**zhyeet bit'
here	здесь	zdyehs'
there	там	tahm
now	теперь	tyee**pyehr'**
then	тогда	tahg**dah**

Arrival

Your passport, please.	Ваш паспорт, пожалуйста.	vahsh **pahs**pahrt pahzhah-loostah
Here it is.	Пожалуйста.	pah**zhah**loostah
Have you anything to declare?	У Вас есть что-либо заявить для таможни?	oo vahs yehst' **shto**leebah zahyah**veet'** dlyah **tah**mahzhnyee
No, nothing at all.	Нет, ничего.	nyeht nyee**chee**vo
Porter!	Носильщик!	nah**seel'**shcheek
Can you help me with my luggage, please?	Пожалуйста возьмите мой багаж?	pah**zhah**loostah vahzmee-tyeh moy bah**gahzh**
That's my suitcase.	Это мой чемодан.	**eh**tah moy cheemah**dahn**
Where's the tourist office?	Где бюро Интуриста?	gdyeh bjoo**ro** eentoo**rees**tah
This way, please.	Сюда, пожалуйста.	syoo**dah** pahzhahloostah

Changing money

| Can you change a traveller's cheque, please? | Можете ли Вы разменять аккредитив? | **mo**zhehtyeh lee vi rahz-myeh**nyaht'** ahkryeh-dyee**tyeev** |
| Where's the nearest bank, please? | Где ближайший банк? | gdyeh blee**zhigh**sheey bahnk |

Car rental

I'd like a car.	Мне нужна машина.	mnyeh noozh**nah** mah-**shee**nah
For how long?	На какое время?	nah kah**ko**yeh **vryeh**myah
A day/Four days/ A week/Two weeks.	На день/на четыре дня/на неделю/на две недели.	nah dyehn'/nah chyeht**ir**yeh dnyah/nah nyeh**dyeh**lyoo/nah dvyeh nyeh**dyeh**lee

Taxi

Where can I get a taxi?	Где я могу найти такси?	gdyeh yah mah**goo** night-**yee** tahk**see**
What's the fare to . . . ?	Сколько стоит доехать до . . . ?	**skol**'kah **stoe**et dah**yeh**khaht' dah
Take me to this address, please.	Довезите меня по этому адресу, пожалуйста.	dahvee**zee**tyeh myeh**nyah** pah **eh**tahmoo **ah**dryehsoo pahzhah**loo**stah
I'm in a hurry.	Я спешу.	yah spee**shoo**
Could you drive more slowly, please?	Могли бы Вы ехать медленнее?	mahg**lee** bi vi **yeh**khaht' **myehd**lyehnnyehyeh

Hotel and other accommodation

My name is . . .	Моя фамилия . . .	mah**yah** fah**mee**leeyah . . .
Have you a reservation?	Вы резервировали номер?	vi ryehzyehr**vee**rahvahlee **no**myehr
Yes, here's the confirmation.	Да, вот подтверждение.	dah vot pahdtvyehr**zhdyeh**nyeeyeh
We reserved a single room/ a double room.	Мы забронировали одинарный / двойной номер.	mi zahbrahn**yee**rahvahlee ahdyee**nahr**niy/dvigh**noy no**myehr
a room with a bath/with a shower	номер с ванной/с душем	**no**myehr s **vahn**nigh/ s **doo**shahm
What's my room number, please?	Какой у меня номер комнаты?	kah**koy** oo myeh**nyah no**myehr **kom**nahti
Number 123.	Номер 123.	**no**myehr 123

Service, please

Who is it?	Кто там?	**kto** tahm
Just a minute, please.	Одну минуту, пожалуйста.	ahd**noo** mee**noo**too pahzhah**loo**stah
Come in! The door's open.	Войдите! Дверь открыта.	vigh**dyee**tyeh! dvyehr' aht**krit**ah
May we have breakfast in our room?	Можно получить завтрак в нашей комнате?	**mozh**nah pahloo**cheet' zahv**trahk v **nah**shay **kom**nahtyeh

RUSSIAN

RUSSIAN

Breakfast

I'll have ...	Я хотел бы ...	yah khah**tyehl** bi
I'll have some fruit juice.	Я хотел бы фруктовый сок.	yah khah**tyehl** bi frookto-viy sok
a boiled egg	варёное яйцо	vahr**yo**nahyeh yight**so**
a fried egg	яичницу	yah**yeech**nyeetsoo
some bacon/some ham	бекон/ветчину	**byeh**kon/veecheen**oo**
some toast	тост	tost
a pot of tea	чай в чайничке	chigh v **chigh**nyeechkyeh
a cup of tea	чашку чая	**chahsh**koo **chah**yah
some coffee	кофе	**ko**fyeh
some chocolate	шоколад	shahkah**lahd**
more butter	больше масла	**bol**'sheh **mahs**lah
some hot water	горячей воды	gah**ryah**chyay vah**di**

Difficulties

The central heating doesn't work.	Центральное отопление не работает.	tsehn**trahl**'nahyeh ah-tah**plyeh** nyeeyeh nyeh rah**bo**tahyeht
the light/the socket	свет/штепсель	svyeht/**shtehp**sehl'
the tap/the toilet	кран/туалет	krahn/tooah**lyeht**
There's no hot water.	Нет горячей воды.	nyeht gah**ryah**chyay vah**di**
May I see the manager, please?	Можно поговорить с администратором?	**mozh**nah pahgahvah**reet**' s ahdmeenyee**strah**tahrom

Telephone—Mail

There's a call for you.	Вас к телефону.	vahs k tyehlyeh**fo**noo
Hold the line, please.	Подождите у телефона.	pahdahzh**dyee**tyeh oo tyehlyeh**fo**nah
Operator, I've been cut off.	Девушка, нас прервали.	**dyeh**vooshkah nahs pryeh**rvah**lee
Did anyone telephone me?	Мне кто-нибудь звонил?	mnyeh **kto**nyeebood' zvah**nyeel**
Is there any mail for me?	Есть для меня почта?	yehst' dlyah myeh**nyah** **poch**tah
Are there any messages for me?	Мне никто не оставил записки?	mnyeh nyee**kto** nyeh ah**stah**veel zah**pee**skee

Checking out

May I have my bill, please?	Могу ли я получить счёт?	mah**goo** lee yah pahloo**cheet'** shchyot
We're in a great hurry.	Мы очень спешим.	mi **o**chehn' spee**shim**
It's been a very enjoyable stay.	Пребывание было очень приятным.	preebi**vah**nyeeyeh **bi**lah **o**chehn' pree**yaht**nim

Eating out

Good evening, sir/ Good evening, madam.	Добрый вечер, господин/ Добрый вечер госпожа.	**dobriy vyeh**chehr gahspah**dyeen**/**dobriy vyeh**chehr gahspah**zhah**
Good evening, I'd like a table for two, please.	Добрый вечер. Я хотел бы столик на двоих.	**dobriy vyeh**chehr. yah khah**tyehl** bi **sto**leek nah dvah**yeekh**
Do you have a fixed-price menu?	У Вас есть меню?	oo vahs yehst' meh**nyoo**
May I see the à la carte menu?	У Вас есть обеденное меню?	oo vahs yehst' ah**byeh**-dyehnnahyeh meh**nyoo**
May we have an ashtray, please?	Можно попросить пепельницу?	**mozh**nah pahprah**seet'** **pyeh**pyehl'nyee tsoo
some bread	хлеб	khlyehb
a fork	вилку	**veel**koo
a knife	нож	nozh
a spoon	ложку	**lozh**koo
a plate	тарелку	tah**ryehl**koo
a glass	стакан	stah**kahn**
a napkin	салфетку	sahl**fyeht**koo
another chair	другой стул	droo**goy** stool
Where's the gentlemen's toilet (men's room)?	Где мужской туалет?	gdyeh moozh**skoy** tooah-**lyeht**
Where's the ladies' toilet (ladies' room)?	Где женский туалет?	gdyeh **zhehn**skeey tooah-**lyeht**

Appetizers

| I'd like some . . . | Я хотел бы . . . | yah khah**tyehl** bi |
| I'd like some assorted appetizers. | Я хотел бы ассорти. | yah khah**tyehl** bi ahsor-**tyee** |

RUSSIAN

orange juice	апельсиновый сок	ahpyehl'**see**nahviy sok
ham	ветчину	veechee**noo**
melon	дыню	**di**nyoo
pâté	паштет	pah**shty**eht
smoked salmon	сёмгу	**syom**goo
shrimps (shrimp)	креветок	kryeh**vyeh**tahk

Soup

Have you any . . . ?	Есть у Вас . . . ?	yehst' oo vahs
Have you any chicken soup?	Есть у Вас суп с курицей?	yehst' oo vahs soop s **koo**reetsay
vegetable soup	овощной суп	ovahshch**noy** soop
onion soup	луковый суп	**loo**kahviy soop

Fish

I'd like some . . .	Я хотел бы . . .	yah khah**tyehl** bi
I'd like some fish.	Я хотел бы рыбу.	yah khah**tyehl** bi riboo
sole	морской язык	mahr**skoy** yah**zik**
trout	форель	fah**rehl'**
lobster	омаров	o**mah**rahv
crayfish	лангуст	lahn**goost**
prawns	креветок	kryeh**vyeh**tahk
I'd like it . . .	Я бы хотел это . . .	yah bi khah**tyehl eh**tah
I'd like it steamed.	Я бы хотел это паровое.	yah bi khah**tyehl eh**tah pah**rah**voyeh
grilled	жареное на рашпере.	**zhah**ryehnahyeh nah rahsh**pyeh**ryeh
boiled	отварное	ahtvahr**noy**eh
baked	печёное	pyeh**chyo**nahyeh
fried	жареное	**zhah**ryehnahyeh

Meat—Poultry—Game

I'd like some . . .	Я бы хотел . . .	yah bi khah**tyehl**
I'd like some beef.	Я бы хотел говядину.	yahbi khah**tyehl** gah**vyah**dyeenoo
a beef steak	бифштекс	beef**shtehks**
some roast beef	ростбиф	rost**beef**
a veal cutlet	телячью котлету	tyeh**lyah**chyoo kaht**lyeh**too

mutton	баранину	bahrahnyeenoo
lamb	мясо барашка	myahsah bahrahshkah
a pork chop	свиную котлету	sveenooyoo kahtlyehtoo
roast pork	жареную свинину	zhahryehnooyoo sveenyeenoo
hare	зайца	zightsah
chicken	цыплёнка	tsiplyonkah
roast chicken	жареного цыплёнка	zhahryehnahvah tsiplyonkah
duck	утку	ootkoo

Vegetables

What vegetables have you got?	Какие овощи у Вас есть?	kahkeeyeh ovahshchee oo vahs yehst'
I'd like some . . .	Я бы хотел . . .	yah bi khahtyehl
I'd like some asparagus.	Я бы хотел спаржу.	yah bi khahtyehl spahrzhoo
green beans	бобы	bobi
mushrooms	грибы	greebi
carrots	морковь	mahrkov'
onions	лук	look
red cabbage	красную капусту	krahsnooyoo kahpoostoo
spinach	шпинат	shpeenaht
rice	рис	rees
peas	горох	gahrokh
tomatoes	помидоры	pahmeedori
green salad	зелёный салат	zyehlyoniy sahlaht
potatoes	картофель	kahrtofyehl'

Desserts

Nothing more, thanks.	Больше ничего, спасибо.	bol'sheh nyeechyehvo spahseebah
Just a small portion, please.	Маленькую порцию, пожалуйста.	mahlyehn'kooyoo portsiyoo pahzhahloostah
Have you any ice-cream?	У Вас есть мороженое?	oo vahs yehst' mahrozhehnahyeh
fruit salad	салат из фруктов	sahlaht eez frooktahv
fresh fruit	свежие фрукты	svyehzhiyeh frookti
cheese	сыр	sir

RUSSIAN

Drink

What would you like to drink?	Что бы вы хотели выпить?	shto bi vi khah**tyeh**lee **vi**peet'
I'll have a beer, please.	Пиво, пожалуйста.	**pee**vah pah**zhah**loostah
I'll have a whisky, please.	Виски, пожалуйста.	**vee**skee pah**zhah**loostah

Wine

I'd like a bottle of wine.	Я бы хотел бутылку вина.	yah bi khah**tyehl** bootil-koo **vee**nah
red wine	красного вина	**krahs**nahvah **vee**nah
rosé wine	розового вина	**ro**zahvahvah **vee**nah
white wine	белого вина	**byeh**lahvah **vee**nah
Cheers!	На здоровье!	nah zdah**ro**vyeh

The bill (check)

May I have the bill (check) please?	Пожалуйста счёт!	pah**zhah**loostahs-chyot
Is service included?	Обслуживание включено?	ahb**sloo**zhivahnyeeyeh vklyoocheh**no**
Everything's included.	Всё включено.	vsyo vklyoocheh**no**
Thank you, that was a very good meal.	Спасибо, всё было очень вкусно.	spah**see**bah, vsyo **bi**lah **o**chehn' **vkoos**nah

Travelling

Where's the railway station, please?	Пожалуйста, где вокзал?	pah**zhah**loostah gdyeh vah**kzal**
Where's the ticket office, please?	Пожалуйста, где касса?	pah**zhah**loostah gdyeh **kah**sah
I'd like a ticket to ...	Мне нужен билет до ...	mnyeh **noo**zhehn bee**lyeht** dah
First or second class?	Первый или второй класс?	**pyeh**rviy **ee**lee vtah**roy** klahss
First class, please.	Первый класс, пожалуйста.	**pyeh**rviy klahss pah**zhah**loostah
Single or return (one way or round-trip)?	В один или оба конца?	v ah**dyeen** **ee**lee **o**bah **kahn**tsah

Do I have to change trains?	Мне надо будет делать пересадку.	mnyeh **nahdah boodyeht dyeh**laht' peeree**sahd**koo
What platform does the train leave from?	С какой платформы отправляется поезд?	s kah**koy** plaht**form**i ahtprahv**lyah**yehtsah **po**yehzd
Where's the nearest underground station?	Где ближайшая станция метро?	gdyeh blee**zhigh**shahyah **stahn**tsiyah myeh**tro**
Where's the bus station, please?	Где автобусная остановка?	gdyeh ahv**to**boosnahyah ahstah**nov**kah
When's the first bus to ... ?	Когда идёт первый автобус в ... ?	kahg**dah** eed**yot pyehr**viy ahv**to**boos v
the last bus	последний автобус	pah**slyehd**nyeey ahv**to**boos
the next bus	следующий автобус	**slyeh**dooosshcheey ahv**to**boos
Please let me off at the next stop.	Дайте мне выйти на следующей остановке, пожалуйста.	**dight**yeh mnyeh **viy**tee nah **slyeh**dooosshchay ahstah**nov**kee pah**zhah**loo-stah

RUSSIAN

Relaxing

What's on at the cinema (movies)?	Что идёт в кино?	shto eed**yot** v **kee**no
What's on at the theatre?	Что идёт в театре?	shto eed**yot** v tyeh**ah**tryeh
What time does the film begin?	Когда начинается фильм?	kahg**dah** nah**chee nah**yehtsah feel'm
And the play?	А пьеса?	ah **pyeh**sah
Are there any tickets for tonight?	Есть билеты на вечер?	yehst' bee**lyeh**ti nah **vyeh**chehr
Where can we go dancing?	Куда можно пойти танцевать?	koo**dah mozh**nah pigh**tyee** tahntsi**vaht'**
Would you like to dance?	Хотите ли вы потанцевать?	kha**tyee**tyeh lee vi pahtahntsi**vaht'**

Introductions

How do you do?	Добрый день?	**dob**riy dyehn'
How are you?	Как поживаете?	kahk pahzhi**vah**yehtyeh
Very well, thank you. And you?	Спасибо, очень хорошо. А Вы?	spah**see**bah **o**chehn' khahrah**sho**. ah vi
May I introduce Miss Philips?	Разрешите представить мисс филипс?	rahzree**shi**tyeh pryehd**stah**veet' Miss Philips
My name is . . .	Меня зовут . . .	myeh**nyah** zah**voot**
I'm very pleased to meet you.	Очень приятно.	**o**chehn' pree**yaht**nah
How long have you been here?	Вы давно уже здесь?	vi dah**vno** oo**zheh** zdyehs'
It was nice meeting you.	Было очень приятно с Вами встретиться.	**bi**lah **o**chehn' pree**yaht**nah s **vah**mee **vstryeh**teetsah

Dating

Would you like a cigarette?	Хотите сигарету?	khah**tyee**tyeh seegah**ryeh**too
May I get you a drink?	Хотите что-нибудь выпить?	khah**tyee**tyeh **shto**nyeebood' **vi**peet'
Do you have a light, please?	У Вас есть спички?	vahs yehst' **speech**kee
Are you free this evening?	Вы свободны сегодня вечером?	vi svah**bod**ni seevod**nyah vyeh**chehrahm
Where shall we meet?	Где мы встретимся?	gdyeh mi **vstryeh**tyeem-syah
What time shall I meet you?	Когда я Вас встречу?	kahg**dah** yah vahs **vstryeh**choo
Thank you, it's been a wonderful evening.	Спасибо, это был чудесный вечер.	spah**see**bah, **eh**tah bil choo**dyehs**niy **vyeh**chehr
What time is your last train?	Когда уходит Ваш последний поезд?	kahg**dah** ook**ho**dyeet vahsh pah**slyehd**nyeey **po**yehzd
Good-night . . .	Доброй ночи . . .	**do**brigh **no**chee

Banks

Where's the nearest bank, please?	Где ближайший банк?	gdyeh bleezhighshiy bahnk
Where can I cash some traveller's cheques?	Где я могу обменять аккредитивы?	gdyeh yah mahgoo ahbmyehnyaht' ahkryehdyeetyeevi
What time does the bank open/What time does it close?	Когда открывается банк/когда он закрывается?	kahgdah ahtkrivahyehtsah bahnk/kahgdah on zahkrivahyehtsah
I'm expecting some money from home. Has it arrived?	Я жду деньги из дому. Они прибыли?	yah zhdoo dyehn'ghee eezdahmoo. ahnyee preebilee
Can you give me some small change, please?	Дайте мне, пожалуйста, мелочью?	dightyeh mnyeh pahzhahloostah myehlahchyo

Shops, stores and services

Where is the nearest chemist (pharmacy)?	Где ближайшая аптека?	gdyeh bleezhighshahyah ahptyehkah
the nearest hairdresser's	ближайшая парикмахерская	bleezhighshahyah pahreekmahkhehrskahyah
the photo shop	фотомагазин	fotomahgahzeen
the jeweller's	ювелирный магазин	yooveeleerniy mahgahzeen
the department store	универмаг	oonyeevyehrmahg
the police station	отделение милиции	ahtdyehlyehnyeeyeh meeleetsiee
the garage	гараж	gahrahzh
How do I get there?	Как мне туда проехать?	kahk mnyeh toodah prahyehkhaht'
Is it within walking distance?	Можно дойти пешком?	mozhnah dightyee peeshkom

Service

Can you help me, please?	Помогите мне, пожалуйста?	pahmahgheetyeh mnyeh pahzhahloostah
Can you show me this? And that, too.	Покажите мне, пожалуйста, это. И то тоже.	pahkahzhityeh mnyeh pahzhahloostah ehtah. ee to tozheh
It's too expensive/too big/too small.	Это слишком дорого/слишком велико/слишком мало.	ehtah sleeshkahm dorahgah/sleeshkahm vyehleeko/sleeshkahm mahlo.

RUSSIAN

Can you show me some more?	Вы мне можете показать еще?	vi mnyeh **mo**zhehtyeh pahkah**zaht'** yeh**shchyo**
something better	Что-нибудь получше	**shto**nyeebood' pah**looch**sheh
something cheaper	Что-нибудь подешевле	**shto**nyeebood' pahdyee**shehv**lee
How much is this? And that?	Сколько стоит это? И то?	skol'kah **sto**eet **eh**tah? ee to?
It's not quite what I want.	Это не совсем то, что я хочу.	**eh**tah nyeh sahv**syehm** to shto yah khah**choo**
I like it.	Это мне нравится.	**eh**tah mnyeh **nrah**veetsah

Chemist's (Pharmacy)

| I'd like something for a cold/for a cough/for travel sickness. | Я хотел бы что-нибудь от простуды/от кашля/от морской болезни. | yah khah**tyehl** bi **shto**nyeebood' aht prah**stoo**di/aht **kahsh**lyah/ aht mar**skoy** bal'**yehz**ni |
| Can you recommend something for hay-fever/for sunburn? | Что Вы мне можете рекомендовать от сенной лихорадки/ от ожогов? | shto vi mnyeh **mo**zhehtyeh ryehkah-myehndah**vaht'** aht **syehn**nigh leekhah**rahd**kee/ aht a**zho**gav |

Toiletry

May I have some razor blades?	У Вас есть лезвия для бритья?	oo vahs yehst' **lyehz**-veeyah dlyah bree**tyah**
some shaving cream	крем для бритья	kryehm dlyah bree**tyah**
some toothpaste	зубная паста	zoob**nah**yah **pahs**tah
I'd like some soap.	Мне нужно мыло.	mnyeh **noo**zhnah milah
some suntan oil	крем для загара	kryehm dlyah zah**gah**rah

At the barber's

I'd like a haircut, please.	Я хотел бы постричься.	yah khah**tyehl** bi pah**streech**syah
Short/Leave it long.	Коротко/оставьте длинные.	**ko**rahtkah/ah**stahv'**tyeh **dleen**niyeh
A razor cut, please.	Бритвой, пожалуйста.	**breet**vigh pah**zhah**loostah

RUSSIAN

At the hairdresser's

I'd like a shampoo and set, please.	Помойте голову и сделайте укладку, пожалуйста.	pah**moy**tyeh **go**lahvoo ee **sdyeh**lightyeh oo**klahd**koo pah**zhah**loostah
I'd like a bleach.	Мне нужно обесцвечивание.	mnyeh **noozh**nah ahbyeh-**stsvyeh**cheevahnyeeyeh.
a permanent	перманент	pyehr**mah**nyehnt
a colour rinse	оттеночное полоскание	aht**tyeh**nahchnahyeh pahlahs**kah**nyeeyeh
a manicure	маникюр	mahnyee**kyoor**

Photography

I'd like a film for this camera.	Мне нужна плёнка для зтого аппарата.	mnyeh noozh**nah plyon**kah dlyah **eh**tahvah ahpah**rah**tah.
This camera doesn't work.	Этот аппарат не работает.	**eh**taht ahpah**raht** nyeh rah**bo**tahyeht.

At the post office

Where's the nearest post office, please?	Где ближайшая почта?	gdyeh blee**zhigh**shahyah **poch**tah
I'd like to send this by express (special delivery)/by air mail.	Я хотел бы послать зто срочно/авиапочтой.	yah khah**tyehl** bi pahs**laht'** ehtah **sroch**nah/ahveeah**poch**tigh

Service stations

Where is the nearest service station, please?	Где ближайшая станция обслуживания?	gdyeh blee**zhigh**shahyah **stahn**tsiyah ahb**sloozh**i-vahnyeeyah
Fill her up, please.	Полный, пожалуйста.	**pol**niy pah**zhah**loostah
Check the oil, please.	Проверьте масло, пожалуйста.	prah**vyehr**'tyeh **mahs**lah pah**zhah**loostah
Would you check the tyres?	Проверьте шины, пожалуйста?	prah**vyehr**'tyeh **shi**ni pah**zhah**loostah

RUSSIAN

Street directions

Can you show me on the map where I am?	Вы мне можете показать на карте, где я?	vi mnyeh **mozhehtyeh** pahkah**zaht'** nah **kahr**tyeh gdyeh yah
You're on the wrong road.	Вы едете неверно.	vi **yeh**dyehtyeh nyeh**vyehr**nah
Go back to . . .	Вернитесь назад к . . .	vyeh**rnyee**tyehs' nah**zahd** k
Go straight ahead.	Вам надо прямо.	vahm **nah**dah **pryah**mah
It's on the left/on the right.	Это слева/справа.	**eh**tah **slyeh**vah/**sprah**vah

Accidents

May I use your telephone?	Можно позвонить по Вашему телефону?	**mozh**nah pahzvah**nyeet'** pah **vah**shehmoo tyehlyeh**fo**noo
Call a doctor quickly.	Быстро вызовите доктора.	**bist**rah vi**zah**veetyeh **dok**tahrah
Call an ambulance.	Вызовите санитарную машину.	vi**zah**veetyeh sahnyee-**tah**rnooyoo mah**shi**noo
Please call the police.	Вызовите милицию.	vi**zha**veetyeh mee**leet**siyoo

Numbers

one	один	ah**dyeen**
two	два	dvah
three	три	tree
four	четыре	chee**tir**yeh
five	пять	pyaht'
six	шесть	shehst'
seven	семь	syehm'
eight	восемь	**vo**syehm'
nine	девять	**dyeh**vyaht'
ten	десять	**dyeh**syaht'
eleven	одиннадцать	ah**dyee**nahtsaht'
twelve	двенадцать	dvee**nahts**aht'
thirteen	тринадцать	tree**nahts**aht'
fourteen	четырнадцать	chyeh**tir**nahtsaht'
fifteen	пятнадцать	pyaht**nah**tsaht'
sixteen	шестнадцать	shehst'**nah**tsaht'
seventeen	семнадцать	syehm**nah**tsaht'
eighteen	восемнадцать	vahseem**nah**tsaht'

nineteen	девятнадцать	dyehvyaht**naht**saht'
twenty	двадцать	**dvaht**saht'
twenty-one	двадцать один	**dvaht**saht' ah**dyeen**
thirty	тридцать	**treet**saht'
forty	сорок	**so**rahk
fifty	пятьдесят	peedyee**syaht**
sixty	шестьдесят	shehs'dyeh**syaht**
seventy	семьдесят	**syehm**'dyehsyaht
eighty	восемьдесят	**vo**syehm'dyehsyaht
ninety	девяносто	dyehvyah**nos**tah
one hundred	сто	sto
one thousand	тысяча	**ti**syahchah
ten thousand	десять тысяч	**dyeh**syaht' **ti**syahch

Days

It's Sunday.	Воскресенье	vahskryeh**syehn**'yeh
Monday	Понедельник	pahnyee**dyehl**'nyeek
Tuesday	Вторник	**vtor**nyeek
Wednesday	Среда	sryeh**dah**
Thursday	Четверг	chyeht**vyehrg**
Friday	Пятница	**pyaht**nyeetsah
Saturday	Суббота	soo**bo**tah
yesterday	вчера	vchyeh**rah**
today	сегодня	syeh**vod**nyah
tomorrow	завтра	**zahv**trah
morning/afternoon	утро/после обеда	**oo**trah/**pos**lyeh ah**byeh**dah
evening/night	вечер/ночь	**vyeh**chyehr/noch'

Months

January	январь	yahn**vahr**'
February	февраль	fyeh**vrahl**'
March	март	mahrt
April	апрель	ah**pryehl**'
May	май	migh
June	июнь	ee**yoon**'
July	июль	ee**yool**'
August	август	**ahv**goost
September	сентябрь	syehn**tyahbr**'
October	октябрь	ahk**tyahbr**'
November	ноябрь	nah**yahbr**'
December	декабрь	dyeh**kahbr**'
Happy New Year!	Счастливого Нового Года!	schah**stlee**vahvah **no**vahvah **go**dah

RUSSIAN

SERBO-CROATIAN

Guide to Pronunciation

Note that Serbo-Croatian has some diacritical letters—with accent marks—which we do not know in English. On the other hand, **q, w, x** and **y** do not exist in Serbo-Croatian. A basic rule for handling Serbo-Croatian might be: pronounce it as it's written—every letter is pronounced, and its pronunciation is always the same, regardless of its position in a word.

Letter	Approximate pronunciation	Symbol	Example	
Consonants				
b	like **b** in **b**rother	b	**brat**	braht
c	like **ts** in **ts**e-**ts**e	ts	**cesta**	**tsehss**tah
č	like **ch** in **ch**urch	ch	**čuti**	**choo**tee
ć	like **ch** in **ch**eap (a little further forward in the mouth than **č**; called a "soft" **č**)	ch	**ćerka**	**chehr**kah
d	like **d** in **d**own	d	**dole**	**dol**eh

dž	like j in June	j	džem	jehm
dj	like j in jeep (a "soft" dž); also written đ	j	djak	jahk
f	like f in father	f	figura	feegoorah
g	like g in go	g	gde	gdeh
h	like h in house	h	hleb	hlehb
j	like y in yoke	y	ja	yah
k	like k in key	k	kuća	koochah
l	like l in lip	l	lep	lehp
lj	like l in failure	lʸ	ljubav	lʸoobahv
m	like m in mouth	m	most	most
n	like n in not	n	ne	neh
nj	like ni in onion	ñ	njegov	ñehgov
p	like p in put	p	policija	poleetseeyah
r	like r in rope	r	reka	rehkah
s	like s in sister	s/ss	sestra	sehsstrah
š	like sh in ship	sh	šta	shtah
t	like t in top	t	tamo	tahmo
v	like v in very	v	vrlo	verlo
z	like z in zip	z	zvezda	zvehzdah
ž	like s in pleasure	zh	želim	zhehleem

Note: The letter r can also act as a vowel, as for example, in the word vrlo or in the name of the island Krk; in this case, it should be pronounced rather like a Scottish r, e.g., Krk is pronounced kerk.

Vowels

a	like a in car	ah	sat	saht
e	like e in get	eh	svet	sveht
i	like i in it	ee	iz	eez
o	like o in hot	o	ovde	ovdeh
u	like oo in boom	oo	put	poot

The alphabet

Two different alphabets are used in Yugoslavia. Our Roman alphabet is in use in Slovenia and Croatia; elsewhere the Cyrillic alphabet (more or less like the Russian one) is dominant. Given below are the characters which the Cyrillic alphabet, as used in Yugoslavia, comprises. The column at left shows the printed capital and small letters while written letters are shown in the center column. At right the corresponding letters are shown in the Roman alphabet which we're using in this book.

Printed		Written		Roman
А	а	𝒜 𝒶		a
Б	б	𝒷 𝒹		b
Ц	ц	𝒰 𝓊		c
Ч	ч	𝒞 𝓇		č
Ћ	ћ	𝓀 𝒽		ć
Д	д	2 𝑔		d
Џ	џ	𝒰 𝓊		dž (cap. **Dž**)
Ђ	ђ	𝒷 𝒿		dj or đ (cap. **Dj** or **Đ**)
Е	е	𝓔 𝓋		e
Ф	ф	𝒻 𝒻		f
Г	г	𝒯 𝒾		g
Х	х	𝒳 𝓍		h
И	и	𝒰 𝓊		i
Ј	ј	𝒥 𝒿		j
К	к	𝒦 𝓀		k
Л	л	𝓛 𝓁		l
Љ	љ	𝓁 𝓁		lj (cap. **Lj**)
М	м	𝓜 𝓂		m
Н	н	𝓗 𝓃		n
Њ	њ	𝓝 𝓃		nj (cap. **Nj**)
О	о	𝒪 𝑜		o
П	п	𝒯 𝓊		p
Р	р	𝒫 𝓅		r
С	с	𝒞 𝒸		s
Ш	ш	𝒰𝓁 𝓊𝓁		š
Т	т	𝒯 𝓊		t
У	у	𝒴 𝓎		u
В	в	𝓑 𝒷		v
З	з	𝒵 𝑔		z
Ж	ж	𝓂 𝓂		ž

Some basic expressions

Yes.	**Da.**	dah
No.	**Ne.**	neh
Please.	**Molim.**	moleem
Thank you.	**Hvala.**	hvahlah
Thank you very much.	**Hvala Vam mnogo.**	hvahlah vahm mnogo
That's all right.	**Molim.**	moleem

Greetings

Good morning.	**Dobro jutro.**	dobro yootro
Good afternoon.	**Dobar dan.**	dobahr dahn
Good evening.	**Dobro veče.**	dobro vehcheh
Good night.	**Laku noć.**	lahkoo noch
Good-bye.	**Zbogom.**	zbogom
See you later.	**Dovidjenja.**	doveejehnyah
This is Mr. . . .	**Ovo je Gospodin . . .**	ovo yeh gospodeen
This is Mrs. . . .	**Ovo je Gospodja . . .**	ovo yeh gospojah
This is Miss . . .	**Ovo je Gospod-jica . . .**	ovo yeh gospojeetsa
I'm very pleased to meet you.	**Milo mi je da sam Vas upoznao.**	meelo mee yeh dah sahm vahss oopoznaho
How are you?	**Kako ste?**	kahko steh
Very well, thank you.	**Hvala, vrlo dobro.**	hvahlah verlo dobro
And you?	**A Vi?**	ah vee
Fine.	**Dobro.**	dobro
Excuse me.	**Izvinite.**	eezveehneehteh

Questions

Where?	**Gde?**	gdeh
Where is . . . ?	**Gde je . . . ?**	gdeh yeh
Where are . . . ?	**Gde su . . . ?**	gdeh soo
When?	**Kad?**	kahd
What?	**Šta?**	shtah

How?	**Kako?**	kahko
How much?	**Koliko?**	koleeko
How many?	**Koliko?**	koleeko
Who?	**Ko?..**	ko
Why?	**Zašto?**	zahshto
Which?	**Koji/Koja/Koje?**	koyee/koyah/koyeh
What do you call this?	**Kako se ovo zove?**	kahko seh ovo zoveh
What do you call that?	**Kako se zove ono?**	kahko seh zoveh ono
What does this mean?	**Šta ovo znači?**	shtah ovo znahchee
What does that mean?	**Šta ono znači?**	shtah ono znahchee

Do you speak . . . ?

Do you speak English?	**Govorite li engleski?**	govoreeteh lee ehnglehskee
Do you speak German?	**Govorite li nemački?**	govoreeteh lee nehmahchkee
Do you speak French?	**Govorite li francuski?**	govoreeteh lee frahntsooskee
Do you speak Spanish?	**Govorite li španski?**	govoreeteh lee shpahnskee
Do you speak Italian?	**Govorite li italijanski?**	govoreeteh lee eetahleeyahnskee
Could you speak more slowly. please?	**Možete li govoriti sporije molim Vas?**	mozhehteh lee govoreetee sporeeyeh moleem vahss
Please point to the phrase in the book.	**Pokažite mi molim Vas tu frazu u knjizi.**	pokahzheeteh mee moleem vahss too frahzoo oo kñeezee
Just a minute. I'll see if I can find it in this book.	**Samo trenutak. Videću da li mogu da je nadjem u knjizi.**	sahmo trehnootahk. veedehchoo dah lee mogoo dah yeh nahjehm oo kñeezee
I understand.	**Razumem.**	rahzoomehm
I don't understand.	**Ne razumem.**	neh rahzoomehm

Can...?

Can I have...?	**Mogu li dobiti...?**	**mo**goo lee **do**beetee
Can we have...?	**Možemo li dobiti...?**	**mozh**ehmo lee **do**beetee
Can you show me...?	**Možete li mi pokazati...?**	**mozh**ehteh lee mee po**kah**zahtee
Can you tell me...?	**Možete li mi reći...?**	**mozh**ehteh lee mee **reh**chee
Can you help me, please?	**Možete li mi pomoći molim Vas?**	**mozh**ehteh lee mee **po**mochee **mo**leem vahss

Wanting

I'd like...	**Želeo bih...**	**zheh**leho beeh
We'd like...	**Želeli bismo...**	**zheh**lehlee **beess**mo
Please give me...	**Molim Vas dajte mi...**	**mo**leem vahss **dah**yteh mee
Give it to me, please.	**Dajte mi to molim Vas.**	**dah**yteh mee to **mo**leem vahss
Please bring me...	**Molim Vas donesite mi...**	**mo**leem vahss do**neh**seeteh mee
Bring it to me, please.	**Donesite mi to molim Vas.**	do**neh**seeteh mee to **mo**leem vahss
I'm hungry.	**Gladan sam.**	**glah**dahn sahm
I'm thirsty.	**Žedan sam.**	**zheh**dahn sahm
I'm tired.	**Umoran sam.**	**oo**morahn sahm
I'm lost.	**Zalutao sam.**	zah**loo**taho sahm
It's important.	**Važno je.**	**vahzh**no yeh
It's urgent.	**Hitno je.**	**heet**no yeh
Hurry up!	**Požurite!**	po**zhoo**reeteh

It is/There is...

It is/It's...	**To je...**	to yeh
Is it...?	**Da li je to...?**	dah lee yeh to
It isn't...	**To nije...**	to **nee**yeh
There is/There are...	**Ima...**	**ee**mah
Is there/Are there...?	**Ima li...?**	**ee**mah lee

| There isn't/There aren't... | **Nema ...** | nehmah |
| There isn't any/There aren't any. | **Nema.** | nehmah |

A few common words

big/small	**veliko/malo**	vehleeko/mahlo
quick/slow	**brzo/sporo**	berzo/sporo
early/late	**rano/kasno**	rahno/kahsno
cheap/expensive	**jeftino/skupo**	yehfteeno/skoopo
near/far	**blizu/daleko**	bleezoo/dahlehko
hot/cold	**vruće/hladno**	vroocheh/hlahdno
full/empty	**puno/prazno**	poono/prahznoh
easy/difficult	**lako/teško**	lahko/tehshko
heavy/light	**teško/lako**	tehshko/lahko
open/shut	**otvoreno/zatvoreno**	otvorehno/zahtvorehno
right/wrong	**tačno/pogrešno**	tahchno/pogreshno
old/new	**staro/novo**	stahro/novo
old/young	**star/mlad**	stahr/mlahd
beautiful/ugly	**lepo/ružno**	lehpo/roozhno
good/bad	**dobro/loše**	dobro/losheh
better/worse	**bolje/lošije**	bolʸeh/losheeyeh

Some prepositions and a few more useful words

at	**kod**	kod
on	**na**	nah
in	**u**	oo
to	**ka**	kah
from	**od**	od
inside	**unutra**	oonootrah
outside	**napolju**	nahpolʸoo
up	**gore**	goreh
down	**dole**	doleh
before	**pre**	preh
after	**posle**	posleh
with	**sa**	sah
without	**bez**	behz
through	**kroz**	kroz
towards	**prema**	prehmah
until	**do**	do
during	**za vreme**	zah vrehmeh
and	**i**	ee
or	**ili**	eelee
not	**ne**	neh
nothing	**ništa**	neeshtah

none	**ni jedan**	nee **yeh**dahn
very	**vrlo**	verlo
also	**takodje**	**tah**kojeh
soon	**uskoro**	**ooss**koro
perhaps	**možda**	**mozh**dah
here	**ovde**	**ov**deh
there	**tamo**	**tah**mo
now	**sada**	**sah**dah
then	**tada**	**tah**dah

Arrival

Your passport, please.	**Vaš pasoš, molim Vas.**	vahsh **pah**sosh **mo**leem vahss
Here it is.	**Izvolite.**	eez**vo**leeteh
Have you anything to declare?	**Imate li nešto za carinu?**	**ee**mahteh lee **neh**shto zah **tsah**reenoo
No, nothing at all.	**Ne, nemam ništa.**	neh **neh**mahm **nee**shtah
Porter!	**Nosač!**	**no**sahch
Can you help me with my luggage, please?	**Možete li mi poneti prtljag, molim Vas?**	**mozh**ehteh lee mee **po**nehtee pert**l^y**ahg **mo**leem vahss
That's my suitcase.	**To je moj kofer.**	to yeh moy **ko**fehr
Where's the bus to the centre of town, please?	**Gde je autobus zà centar grada, molim Vas?**	gdeh yeh ahoo**to**booss zah **tsehn**tar **grah**dah **mo**leem vahss
This way, please.	**Ovuda, izvolite.**	o**voo**dah eez**vo**leeteh

Changing money

| Can you change a traveller's cheque, please? | **Možete li promeniti putni ček, molim Vas?** | **mozh**ehteh lee pro-**meh**neetee **poot**nee chehk **mo**leem vahss |
| Where's the nearest bank, please? | **Gde je najbliža banka, molim Vas?** | gdeh yeh **nahy**bleezhah **bahn**kah **mo**leem vahss |

Car rental

I'd like a car.	**Želeo bih kola.**	**zheh**leho beeh **ko**lah
For how long?	**Za koliko dugo?**	zah **ko**leeko **doo**go
A day/Four days/ A week/Two weeks.	**Jedan dan/Četiri dana/Nedelju dana/Dve nedelje.**	**yeh**dahn dahn/**cheh**teeree **dah**nah/**neh**dehl^y oo **dah**nah/dveh **neh**dehl^{y}eh

Taxi

Where can I get a taxi?	**Gde mogu da dobijem taksi?**	gdeh mogoo dah dobeeyehm tahksee
What's the fare to...?	**Koliko staje do...?**	koleeko stahyeh do
Take me to this address, please.	**Odvezite me na ovu adresu, molim Vas.**	odvehzeeteh meh nah ovoo ahdrehssoo moleem vahss
I'm in a hurry.	**Žurim se.**	zhooreem seh
Could you drive more slowly, please?	**Da li biste mogli da vozite malo sporije, molim Vas?**	dah lee beesteh moglee dah vozeeteh mahlo sporeeyeh moleem vahss

Hotel and other accommodation

My name is...	**Ja se zovem...**	yah seh zovehm
Have you a reservation?	**Imate li rezervaciju?**	eemahteh lee rehzehrvahtseeyoo
Yes, here's the confirmation.	**Da, izvolite potvrdu.**	dah eezvoleeteh potverdoo
I'd like...	**Želeo bih...**	zhehleho beeh
I'd like a single room/a double room.	**Želeo bih sobu sa jednim krevetom/sa dva kreveta.**	zhehleho beeh soboo sah yehdneem krehvehtom/ sah dvah krehvehtah
a room with a bath/ with a shower	**sobu sa kupatilom/ sa tušem**	soboo sah koopahteelom/ sah tooshehm

How much?

What's the price per night/per week/per month?	**Koliko staje za jednu noć/jednu nedelju/mesec?**	koleeko stahyeh zah yehdnoo noch/yehdnoo nehdeh^l'oo/mehssehts
May I see the room?	**Mogu li da vidim sobu?**	mogoo lee dah veedeem soboo
I'm sorry, I don't like it.	**Nažalost ne dopada mi se.**	nahzhahlost neh dopahdah mee seh
Yes, that's fine. I'll take it.	**Da, dobra je, uzeću je.**	dah dobrah yeh oozehchoo yeh
What's my room number, please?	**Koji je broj moje sobe?**	koyee yeh broy moyeh sobeh
Number 123.	**Broj 123.**	broy 123

Service, please

Who is it?	Ko je?	ko yeh
Just a minute.	Samo jedan trenutak.	sahmo yehdahn trehnootahk
Come in! The door's open.	Udjite! Vrata su otvorena.	oojeeteh. vrahtah soo otvorehnah
May we have breakfast in our room?	Možemo li dobiti doručak u sobi?	mozhehmo lee dobeetee doroochahk oo sobee

Breakfast

I'll have . . .	Želeo bih . . .	zhehleho beeh
I'll have some fruit juice.	Želeo bih voćni sok.	zhehleho beeh vochnee sok
a boiled egg	jedno kuvano jaje	yehdno koovahno yahyeh
a fried egg	jedno prženo jaje	yehdno perzhehno yahyeh
some bacon/some ham	slaninu/šunku	slahneenoo/shoonkoo
some toast	tost	tost
a pot of tea	lonče čaja	loncheh chahyah
a cup of tea	šoljicu čaja	shol'yeetsoo chahyah
some coffee	hafu	kahfoo
some chocolate	čokoladu	chokolahdoo
more butter	još malo putera	yosh mahlo pootehrah
some hot water	vruće vode	vroocheh vodeh

Difficulties

The central heating doesn't work.	Centralno grejanje ne rađi.	tsentrahlno grehyahñeh neh rahdee
the light/the socket the tap/the toilet	svetlo/utikač slavina (pipa)/toalet	svehtlo/ooteekahch slahveenah (peepah)/ toahleht
There's no hot water.	Nema tople vode.	nehmah topleh vodeh
May I see the manager, please?	Želeo bih da govorim sa šefom, molim Vas.	zhehleho beeh dah govoreem sah shehfom, moleem vahss

Telephone—Mail

| There's a call for you. | Imate telefonski poziv. | eemahteh tehlehfonskee pozeev |
| Hold the line, please. | Ostanite na telefonu, molim Vas. | ostahneeteh nah tehlehfonoo moleem vahss |

Operator, I've been cut off.	**Gospodjice, veza se prekinula.**	**goss**pojeetseh **veh**zah seh **prehk**eenoolah
Did anyone telephone me?	**Da li me neko tražio telefonom?**	dah lee meh **neh**ko trah**zhee**o tehleh**fo**nom
Is there any mail for me?	**Ima li pošte za mene?**	**ee**mah lee **po**shteh zah **meh**neh
Are there any messages for me?	**Ima li neka poruka za mene?**	**ee**mah lee **neh**kah po**roo**kah zah **meh**neh

Checking out

May I have my bill, please?	**Molim Vas račun.**	**mo**leem vahss **rah**choon
We're in a great hurry.	**Jako se žurimo.**	**yah**ko seh **zhoo**reemo
It's been a very enjoyable stay.	**Boravak je bio vrlo prijatan.**	bo**rah**vahk yeh **bee**o **ver**lo **pree**yahtahn

Eating out

Good evening, sir/ Good evening, madam.	**Dobro veče Gospodine/Dobro veče Gospodjo.**	**do**bro **veh**cheh gos**po**deeneh/**do**bro **veh**cheh gos**po**jo
Good evening. I'd like a table for two, please.	**Dobro veče. Hteo bih sto za dvoje molim Vas.**	**do**bro **veh**cheh. **hteh**o beeh sto zah **dvo**yeh **mo**leem vahss
Do you have a fixed-price menu?	**Imate li meni?**	ee**mah**teh lee **meh**nee
May I see the à la carte menu?	**Mogu li da dobijem jelovnik?**	**mo**goo lee dah do**bee**yehm **yeh**lovneek
May we have an ashtray, please?	**Molim Vas pepeljaru.**	**mo**leem vahss peh**pehl**^yahroo
some bread	**hleb**	hlehb
a fork	**viljušku**	veel^y**oo**shkoo
a knife	**nož**	nozh
a spoon	**kašiku**	kah**shee**koo
a plate	**tanjir**	tah**ñee**r
a glass	**čašu**	**chah**shoo
a napkin	**salvetu**	sahl**veh**too
another chair	**još jednu stolicu**	yosh **yehd**noo sto**lee**tsoo
Where's the gentlemen's toilet (men's room)?	**Gde je toalet za muškarce?**	gdeh yeh toah**leht** zah **moosh**kahrtseh
Where's the ladies' toilet (ladies' room)?	**Gde je toalet za žene?**	gdeh yeh toah**leht** zah **zheh**neh

Appetizers

I'd like some . . .	**Hteo bih . . .**	hteho beeh
I'd like some assorted appetizers.	**Hteo bih mešano predjelo.**	hteho beeh mehshahno prehdyehlo
orange juice	**sok od pomorandže**	sok od pomorahnjeh
ham	**šunku**	shoonkoo
melon	**dinju**	deeñoo
pâté	**paštetu**	pahshtehtoo
smoked salmon	**dimljenog lososa**	deeml^yehnog lossossah
shrimps (shrimp)	**račiće**	rahcheecheh

Soup

Have you any . . . ?	**Imate li . . . ?**	eemahteh lee
Have you any chicken soup?	**Imate li pileću čorbu?**	eemahteh lee peelehchoo chorboo
vegetable soup	**čorbu od povrća**	chorboo od poverchah
onion soup	**čorbu od luka**	chorboo od lookah

Fish

I'd like some . . .	**Hteo bih . . .**	hteho beeh
I'd like some fish.	**Hteo bih ribu.**	hteho beeh reeboo
sole	**tabinju**	tahbeeñoo
trout	**pastrmku**	pahstermkoo
lobster	**jastoga**	yahstogah
crayfish	**rak**	rahk
prawns	**kozice**	kozeetseh
I'd like it . . .	**Želeo bih . . .**	zhehleho beeh
I'd like it steamed.	**Spremljenu na pari.**	sprehml^yehnoo nah pahree
grilled	**na roštilju**	nah roshteel^yoo
boiled	**kuvanu**	koovahnoo
baked	**pečenu**	pehchehnoo
fried	**prženu**	perzhehnoo

Meat—Poultry—Game

I'd like some . . .	**Želeo bih . . .**	zhehleho beeh
I'd like some beef.	**Želeo bih govedinu.**	zhehleho beeh govehdeenoo
a beef steak	**govedju šniclu**	govehjoo shneetsloo
some roast beef	**govedje pečenje**	govehjeh pehchehñeh

a veal cutlet	teleći kotlet	tehlehchee kotleht
mutton	ovčetinu	ovchehteenoo
lamb	jagnjetinu	yahgñehteenoo
a pork chop	svinjski kotlet	sveeñskee kotleht
roast pork	svinjsko pečenje	sveeñsko pehchehñeh
hare	zečetinu	zehchehteenoo
chicken	piletinu	peelehteenoo
roast chicken	pečenu piletinu	pehchehnoo peelehteenoo
duck	patku	pahtkoo

How do you like your meat?	Kako pečeno želite meso?	kahko pehchehno zhehleeteh mehsso
rare	polu-pečeno	poloo pehchehno
medium	srednje pečeno	srehdñeh pehchehno
well done	dobro pečeno	dobro pehchehno

Vegetables

What vegetables have you got?	Kakvo povrće imate?	kahkvo povercheh eemahteh
I'd like some ...	Želeo bih ...	zhehleho beeh
I'd like some asparagus.	Želeo bih špargle.	zhehleho beeh shpahrgleh
green beans	boraniju (mahune)	borahneeyoo (mahhooneh)
mushrooms	pečurke	pehchoorkeh
carrots	šargarepu	shahrgahrehpoo
onions	luk	look
red cabbage	crveni kupus	tservehnee koopooss
spinach	spanać (špinat)	spahnahch (shpeenaht)
rice	pirinač (rižu)	peereenahch (reezhoo)
peas	grašak	grahshahk
tomatoes	paradajz	pahrahdahyz
green salad	zelenu salatu	zehlehnoo sahlahtoo
potatoes	krompir	krompeer

Desserts

Nothing more, thanks.	Ništa više, hvala lepo.	neeshtah veesheh hvahlah lehpo
Just a small portion, please.	Jednu malu porciju, molim.	vehdnoo mahloo portseeyoo moleem
Have you any ice-cream?	Imate li sladoleda?	eemahteh lee slahdolehdah
fruit salad	voćnu salatu	vochnoo sahlahtoo
fresh fruit	sveže voće	svehzheh vocheh
cheese	sir	seer

Drink

What would you like to drink?	**Šta biste želeli da pijete?**	shtah **bee**steh zhehlehlee dah **pee**yehteh
I'll have a beer, please.	**Ja bih pivo, molim.**	yah beeh **pee**vo mo**leem**
I'll have a whisky, please.	**Ja bih viski, molim.**	yah beeh **vee**skee mo**leem**

Wine

I'd like a bottle of wine.	**Hteo bih jednu flašu vina.**	**hte**ho beeh **yeh**dnoo **flah**shoo **vee**nah
red wine	**crvenog vina**	**tser**vehnog **vee**nah
rosé wine	**ružice**	**roo**zheetseh
white wine	**belog vina**	**beh**log **vee**nah
Cheers!	**Živeli.**	**zhee**vehlee

The bill (check)

May I have the bill (check) please?	**Molim Vas račun.**	mo**leem** vahss **rah**choon
Is service included?	**Da li je servis uračunat?**	dah lee yeh **seh**rveess oo**rah**choonaht
Everything's included.	**Sve je uračunato.**	sveh yeh oo**rah**choonahto
Thank you, that was a very good meal.	**Hvala lepo, jelo je bilo vrlo dobro.**	**hvah**lah **leh**po **yeh**lo yeh **bee**lo **ver**lo **do**bro

Travelling

Where's the railway station, please?	**Gde je železnička stanica (kolodvor), molim Vas?**	gdeh yeh **zheh**lehzneech-kah **stah**neetsah (kolod-vor) mo**leem** vahss
Where's the ticket office, please?	**Gde je šalter za karte, molim Vas?**	gdeh yeh **shah**ltehr zah **kah**rteh mo**leem** vahss
I'd like a ticket to . . .	**Želeo bih kartu do . . .**	**zheh**leho beeh **kah**rtoo do
First or second class?	**Prvu ili drugu klasu?**	**per**voo eelee **droo**goo **klah**ssoo
First class, please.	**Prvu klasu molim.**	**per**voo **klah**ssoo mo**leem**
Single or return (one way or round-trip)?	**U jednom pravcu ili povratnu?**	oo **yehd**nom **prah**vtsoo eelee po**vrah**tnoo

Do I have to change trains?	**Moram li presedati?**	morahm lee **preh**-sehdahtee
What platform does the train leave from?	**Sa koga perona polazi voz (vlak)?**	sah **ko**gah pehronah **po**lahzee voz (vlahk)
Where's the nearest underground (subway) station?	**Gde je najbliža stanica podzemne železnice?**	gdeh yeh **nahy**bleezhah **stah**neetsah **pod**zehmneh **zheh**lehzneetseh
Where's the bus station, please?	**Gde je autobuska stanica, molim Vas?**	gdeh yeh ahootoobooskah **stah**neetsah **mo**leem vahss
When's the first bus to . . . ?	**Kad polazi prvi autobus za . . . ?**	kahd **po**lahzee **per**vee ahootoobooss zah
the last bus	**poslednji autobus**	po**slehd**ñee ahootoobooss
the next bus	**sledeći autobus**	**sleh**dehchee ahootoobooss
Please let me off at the next stop.	**Sišao bih na sledećoj stanici.**	**see**shaho beeh nah **sleh**dehchoy **stah**neetsee

Relaxing

What's on at the cinema (movies)?	**Šta se daje u bioskopu (kinu)?**	shtah seh **dah**yeh oo **bee**oskopoo (**kee**noo)
What's on at the theatre?	**Šta se daje u pozorištu (kazalištu)?**	shtah seh **dah**yeh oo **po**zoreeshtoo (**kah**zahleeshtoo)
What time does the film begin?	**U koliko sati počinje film?**	oo **ko**leeko **sah**tee **po**cheeñeh feelm
And the play?	**A komad?**	ah **ko**mahd
Are there any tickets for tonight?	**Ima li karata za večeras?**	**ee**mah lee **kah**rahtah zah veh**cheh**rahss
Where can we go dancing?	**Gde možemo da idemo na ples?**	gdeh **mo**zhehmo dah **ee**dehmo nah plehss
Would you like to dance?	**Želite li da igrate (plešete)?**	**zheh**leeteh lee dah **ee**grahteh (**pleh**shehteh)

Introductions

How do you do?	**Dobar dan.**	**do**bahr dahn
How are you?	**Kako ste?**	**kahk**o steh
Very well, thank you. And you?	**Hvala, vrlo dobro. A Vi?**	**hvah**lah **ver**lo **do**bro. ah vee
May I introduce Miss Philips?	**Mogu li da Vam predstavim Gospodjicu Filips.**	**mo**goo lee dah vahm **prehd**stahveem **go**spojeetsoo Philips

SERBO-CROATIAN

My name is...	Ja se zovem...	yah seh zovehm
I'm very pleased to meet you.	Drago mi je da sam Vas upoznao.	drahgo mee yeh dah sahm vahss oopoznaho
How long have you been here?	Od kad ste ovde?	od kahdah steh ovdeh
It was nice meeting you.	Bilo mi je zadovoljstvo.	beelo mee yeh zahdovol'stvo

Dating

Would you like a cigarette?	Želite li cigaretu?	zhehleeteh lee tseegahrehtoo
May I get you a drink?	Da li Vam mogu doneti jedno piće?	dah lee vahm mogoo donehtee yehdno peecheh
Do you have a light, please?	Imate li šibicu, molim Vas?	eemahteh lee sheebeetsoo moleem vahss
Are you waiting for someone?	Da li čekate nekoga?	dah lee chehkahteh nehkogah
Are you free this evening?	Da li ste slobodni večeras?	dah lee steh slobodnee vehchehrahss
Where shall we meet?	Gde ćemo se sastati?	gdeh chehmo seh sahstahtee
What time shall I meet you?	Kad ćemo se videti?	kahd chehmo seh veedehtee
May I take you home?	Smem li Vas otpratiti kući?	smehm lee vahss otprahteetee koochee
Thank you, it's been a wonderful evening.	Hvala Vam, bilo je divno veče.	hvahlah vahm beelo yeh deevno vehcheh
What's your telephone number?	Koji je broj Vašeg telefona?	koyee yeh broy vahshehg tehlehfonah
Do you live alone?	Da li živite sami?	dah lee zheeveeteh sahmee
What time is your last train?	Kad ide Vaš poslednji voz (vlak)?	kahd eedeh vahsh poslehdnee voz (vlahk)
Good-night...	Laku noć...	lahkoo noch

Banks

Where's the nearest bank, please?	Gde je najbliža banka, molim Vas?	gdeh yeh nahybleezhah bahnkah moleem vahss
Where can I cash some traveller's cheques?	Gde mogu da unovčim putne čekove?	gdeh mogoo dah oonovcheem pootneh chehkoveh

What time does the bank open/What time does it close?	**Kad se banka otvara/Kad se zatvara?**	kahd seh **bahn**kah otvahrah/kahd seh **zaht**vahrah
I'm expecting some money from home. Has it arrived?	**Očekujem novac od kuće. Da li je stigao?**	o**cheh**kooyehm no**vahtss** od **koo**cheh. dah lee yeh **stee**gaho
Can you give me some small change, please?	**Možete li mi dati malo sitnine, molim Vas?**	**mo**zhehteh lee mee **dah**tee **mah**lo **seet**neeneh **mo**leem vahss

Shops, stores and services

Where is the nearest chemist's (pharmacy)?	**Gde je najbliža apoteka?**	gdeh yeh **nahy**bleezhah ahpo**teh**kah
the nearest hair-dresser's	**najbliži frizer**	**nahy**bleezhee **free**zehr
the photo shop	**radnja sa foto materijalom**	**rahd**ñah sah **foto** mahtehree**yah**lom
the jeweller's	**juvelir**	yoo**veh**leer
the department store	**robna kuća**	**robnah koo**chah
the police station	**policijska stanica**	po**leet**seeyskah **stah**neetsah
the garage	**garaža**	gah**rah**zhah
How do I get there?	**Kako mogu da dodjem do tamo?**	**kahko mo**goo dah **do**jehm do **tah**mo
Is it within walking distance?	**Da li se tamo može stići pešice?**	dah lee seh **tah**mo **mo**zheh **stee**chee peh**sheet**seh

Service

Can you help me, please?	**Možete li mi pomoći, molim Vas?**	**mo**zhehteh lee mee po**mo**chee **mo**leem vahss
Can you show me this? And that, too.	**Možete li mi pokazati ovo? I ono takodje.**	**mo**zhehteh lee mee po**kah**zahtee **ovo**? ee ono tah**ko**jeh
It's too expensive/ too big/too small.	**To je suviše skupo/suviše veliko/suviše malo.**	to yeh **soo**veesheh **skoo**po/**soo**veesheh **veh**leeko/**soo**veesheh **mah**lo
Can you show me some more?	**Možete li mi pokazati još nekoliko?**	**mo**zhehteh lee mee po**kah**zahtee yosh **neh**koleeko
something better	**nešto bolje**	**neh**shto **bol**^yeh
something cheaper	**nešto jevtinije**	**neh**shto **yehv**teeneeyeh

How much is this? And that?	Koliko staje ovo? A ono?	koleeko stahyeh ovo? ah ono
It's not quite what I want.	To baš nije ono što ja želim.	to bahsh neeyeh ono shto yah zhehleem
I like it.	Dopada mi se.	dopahdah mee seh

Chemist's (Pharmacy)

| I'd like something for a cold/for a cough/for travel sickness. | Imate li nešto za nazeb/kašalj/putnu bolest? | eemahteh lee nehshto zah nahzehb/kahshahl^y/pootnoo bolehst |
| Can you recommend something for hay-fever/for sunburn? | Možete li pre-poručiti nešto za polensku groznicu/za opekotine od sunca? | mozhehteh lee prehpo-roocheetee nehshto zah polehnskoo grozneetsoo/zah opehkoteeneh od soontsah |

Toiletry

May I have some razor blades?	Molim Vas žilete.	moleem vahss zheelehteh
some shaving cream some toothpaste	pastu za brijanje pastu za zube	pahstoo zah breeyahñeh pahstoo zah zoobeh
I'd like some soap.	Molim Vas sapun.	moleem vahss sapoon
some suntan oil	ulje za sunčanje	ool^{y}eh zah soonchahñeh

At the barber's

I'd like a haircut, please.	Šišanje, molim Vas.	sheeshahñeh moleem vahss
Short/Leave it long.	Kratko/Ostavite malo duže.	krahtko/ostahveeteh mahlo doozheh
A razor cut, please.	Šišanje, molim, bri-jačem.	sheeshahñeh moleem breeyahchehm

At the hairdresser's

| I'd like a shampoo and set, please. | Operite mi kosu i počešljajte me, molim Vas. | opehreeteh mee kosoo ee pochehshl^{y}ahyteh meh moleem vahss |

I'd like a bleach.	**Molim Vas blaj-hanje.**	**mo**leem vahss **blahy**hahñeh
a permanent	**trajnu ondulaciju**	**trahy**noo ondoo**lahts**eeyoo
a colour rinse	**preliv**	**prehl**eev
a manicure	**manikir**	mah**nee**keer

Photography

I'd like a film for this camera.	**Hteo bih film za ovaj aparat.**	**hteh**o beeh feelm zah ovahy ah**pah**raht
This camera doesn't work.	**Ovaj aparat je pokvaren.**	ovahy ah**pah**raht yeh pok**vah**rehn

At the post office

Where's the nearest post office, please?	**Gde je najbliža pošta, molim Vas?**	gdeh yeh **nahy**bleezhah **po**shtah **mo**leem vahss
I'd like to send this by express (special delivery)/by air mail.	**Želeo bih da pošaljem ovo ekspres/avionom.**	**zheh**leho beeh dah posha**l**ᵛehm ovo ehks**prehss**/ahveeonom

Service stations

Where is the nearest service station, please?	**Gde je najbliža servisna stanica?**	gdeh yeh **nahy**bleezhah **sehr**veessnah **stah**neetsah
Fill her up, please.	**Napunite rezervoar, molim Vas.**	**nah**pooneeteh rehzehr**voahr mo**leem vahss
Check the oil, please.	**Proverite ulje, molim Vas.**	pro**veh**reeteh ool**ᵛ**eh **mo**leem vahss
Would you check the tyres?	**Da li biste hteli da proverite gume?**	dah lee **bee**steh **hteh**lee dah pro**veh**reeteh **goo**meh

Street directions

Can you show me on the map where I am?	**Možete li mi pokazati na karti gde se nalazim?**	mo**zheh**teh lee mee poka**zah**teh nah **kahr**tee gdeh seh **nah**lahzeem
You're on the wrong road.	**Vi ste na pog-rešnom putu.**	vee steh nah **pog**reh-shnom **poo**too
Go back to . . .	**Vratite se do . . .**	**vrah**teeteh seh do
Go straight ahead.	**Idite pravo napred.**	**ee**deeteh **prah**voo **nah**prehd
It's on the left/on the right.	**Na levoj je strani/na desnoj.**	nah **leh**voy yeh **strah**nee/nah **deh**snoy

Accidents

May I use your telephone?	**Mogu li se poslužiti Vašim telefonom?**	mogoo lee seh posloozheetee vahsheem tehlehfonom
Call a doctor quickly.	**Pozovite brzo doktora.**	pozoveeteh berzo doktorah
Call an ambulance.	**Pozovite kola za hitnu pomoć.**	pozoveeteh kolah zah heetnoo pomoch
Please call the police.	**Pozovite, molim Vas, policiju.**	pozoveeteh moleem vahss poleetseeyoo

Numbers

one	**jedan**	yehdahn
two	**dva**	dvah
three	**tri**	tree
four	**četiri**	chehteeree
five	**pet**	peht
six	**šest**	shehst
seven	**sedam**	sehdahm
eight	**osam**	ossahm
nine	**devet**	dehveht
ten	**deset**	dehseht
eleven	**jedanaest**	yehdahnahehst
twelve	**dvanaest**	dvahnahehst
thirteen	**trinaest**	treenahehst
fourteen	**četrnaest**	chehternahehst
fifteen	**petnaest**	pehtnahehst
sixteen	**šesnaest**	shehssnahehst
seventeen	**sedamnaest**	sehdahmnahehst
eighteen	**osamnaest**	osahmnahehst
nineteen	**devetnaest**	dehvehtnahehst
twenty	**dvadeset**	dvahdehseht
twenty-one	**dvadeset jedan**	dvahdehseht yehdahn
thirty	**trideset**	treedehseht
forty	**četrdeset**	chehterdehseht
fifty	**pedeset**	pehdehseht
sixty	**šezdeset**	shehzdehseht
seventy	**sedamdeset**	sehdahmdehseht
eighty	**osamdeset**	osahmdehseht
ninety	**devedeset**	dehvehdehseht
one hundred	**sto**	sto
one thousand	**hiljadu**	heel^{y}ahdoo
ten thousand	**deset hiljada**	dehseht heel^{y}ahdah

Days

It's Sunday.	**Nedelja je.**	**neh**dehl^yah yeh
Monday	**ponedeljak**	ponehdehl^yahk
Tuesday	**utorak**	**oo**torahk
Wednesday	**sreda**	**sreh**dah
Thursday	**četvrtak**	cheht**ver**tahk
Friday	**petak**	**peh**tahk
Saturday	**subota**	**soo**botah
yesterday	**juće**	**yoo**cheh
today	**danas**	**dah**nahss
tomorrow	**sutra**	**soo**trah
morning/afternoon	**jutro/posle podne**	**yoo**tro/**posleh** podneh
evening/night	**veče/noć**	**veh**cheh/noch

Months

January	**januar**	**yah**nooahr
February	**februar**	**fehb**rooahr
March	**mart**	mahrt
April	**april**	**ah**preel
May	**maj**	**mahy**
June	**jun**	yoon
July	**juli**	**yoo**lee
August	**avgust**	**ahv**goost
September	**septembar**	sehp**tehm**bahr
October	**oktobar**	ok**to**bahr
November	**novembar**	no**vehm**bahr
December	**decembar**	deht**sehm**bahr
Merry Christmas!	**Srećan Božić!**	**sreh**chahn **bo**zheech!
Happy New Year!	**Srećna Nova godina!**	**sreh**chnah **no**vah **go**deenah

SPANISH

Guide to Pronunciation

Letter	Approximate pronunciation	Symbol	Example	
Consonants				
f, k, l, m, n, p, t, y	as in English			
b	1) generally as in English	b	**bueno**	**bway**noa
	2) between vowels, a sound between **b** and **v**	bh	**bebida**	bayb**hee**dhah
c	1) before **e** and **i** like **th** in **th**in	th	**centro**	**thayn**troa
	2) otherwise, like **k** in **k**it	k	**como**	**koa**moa
ch	as in English	ch	**mucho**	**moo**choa
d	1) generally as in **d**og, although less decisive	d	**donde**	**don**day
	2) between vowels and at the end of a word, like **th** in **th**is	dh	**edad**	ay**dhahdh**

SPANISH

270

g	1) before e and i, like ch in Scottish lo**ch**	kh	**urgente**	oor**kh**ayntay
	2) between vowels and sometimes inside a word, a weak, voiced version of the ch in lo**ch**	ġ	**agua**	ah**ġ**wah
	3) otherwise, like g in go	g	**ninguno**	neen**gg**oonoa
h	always silent		**hombre**	**o**mbray
j	like ch in Scottish lo**ch**	kh	**bajo**	bah**kh**oa
ñ	like ni in onion	ñ	**señor**	say**ñ**or
qu	like k in kit	k	**quince**	**k**eenthay
r	more strongly trilled (like a Scottish r), especially at the beginning of a word	r	**rio**	**r**eeoa
rr	strongly trilled	rr	**arriba**	ah**rr**eebhah
s	always like the s in sit, often with a slight lisp	s/ss	**vista** **cuantos**	bee**s**tah kwahnto**ass**
v	1) tends to be like b in bad, but less tense	b	**viejo**	**b**yaykhoa
	2) between vowels, more like English v	bh	**rival**	ree**bh**ahl
z	like th in thin	th	**brazo**	brah**th**oa

Vowels

a	like a in car, but fairly short	ah	**gracias**	gr**ah**thyahss
e	1) sometimes like a in late	ay	**de**	d**ay**
	2) less often, like e in get	eh	**llover**	lyoabh**ehr**
i	like ee in feet	ee	**si**	s**ee**
o	1) sometimes fairly like o in rope	oa	**sopa**	s**oa**pah
	2) sometimes like o in got	o	**dos**	d**o**ss
u	like oo in loot	oo	**una**	**oo**nah
y	only a vowel when alone or at the end of a word; like ee in feet	ee	**y**	**ee**

N.B. 1) In forming diphthongs, **a**, **e**, and **o** are strong vowels, and **i** and **u** are weak vowels. This means that in diphthongs the strong vowels are pronounced more strongly than the weak ones. If two weak vowels form a diphthong, the second one is pronounced more strongly.
2) The acute accent (´) is used to indicate a syllable that is stressed, e.g., *río* = **ree**oa.
3) In words ending with a consonant, the last syllable is stressed, e.g., *señor* = say**nor**.
4) In words ending with a vowel, the next to the last syllable is stressed, e.g., *mañana* = mah**ñah**nah.

Some basic expressions

Yes.	**Sí.**	see
No.	**No.**	noa
Please.	**Por favor.**	por fah**bhor**
Thank you.	**Gracias.**	**grah**thyahss
Thank you very much.	**Muchas gracias.**	**moo**chahss **grah**thyahss
That's all right.	**No hay de qué.**	noa igh day kay

Greetings

Good morning.	**Buenos días.**	bway**noass dee**eahss
Good afternoon.	**Buenas tardes.**	bway**nahss tahr**dhayss
Good evening.	**Buenas tardes.**	bway**nahss tahr**dhayss
Good night.	**Buenas noches.**	bway**nahss noa**chayss
Good-bye.	**Adiós.**	ahd**hyoss**
See you later.	**Hasta luego.**	**ahss**tah **lway**goa
This is Mr....	**Este es el Señor...**	**ayss**tay ayss ehl say**ñor**
This is Mrs....	**Esta es la Señora...**	**ayss**tah ayss lah say**ñoa**rah
This is Miss...	**Esta es la Señorita...**	**ayss**tah ayss lah say**ñoa**-reetah
I'm very pleased to meet you.	**Encantado de conocerle.**	ayngkahn**tah**dhoa day koanoa**thayr**lay
How are you?	**Cómo está usted?**	**koa**moa ayss**tah** ooss**taydh**
Very well, thank you. And you?	**Muy bien, gracias. ¿Y usted?**	mwee byayn **grah**thyahss. ee ooss**taydh**
Fine.	**Bien. Gracias.**	byayn **grah**thyahss
Excuse me.	**Dispénseme.**	deess**payn**saymay

Questions

Where?	**¿Dónde?**	**don**day
Where is...?	**¿Dónde está...?**	**don**day ayss**tah**
Where are...?	**¿Dónde están...?**	**don**day ayss**tahn**
When?	**¿Cuándo?**	**kwahn**doa

SPANISH

SPANISH

What?	¿Qué?	kay
How?	¿Cómo?	koamoa
How much?	¿Cuánto?	kwahntoa
How many?	¿Cuántos?	kwahntoass
Who?	¿Quién?	kyayn
Why?	¿Por qué?	por kay
Which?	¿Cuál?	kwahl
What do you call this?	¿Cómo se llama esto?	koamoa say lyahmah aysstoa
What do you call that?	¿Cómo se llama eso?	koamoa say lyahmah aysoa
What does this mean?	¿Qué quiere decir esto?	kay kyayray daytheer aysstoa
What does that mean?	¿Qué quiere decir eso?	kay kyayray daytheer aysoa

Do you speak ... ?

Do you speak English?	¿Habla usted inglés?	ahbhlah oosstaydh eengglayss
Do you speak German?	¿Habla usted alemán?	ahbhlah oosstaydh ahlaymahn
Do you speak French?	¿Habla usted francés?	ahbhlah oosstaydh frahnthayss
Do you speak Spanish?	¿Habla usted español?	ahbhlah oosstaydh aysspahñol
Do you speak Italian?	¿Habla usted italiano?	ahbhlah oosstaydh eetahlyahnoa
Could you speak more slowly, please?	¿Puede usted hablar más despacio, por favor?	pwaydhay oosstaydh ahbhlahr mahss dayspahthyoa por fahbhor
Please point to the phrase in the book.	Por favor, señale la frase en el libro.	por fahbhor sayñahlay lah frahsay ayn ehl leebhroa
Just a minute. I'll see if I can find it in this book.	Un momento. Veré si lo puedo encontrar en este libro.	oon moamayntoa. bayray see loa pwaydhoa ayngkontrahr ayn aysstay leebroa
I understand.	Comprendo.	komprayndoa
I don't understand.	No comprendo.	noa komprayndoa

Can...?

Can I have...?	¿Puede darme...?	pwaydhay dahrmay
Can we have...?	¿Puede darnos...?	pwaydhay dahrnoss
Can you show me...?	¿Puede usted enseñarme...?	pwaydhay oosstaydh aynsayñahrmay
Can you tell me...?	¿Puede usted decirme...?	pwaydhay oosstaydh daytheermay
Can you help me, please?	¿Puede usted ayudarme, por favor?	pwaydhay oosstaydh ahyoodahrmay por fahbhor

Wanting

I'd like...	Quisiera...	keesyayrah
We'd like...	Quisiéramos...	keesyayrahmoss
Please give me...	Por favor, déme...	por fahbhor daymay
Give it to me, please.	Démelo, por favor.	daymayloa por fahbhor
Please bring me...	Por favor, tráigame...	por fahbhor trighgahmay
Bring it to me, please.	Tráigamelo, por favor.	trighgahmayloa por fahbhor
I'm hungry.	Tengo hambre.	taynggoa ahmbray
I'm thirsty.	Tengo sed.	taynggoa saydh
I'm tired.	Estoy cansada.	aysstoy kahnsahdhah
I'm lost.	Me he perdido.	may ay pehrdheedhoa
It's important.	Es importante.	ayss eempoartahntay
It's urgent.	Es urgente.	ayss oorkhayntay
Hurry up!	¡Dése prisa!	daysay preesah

It is/There is...

It is/It's...	Es...	ayss
Is it...?	¿Es...?	ayss
It isn't...	No es...	noa ayss
There is/There are...	Hay...	igh
Is there/Are there...?	¿Hay...?	igh

SPANISH

| There isn't/There aren't... | **No hay ...** | noa igh |
| There isn't any/ There aren't any. | **No hay ninguno/No hay ningunos (No hay ninguna/No hay ningunas).** | noa igh neenggoonoa/noa igh neenggoonoss (noa igh neenggoonah/noa igh neenggoonahss) |

A few common words

big/small	**grande/pequeño**	grahnday/paykayñoa
quick/slow	**rápido/lento**	rahpeedhoa/layntoa
early/late	**temprano/tarde**	taymprahnoa/tahrdhay
cheap/expensive	**barato/caro**	bahrahtoa/kahroa
near/far	**cerca/lejos**	thehrkah/laykhoass
hot/cold	**caliente/frío**	kahlyayntay/freeoa
full/empty	**lleno/vacío**	lyaynoa/bahtheeoa
easy/difficult	**fácil/difícil**	fahtheel/deefeetheel
heavy/light	**pesado/ligero**	paysahdhoa/leekhayroa
open/shut	**abierto/cerrado**	ahbyehrtoa/thayrrahdhoa
right/wrong	**correcto/incorrecto**	korrehktoa/eengkorrehktoa
old/new	**viejo/nuevo**	byaykhoa/nwaybhoa
old/young	**viejo/joven**	byaykhoa/khoabhayn
beautiful/ugly	**bonito/feo**	boaneetoa/fayoa
good/bad	**bueno/malo**	bwaynoa/mahloa
better/worse	**mejor/peor**	mehkhor/payor

Some prepositions and a few more useful words

at	**a**	ah
on	**sobre**	soabhray
in	**en**	ayn
to	**para**	pahrah
from	**desde**	dayzday
inside	**dentro**	dayntroa
outside	**fuera**	fwayrah
up	**arríba**	ahrreebhah
down	**abajo**	ahbhahkhoa
before	**antes**	ahntayss
after	**después**	daysspwayss
with	**con**	kon
without	**sin**	seen
through	**a través**	ah trahbhayss
towards	**hacia**	ahthyah
until	**hasta**	ahsstah
during	**durante**	doorahntay
and	**y**	ee
or	**o**	oa

SPANISH

not	**no**	noa
nothing	**nada**	**nah**dhah
none	**ninguno**	neeng**goo**noa
very	**muy**	mwee
also	**también**	tahm**bhyayn**
soon	**pronto**	**pront**oa
perhaps	**tal vez**	tal bayth
here	**aquí**	ah**kee**
there	**allí**	ah**lyee**
now	**ahora**	a**hor**ah
then	**entonces**	ayn**ton**thayss

Arrival

Your passport, please.	**Su pasaporte, por favor.**	soo pahsah**por**tay por **fah**bhor
Here it is.	**Aquí está.**	ah**kee** ayss**tah**
Have you anything to declare?	**¿Tiene usted algo que declarar?**	**tyay**nay ooss**taydh ahl**goa kay dayklah**rahr**
No, nothing at all.	**No, nada en absoluto.**	noa **nah**dhah ayn ahb-soa**loo**toa
Porter!	**¡Mozo!**	**moa**thoa
Can you help me with my luggage, please?	**¿Puede usted ayudarme con mi equipaje, por favor?**	**pway**dhay ooss**taydh** ahyoo**dhahr**may kon mee aykee**pahk**hay por **fah**bhor
That's my suitcase.	**Esa es mi maleta.**	**ay**sah ayss mee mah**lay**tah
Where's the bus to the centre of town, please?	**¿Dónde está el autobús que va al centro, por favor?**	**don**day ayss**tah** ehl ow-toa**booss** kay bah ahl **thayn**troa por **fah**bhor
This way, please.	**Por aquí, por favor.**	por ah**kee** por **fah**bhor

Changing money

| Can you change a traveller's cheque, please? | **¿Puede usted cambiarme un traveller's cheque, por favor?** | **pway**dhay ooss**taydh** kahm**byahr**may oon ''traveller's cheque'' por **fah**bhor |
| Where's the nearest bank, please? | **¿Dónde está el banco más cercano, por favor?** | **don**day ayss**tah** ehl **bahng**koa mahss thehr**kah**noa por **fah**bhor |

Car rental

I'd like a car.	**Quisiera un coche.**	keesyayrah oon koachay
For how long?	**¿Para cuánto tiempo?**	pahrah kwahntoa tyaympoa
A day/Four days/ A week/Two weeks.	**Un día/Cuatro días/Una semana/ Dos semanas.**	oon deeah/kwahtroa deeahss/oonah saymah-nah/doss saymahnahss

Taxi

Where can I get a taxi?	**¿Dónde puedo coger (conseguir) un taxi?**	donday pwaydhoa kokhehr (koansaygeer) oon tahksee
What's the fare to . . . ?	**¿Cuánto es la tarifa a . . . ?**	kwahntoa ayss lah tahreefah ah
Take me to this address, please.	**Lléveme a esta dirección, por favor.**	lyaybhamay ah aysstah deerehğthyon por fahbhor
I'm in a hurry.	**Tengo mucha prisa.**	taynggoa moochah preesah
Could you drive more slowly, please?	**¿Puede usted ir mas despacio, por favor?**	pwaydhay oosstaydh eer mahss daysspahthyoa por fahbhor

Hotel and other accommodation

My name is . . .	**Me llamo . . .**	may lyahmoa
Have you a reservation?	**¿Ha hecho usted una reserva?**	ah aychoa oosstaydh oonah rrehsehrbhah
Yes, here's the confirmation.	**Si, aqui está la confirmación.**	see ahkee aysstah lah konfeermahthyon
I'd like . . .	**Quisiera . . .**	keesyayrah
I'd like a single room/a double room.	**Quisiera una habitación sencilla/una habitación doble.**	keesyayrah oonah ah-bheetahthyon sayntheelyah/oonah ah-bheetahthyon doabhlay
a room with a bath/ with a shower	**una habitación con baño/con ducha**	oonah ahbheetahthyon kon bahñoa/kon doochah

How much?

What's the price per night/per week/per month?	**¿Cuánto cuesta por noche/por semana/ por mes?**	kwahntoa kwaysstah por noachay/por saymahnah/ por mayss

May I see the room?	¿Puedo ver la habitación?	pwaydhoa bayr lah ahbheetahthyon
I'm sorry, I don't like it.	Lo siento, no me gusta.	loa syayntoa noa may goosstah
Yes, that's fine. I'll take it.	Muy bien, la tomaré.	mwee byayn lah toamahray
What's my room number, please?	¿Cuál es el número de mi habitación, por favor?	kwahl ayss ehl noomayroa day mee ahbheetahthyon por fahbhor
Number 123.	Número 123.	noomayroa 123.

Service, please

Who is it?	¿Quién es?	kyayn ayss
Just a minute.	Un momento, por favor.	oon moamayntoa por fahbhor
Come in! The door's open.	¡Adelante! la puerta está abierta.	ahdhaylahntay! lah pwehrtah aysstah ahbhyehrtah
May we have breakfast in our room?	¿Podemos desayunar en nuestra habitación?	poadhaymoass daysahyoonahr ayn nwaysstrah ahbheetahthyon

Breakfast

I'll have . . .	Quisiera . . .	keesyayrah
I'll have some fruit juice.	Quisiera un zumo de fruta.	keesyayrah oon thoomoa day frootah
a boiled egg	un huevo cocido	oon waybhoa koatheedhoa
a fried egg	un huevo frito	oon waybhoa freetoa
some bacon/some ham	un poco de tocino/un poco de jamón	oon poakoa day toatheenoa/oon poakoa day khahmon
some toast	un poco de pan tostado	oon poakoa day pahn toasstahdhoa
a pot of tea	una tetera de té	oonah taytayrah day tay
a cup of tea	una taza de té	oonah tahthah day tay
some coffee	un poco de café	oon poakoa day kahfay
some chocolate	un poco de chocolate	oon poakoa day choakoalahtay
more butter	más mantequilla	mahss mahntaykeelyah
some hot water	un poco de agua caliente	oon poakoa day ahġwah kahlyayntay

Difficulties

The central heating doesn't work.	La calefacción central no funciona.	lah kahlayfahkthyon thayntrahl noa foonthyoanah
the light/the socket the tap/the toilet	la luz/el enchufe el grifo/el water	lah looth/ehl aynchoofay ehl greefoa/ehl vahtehr
There's no hot water.	No hay agua caliente.	noa igh ahgwah kahlyayntay
May I see the manager, please?	¿Puedo ver al director, por favor?	pwaydhoa behr ahl deerehktor por fahbhor

Telephone—Mail

There's a call for you.	Hay una llamada para usted.	igh oonah lyahmahdhah pahrah oosstaydh
Hold the line, please.	Espere un momento, por favor.	aysspayray oon moamayntoa por fahbhor
Operator, I've been cut off.	Telefonista, me han cortado.	taylayfoaneesstah may ahn kortahdhoa
Did anyone telephone me?	¿Me ha llamado alguien?	may ah lyahmahdhoa ahlgyayn
Is there any mail for me?	¿Hay correo para mí?	igh korrayoa pahrah mee
Are there any messages for me?	¿Hay algún recado para mi?	igh ahlgoon raykahdhoa pahrah mee

Checking out

May I have my bill, please?	¿Puede darme mi cuenta, por favor?	pwaydhay dahrmay mee kwayntah por fahbhor
We're in a great hurry.	Tenemos mucha prisa.	taynaymoss moochah preesah
It's been a very enjoyable stay.	Ha sido una estancia muy agradable.	ah seedhoa oonah aysstahnthyah mwee ahgrahdhahbhlay

Eating out

Good evening, sir/ Good evening, madam.	Buenas noches, señor/Buenas noches, señora.	bwaynahss noachayss sayñor bwaynahss noachayss sayñoarah
Good evening. I'd like a table for two, please.	Buenas noches. Quisiera una mesa para dos, por favor.	bwaynahss noachayss. keesayrah oonah maysah pahrah doss por fahbhor

Do you have a fixed-price menu?	¿Tiene usted un menu de precio fijo?	tyaynay oosstaydh oon maynoo day praythyoa feekhoa
May I see the à la carte menu?	¿Puedo ver la carta?	pwaydhoa behr lah kahr-tah
May we have an ashtray, please?	¿Nos puede traer un cenicero, por favor?	noss pwaydhay trahehr oon thayneethayroa por fahbhor
some bread	un poco de pan	oon poakoa day pan
a fork	un tenedor	oon taynaydhor
a knife	un cuchillo	oon koocheelyoa
a spoon	una cuchara	oonah koochahrah
a plate	un plato	oon plahtoa
a glass	un vaso	oon bahsoa
a napkin	una servilleta	oonah sehrbheelyaytah
another chair	otra silla	oatra seelyah
Where's the gentle-men's toilet (men's room)?	¿Dónde está el lavabo de caballeros?	donday aysstah ehl lah-bhahbhoa day kahbhahlyayross
Where's the ladies' toilet (ladies' room)?	¿Dónde está el lavabo de señoras?	donday aysstah ehl lah-bhahbhoa day sayñoarahss

Appetizers

I'd like some . . .	Quisiera . . .	keesyayrah
I'd like some assorted appetizers.	Quisiera unos en-tremeses variados.	keesyayrah oonoss ayn-traymaysayss bahreeah-dhoss
orange juice	un jugo de naranja	oon khooğoa day nahrahnkhah
ham	jamón	khahmon
melon	melón	maylon
pâté	pastel de carne	pahsstehl day kahrnay
smoked salmon	salmón ahumado	sahlmon ahoomahdhoa
shrimps (shrimp)	quisquillas	keesskeelyahss

Soup

Have you any . . . ?	¿Tiene usted . . . ?	tyaynay oosstaydh
Have you any chicken soup?	¿Tiene usted sopa de pollo?	tyaynay oosstaydh soapah day poalyoa
vegetable soup	sopa de verduras	soapah day behrdhoo-rahss
onion soup	sopa de cebollas	soapah day thaybhoa-lyahss

SPANISH

Fish

I'd like some . . .	Quisiera . . .	kee**syay**rah
I'd like some fish.	Quisiera pescado.	kee**syay**rah pays**skah**dhoa
sole	lenguado	layng**gwah**dhoa
trout	trucha	**troo**chah
lobster	langosta	lang**gosst**ah
crayfish	cangrejos	kahng**gray**khoss
prawns	gambas	**gahm**bahss
I'd like it . . .	Me gustaría . . .	may goosta**ree**ah
I'd like it steamed.	Me gustaria al vapor.	may goosta**ree**ah ahl bah**por**
grilled	a la parrilla	ah lah pah**ree**lyah
boiled	cocido	koa**thee**dhoa
baked	asado	ah**sah**dhoa
fried	frito	**free**toa

Meat—Poultry—Game

I'd like some . . .	Quisiera . . .	kee**syay**rah
I'd like some beef.	Quisiera carne de vaca.	kee**syay**rah **kahr**nay day **bah**kah
a beef steak	un bistec	oon bees**stehk**
some roast beef	rosbif	rroz**bheef**
a veal cutlet	una chuleta de ternera	**oo**nah choo**lay**tah day tehr**nay**rah
mutton	carnero	kahr**nay**roa
lamb	cordero	kor**dhay**roa
a pork chop	una chuleta de cerdo	**oo**nah choo**lay**tah day **thehr**dhoa
roast pork	cerdo asado	**thehr**dhoa ah**sah**dhoa
hare	liebre	**lyay**bhray
chicken	pollo	**poa**lyoa
roast chicken	pollo asado	**poa**lyoa ah**sah**dhoa
duck	pato	**pah**toa
How do you like your meat?	¿Cómo le gusta la carne?	**koa**moa lay **goos**stah lah **kahr**nay
rare	poco asada	**poa**koa ah**sah**dhah
medium	medio asada	**may**dhyoa ah**sah**dhah
well done	bien hecha	byayn **ay**chah

Vegetables

| What vegetables have you got? | ¿Qué verduras tiene usted? | kay behr**dhoo**rahss **tyay**nah ooss**taydh** |
| I'd like some . . . | Quisiera . . . | kee**syay**rah |

I'd like some asparagus.	Quisiera unos espárragos.	keesyayrah oonoss aysspahrrahģoss
green beans	unas judías verdes	oonahss khoodhyahss behrdhayss
mushrooms	unas setas	oonahss saytahss
carrots	unas zanahorias	oonahss thahnahoryahss
onions	unas cebollas	oonahss thaybhoalyahss
red cabbage	lombarda	loambahrdhah
spinach	unas espinacas	oonahss aysspeenahkahss
rice	un poco de arroz	oon poakoa day ahrroth
peas	unos guisantes	oonos geesahntayss
tomatoes	unos tomates	oonos toamahtayss
green salad	ensalada de lechuga	aynsahlahdhah day laychooģah
potatoes	unas patatas	oonahss pahtahtahss

Desserts

Nothing more, thanks.	Nada más, gracias.	nahdhah mahss grahthyahss
Just a small portion, please.	Una pequeña porción, por favor.	oonah paykayñah porthyon por fahbhor
Have you any ice-cream?	¿Tiene usted helado?	tyaynay oosstaydh aylahdhoa
fruit salad	ensalada de fruta	aynsahlahdhah day frootah
fresh fruit	fruta fresca	frootah fraysskah
cheese	queso	kaysoa

Drink

What would you like to drink?	¿Qué le gustaría beber?	kay lay goosstahreeah baybhayr
I'll have a beer, please.	Tomaré una cerveza, por favor.	toamahray oonah thehrbhaythah por fahbhor
I'll have a whisky, please.	Tomaré un whisky, por favor.	toamahray oon weeskee por fahbhor

Wine

I'd like a bottle of wine.	Quisiera una botella de vino.	keesyayrah oonah boatay-lyah day beenoa
red wine	vino tinto	beenoa teentoa
rosé wine	vino clarete	beenoa klahraytay
white wine	vino blanco	beenoa blahngkoa
Cheers!	¡A su salud!	ah soo sahloodh

The bill (check)

May I have the bill (check) please?	¿Podría darme la cuenta, por favor?	poadhreeah dahrmay lah kwayntah por fahbhor
Is service included?	¿Está incluído el servicio?	aysstah eengklooeedhoa ehl sehrbheethyoa
Everything's included.	Todo está incluído.	toadhoa aysstah eeng-klooeedhoa
Thank you, that was a very good meal.	Gracias. Ha sido una comida muy buena.	grahthyahss. ah seedhoa oonah koameedhah mwee bwaynah

Travelling

Where's the railway station, please?	¿Dónde está la estación de ferrocarril, por favor?	donday aysstah lah aysstahthyon day fehrrokahrreel por fahbhor
Where's the ticket office, please?	¿Dónde está la taquilla, por favor?	donday aysstah lah tah-keelyah por fahbhor
I'd like a ticket to ...	Quisiera un billete para ...	keesyayrah oon beelyay-tay pahrah
First or second class?	¿Primera o segunda clase?	preemayrah o saygoon-dah klahsay
First class, please.	Primera clase, por favor.	preemayrah klahsay por fahbhor
Single or return (one way or round-trip)?	¿Ida, o ida y vuelta?	eedhah o eedhah ee bwehltah
Do I have to change trains?	¿Tengo que hacer transbordo?	taynggoa kay ahthehr trahnzbhoardhoa
What platform does the train leave from?	¿De qué andén sale el tren?	day kay ahndayn sahloy ehl trayn
Where's the nearest underground (subway) station?	¿Dónde está la próxima estación de metro?	donday aysstah lah prog-seemah aysstahthyon day maytroa

Where's the bus station, please?	¿Dónde está la estación de auto- buses, por favor?	donday aysstah lah ayss- tahthyon day owtoa- boossayss por fahbhor
When's the first bus to . . . ?	¿Cuándo sale el primer autobús para . . . ?	kwahndoa sahlay ehl preemehr owtoabooss pahrah
the last bus	el último autobús	ehl oolteemoa owtoa- booss
the next bus	el próximo autobús	ehl progseemoa owtoa- booss
Please let me off at the next stop.	Por favor, pare en la próxima parada.	por fahbhor pahray ayn lah progseemah pahrah- dhah

Relaxing

What's on at the cinema (movies)?	¿Qué dan en el cine?	kay dahn ayn ehl theenay
What's on at the theatre?	¿Qué dan en el teatro?	kay dahn ayn ehl tayah- troa
What time does the film begin? And the play?	¿A qué hora em- pieza la película? ¿Y la obra?	ah kay oarah aympyay- thah lah payleekoolah? ee lah oabhrah
Are there any tickets for tonight?	¿Quedan entradas para esta noche?	kaydhahn ayntrahdhahss pahrah aysstah noachay
Where can we go dancing?	¿Dónde se peude ir a bailar?	donday say pwaydhay eer ah bighlahr
Would you like to dance?	¿Quiere usted bailar?	kyayray oosstaydh bighlahr

Introductions

How do you do?	Buenos días.	bwaynoss deeahss
How are you?	¿Cómo está usted?	koamoa aysstah ooss- taydh
Very well, thank you. And you?	Muy bien, gracias. ¿Y usted?	mwee byayn grahthyahss. ee oosstaydh
May I introduce Miss Philips?	¿Me permite pre- sentarle la Señorita Philips?	may pehrmeetay pray- sayntahrlay lah sayñoa- reetah Philips
My name is . . .	Me llamo . . .	may lyahmoa
I'm very pleased to meet you.	Tanto gusto (en conocerle).	tahntoa goosstoa (ayn koanoathehrlay)

SPANISH

How long have you been here?	¿Cuánto tiempo lleva usted aquí?	kwahntoa tyaympoa lyaybhah oosstaydh ahkee
It was nice meeting you.	Ha sido un placer conocerle.	ah seedhoa oon plahthehr koanoathehrlay

Dating

Would you like a cigarette?	¿Quiere usted un cigarrillo?	kyayray oosstaydh oon theegahreelyoa
May I get you a drink?	¿Me permite invitarlo a una bebida?	may pehrmeetay eenbheetahrloa ah oonah baybheedhah
Do you have a light, please?	¿Tiene usted fuego, por favor?	tyaynay oosstaydh fwayǧoa por fahbhor
Are you waiting for someone?	¿Está usted esperando a alguien?	aysstah oosstaydh aysspayrahndoa ah ahlgyayn
Are you free this evening?	¿Está usted libre esta noche?	aysstah oosstaydh leebhray aysstah noachay
Where shall we meet?	¿Dónde quedamos citados?	donday kaydhahmoss theetahdhoss
What time shall I meet you?	¿A qué hora puedo verla?	ah kay oarah pwaydhoa behrlah
May I take you home?	¿Puedo acompañarla a su casa?	pwaydhoa ahkoampahñahrlah ah soo kahsah
Thank you, it's been a wonderful evening.	Gracias, he pasado una velada maravillosa.	grahthyahss ay pahsahdhoa oona bay lahdhah mahrahbheelyoasah
What's your telephone number?	¿Cuál es su número de teléfono?	kwahl ayss soo noomayroa day taylayfoanoa
Do you live alone?	Vive usted sola?	beebhay oosstaydh soalah
What time is your last train?	¿A qué hora sale su último tren?	ah kay oarah sahlay soo oolteemoa trayn
Good-night...	Buenas noches...	bwaynahss noachayss

Banks

Where's the nearest bank, please?	¿Dónde está el banco más cercano, por favor?	donday aysstah ehl bahngkoa mahss thehrkahnoa por fahbhor
Where can I cash some traveller's cheques?	¿Dónde puedo cambiar unos traveller's cheques?	donday pwaydhoa kahmbyahr oonoss "traveller's cheques"

What time does the bank open/What time does it close?	¿A qué hora abren el banco/A qué hora lo cierran?	ah kay oarah ahbrayn ehl bahngkoa/ah kay oarah loa thyehrrahn
I'm expecting some money from home. Has it arrived?	¿Estoy esperando dinero de casa. Ha llegado?	aysstoy aysspayrahndoa deenayroa day kahsah, ah yayḡahdoa
Can you give me some small change, please?	Puede usted darme algún dinero suelto, por favor?	pwaydhay oosstaydh dahrmay ahlgoon deenayroa swehltoa por fahbhor

Shops, stores and services

Where is the nearest chemist (pharmacy)?	¿Dónde está la farmacia más cercana?	donday aysstah lah fahrmahtheeah mahss thehrkahnah
the nearest hairdresser's	la peluquería más cercana	lah paylookayreeah mahss thehrkahnah
the photo shop	la tienda fotográfica	lah tyayndha foatoaḡrahfeekah
the jeweller's	la joyería	lah khoayayreeah
the department store	los grandes almacenes	loss grahndayss ahlmahthaynayss
the police station	la comisaría	lah koameesahreeah
the garage	el garaje	ehl gahrahkhay
How do I get there?	¿Cómo podría ir allí?	koamoa poadhreeah eer ahlyee
Is it within walking distance?	¿Se puede ir andando?	say pwaydhay eer ahndahndoa

Service

Can you help me, please?	¿Puede usted atenderme, por favor?	pwaydhay oosstaydh ahtayndehrmay por fahbhor
Can you show me this? And that, too.	¿Puede usted enseñarme esto? ¿Y aquello también?	pwaydhay oosstaydh aynsayñahrmay aysstoa? ee ahkwaylyoa tahmbyyayn
It's too expensive/too big/too small.	Es demasiado caro/demasiado grande/demasiado pequeño.	ayss daymahsyahdhoa kahroa/daymahsyahdhoa grahnday/daymahsyahdhoa paykayñoa
Can you show me some more?	¿Puede usted enseñarme algo más?	pwaydhay oosstaydh aynsayñahrmay ahlgoa mahss
something better	algo mejor	ahlgoa maykhor
something cheaper	algo más barato	ahlgoa mahss bahrahtoa

SPANISH

How much is this? And that?	¿Cuánto es éste? ¿Y ése?	kwahntoa ayss aaysstay? ee aysay
It's not quite what I want.	No es exactamente lo que quiero.	noa ayss ehġsahktah-mayntay loa kay kyayroa
I like it.	Me gusta.	may goosstah

Chemist's (Pharmacy)

I'd like something for a cold/for a cough/for travel sickness.	Desearía algo para el catarro/para la tos/contra el mareo.	daysayahreeah ahlgoa pahrah ehl kahtahrroa/pahrah lah toss/kontrah ehl mahrayoa
Can you recommend something for hay-fever/for sunburn?	¿Podría recomen-darme algo para la fiebre del heno/para las quema-duras del sol?	poadhreeah raykoamayn-dahrmay ahlgoa pahrah lah fyaybhray dehl ay-noa/pahrah lahss kaymah-dhoorahss dehl sol

Toiletry

May I have some razor blades?	¿Puede darme unas cuchillas para afeitar?	pwaydhay dahrmay oo-nahss koocheelyahss pah-rah ahfaytahr
some shaving cream	una crema para afeitar	oonah kraymah pahrah ahfaytahr
some toothpaste	una pasta de dientes	oonah pahsstah day dyayntayss
I'd like some soap.	Quisiera jabón.	keesyayrah khahbhon
some suntan oil	aceite bronceador	ahthaytay bronthayahdhor

At the barber's

I'd like a haircut, please.	Quisiera cortarme el pelo, por favor.	keesyayrah kortahrmay ehl payloa por fahbhor
Short/Leave it long.	Corto/Déjemelo largo.	kortoa/daykhaymayloa lahrgoa
A razor cut, please.	Un corte a navaja, por favor.	oon kortay ah nahbhah-khah por fahbhor

At the hairdresser's

I'd like a shampoo and set, please.	Quiero un lavado y marcado por favor.	kyayroa oon lahbhahdhoa ee mahrkahdhoa por fahbhor

I'd like a bleach.	**Desearía un aclarado.**	daysayahreeah oon ahklahrahdhoa
a permanent	**una permanente**	oonah pehrmahnayntay
a colour rinse	**un reflejo**	oon rayflaykhoa
a manicure	**una manicura**	oonah mahneekoorah

Photography

| I'd like a film for this camera. | **Desearía un carrete para esta máquina.** | daysayahreeah oon kahrraytay pahrah aysstah mahkeenah |
| This camera doesn't work. | **Esta cámera no funciona.** | aysstah kahmayrah noa foonthyoanah |

At the post office

| Where's the nearest post office, please? | **¿Dónde está la oficina de correos más cercana, por favor?** | donday aysstah lah oafeetheenah day korrehoss mahss thehrkahnah por fahbhor |
| I'd like to send this by express (special delivery)/by air mail. | **Quisiera enviar esto por correo urgente/ por avión.** | keesyayrah aybhyahr aysstoa por korrehoa oorkhayntay/ por ahbhyon |

Service stations

Where is the nearest service station, please?	**¿Dónde está la estación de servicio más cercana?**	donday aysstah lah aysstahthyon day sehrbheethyoa mahss thehrkahnah
Fill her up, please.	**Llénemelo por favor.**	lyaynaymayloa por fahbhor
Check the oil, please.	**Compruebe el aceite, por favor.**	komprwaybhay ehl ahthaytay por fahbhor
Would you check the tyres?	**¿Quiere comprobar los neumáticos?**	kyayray komproabhahr loss nehwmahteekoss

Street directions

| Can you show me on the map where I am? | **¿Puede enseñarme en el mapa donde estoy?** | pwaydhay aynsaynahrmay ayn ehl mahpah donday aysstoy |
| You're on the wrong road. | **Está usted equivocado de camino.** | aysstah oosstaydh aykeebhoakahdhoa day kahmeenoa |

SPANISH

Go back to ...	**Vuelva a ...**	**bwehl**bha a
Go straight ahead.	**Siga todo derecho.**	**see**ġah **toa**dhoa dayray-choa
It's on the left/on the right.	**Está a la izquierda/ a la derecha.**	ays**stah** ah lah eeth**kyehr**-dhah/ah lah dayraychah

Accidents

May I use your telephone?	**¿Puedo utilizar su teléfono?**	**pway**dhoa ooteeleethar soo taylayfoanoa
Call a doctor quickly.	**Lláme a un médico rápidamente.**	**lyah**may ah oon maydee-koa **rah**peedhamayntay
Call an ambulance.	**Lláme a una ambulancia.**	**lyah**may ah **oo**nah ahm-boolahnthyah
Please call the police.	**Lláme a la policia, por favor.**	**lyah**may ah lah polee-**thee**ah por fahbhor

Numbers

one	**uno**	**oo**noa
two	**dos**	doss
three	**tres**	trayss
four	**cuatro**	**kwah**troa
five	**cinco**	**theeng**koa
six	**seis**	**seh**eess
seven	**siete**	**syay**tay
eight	**ocho**	**oa**choa
nine	**nueve**	**nway**bhay
ten	**diez**	dyayth
eleven	**once**	**on**thay
twelve	**doce**	**doa**thay
thirteen	**trece**	**tray**thay
fourteen	**catorce**	kah**tor**thay
fifteen	**quince**	**keen**thay
sixteen	**dieciséis**	dyehthee**seh**eess
seventeen	**diecisiete**	dyehthee**syay**tay
eighteen	**dieciocho**	dyehthee**oa**choa
nineteen	**diecinueve**	dyehthee**nway**bhay
twenty	**veinte**	**bayn**tay
twenty-one	**veintiuno**	baynti**oo**noa
thirty	**treinta**	**trayn**tah
forty	**cuarenta**	kwah**rayn**tah
fifty	**cincuenta**	theeng**kwayn**tah
sixty	**sesenta**	say**sayn**tah
seventy	**setenta**	say**tayn**tah

eighty	**ochenta**	oa**chayn**tah
ninety	**noventa**	noab**hayn**tah
one hundred	**ciento**	**thyayn**toa
one thousand	**mil**	meel
ten thousand	**diez mil**	dyayth meel

Days

It's Sunday.	**Es domingo.**	ayss doa**meeng**goa
Monday	**lunes**	**loo**nayss
Tuesday	**martes**	**mahr**tayss
Wednesday	**miércoles**	**myehr**koalayss
Thursday	**jueves**	**khway**bhayss
Friday	**viernes**	**byehr**nayss
Saturday	**sábado**	**sah**bhahdhoa
yesterday	**ayer**	ah**yehr**
today	**hoy**	oy
tomorrow	**mañana**	mah**ñah**nah
morning/afternoon	**mañana/media tarde**	mah**ñah**nah/**may**dhyah **tahr**dhay
evening/night	**tarde/noche**	**tahr**dhay/**noa**chay

Months

January	**enero**	ay**nay**roa
February	**febrero**	fayb**hray**roa
March	**marzo**	**mahr**thoa
April	**abril**	ahb**hreel**
May	**mayo**	**mah**yoa
June	**junio**	**khoo**nyoa
July	**julio**	**khoo**lyoa
August	**agosto**	ah**goss**toa
September	**septiembre**	sayp**tyaym**bray
October	**octubre**	ok**toob**hray
November	**noviembre**	noab**hyaym**bray
December	**diciembre**	deeth**yaym**bray
Merry Christmas!	**Felices Pascuas!**	fay**lee**thayss **pahss**kwahss!
Happy New Year!	**Feliz Año Nuevo!**	fay**leeth** ah**ñoa** **nway**bhoa

SPANISH

SWEDISH

Guide to Pronunciation

Letter	Approximate pronunciation	Symbol	Example	

Consonants

b, c, d, f, h, l, m, n, p, v, w, x	as in English			
ch	at the beginning of words borrowed from French, like **sh** in **sh**ut	sh	**chef**	shayf
g	1) before stressed **i, e, y, ä, ö** and sometimes after **l** or **r**, like **y** in **y**et	y	**genast**	**yay**nahst
	2) before **e** and **i** in many words of French origin, like **sh** in **sh**ut	sh	**generös**	shaynerr**urss**
	3) elsewhere, generally like **g** in **go**	g	**gammal**	**gah**mahl
j, dj, gj, lj	like **y** in **y**et	y	**ja**	yar
k	1) before stressed **i, e, y, ä, ö** generally like **ch** in Scottish lo**ch**, but pronounced in the front of the mouth	kh	**köpa**	**khur**pah
	2) elsewhere, like **k** in **k**it	k	**kål**	koal

kj	like **ch** in Scottish lo**ch**, but pronounced in the front of the mouth	kh	**kjol**	**kh**ool
qu	like **k** in **k**it followed by **v** in **v**at	kv	**Lindquist**	lind**kv**ist
r	slightly rolled near the front of the mouth	r	**råd**	road
s	1) in the ending **-sion** like **sh** in **sh**ut	sh	**mission**	mi**sh**oon
	2) elsewhere, like **s** in **s**o	s/ss	**smak**	smark
	3) the groups **sch**, **skj**, **stj** are pronounced like **sh** in **sh**ut	sh	**schema**	**sh**aymah
sk	1) before stressed **e**, **i**, **y**, **ä**, **ö**, like **sh** in **sh**ut	sh	**skepp**	**sh**ehp
	2) elsewhere, like **sk** in **sk**ip	sk	**handske**	hahnd**sk**er
t	1) **ti** in the ending **-tion**, is pronounced like **sh** in **sh**ut or like **ch** in **ch**at	sh	**station**	stah**sh**oon
		tsh	**nation**	nah**tsh**oon
	2) elsewhere, like **t** in **t**op	t	**talk**	**t**ahlk
tj	like **ch** in Scottish lo**ch**, but pronounced in the front of the mouth; sometimes with a t-sound at the beginning	kh	**tjäna**	**kh**ainah
z	like **s** in **s**o	s	**zon**	**s**oon

N.B. In the groups **rd**, **rl**, **rn**, **rs** and **rt**, the letter **r** is generally not pronounced but influences the pronunciation of the **d**, **l**, **n**, **s** or **t**, which is then pronounced with the end of the tongue *not* on the upper front teeth, but behind the gums of the upper teeth.

Vowels

Vowels in stressed syllables are long if followed at most by one consonant, but are short if followed by two or more consonants. Vowels in unstressed syllables are short.

a	1) when long, like **a** in c**a**r	ar	**dag**	darg
	2) when short, something like the **u** in c**u**t or **o** in American c**o**llege	ah	**tack**	tahk
e	1) when long, like **ay** in s**ay**, but a *pure* vowel, not a diphthong	ay	**blek**	blayk
	2) in the stressed prefix er-, like **a** in m**a**n, but longer	ææ	**erfara**	**ææ**rfarrah
	3) when short, like **e** in g**e**t	eh	**penna**	p**eh**na
	4) when unstressed, like **a** in **a**bout	er	**betala**	bert**ar**lah
ej	like **a** in m**a**te	ay	**nej**	n**ay**

i	1) when long, like **ee** in b**ee**	ee	**vit**	veet
	2) when short, between **ee** in m**ee**t and **i** in h**i**t	i	**bild**	bild
o	1) when long, often like **oo** in s**oo**n, but with the lips more tightly rounded, and with a puff of breath at the end	oo	**sko**	skoo
	2) the same sound can be short	oo	**ost**	oost
	3) when long, it is also some-times pronounced like **oa** in m**oa**n	oa	**son**	soan
	4) when short, sometimes like **o** in h**o**t	o	**socker**	**so**kkerr
u	1) when long, like Swedish **y**, but with the tongue a little lower in the mouth, and with a puff of breath at the end	ew	**hus**	hewss
	2) when short, a little more like the **u** of p**u**t; a very difficult sound	ew	**ung**	ewng
y	pronounce the **ee** of b**ee** and then round your lips without moving your tongue; the sound can be long or short	ew	**vy**	vew
			syster	**sew**sterr
å	1) when long, like **aw** in r**aw**, but with the tongue a little higher in the mouth	oa	**gå**	goa
	2) when short, like **o** in h**o**t	o	**sång**	song
ä	1) when followed by **r**, like **a** in m**a**n, long or short	ææ	**ära**	**ææ**rah
		æ	**värka**	**væ**rkah
	2) elsewhere, like **e** in g**e**t; long or short	ai	**läsa**	**lai**sah
		eh	**bäst**	behst
ö	like **u** in f**u**r, long or short; when followed by **r**, it is pronounced with the mouth a little more open	ur	**röd**	rurd
			höst	hurst
			öra	**u**rrah

N.B. The principal stress is generally on the *first* syllable of a word, unless it comes from Latin or French.

SWEDISH

Some basic expressions

Yes.	**Ja.**	yar
No.	**Nej.**	nay
Please.	**Varsågod.**	**vahr**soagood
Thank you.	**Tack.**	tahk
Thank you very much.	**Tack så mycket.**	tahk soa **mew**ker(t)
That's all right.	**Ingen orsak.**	**ingern oor**shark

Greetings

Good morning.	**God morgon.**	goo **mo**ron
Good afternoon.	**God middag.**	goo **midd**ah(g)
Good evening.	**God afton.**	goo **ahf**ton
Good night.	**God natt.**	goo naht
Good-bye.	**Adjö.**	a**hyur**
See you later.	**Vi ses.**	vee sayss
This is Mr. . . .	**Det här är herr . . .**	day hæær æær hær
This is Mrs. . . .	**Det här är fru . . .**	day hæær æær frew
This is Miss . . .	**Det här är fröken . . .**	day hæær æær **frur**kern
I'm very pleased to meet you.	**Angenämt.**	ahnyer**nehmt**
How are you?	**Hur står det till?**	hewr stoar deht til
Very well, thank you. And you?	**Tack bara bra. Och Ni själv?**	tahk **barr**ah brar. o(k) nee shehlv
Fine.	**Fint.**	fint
Excuse me.	**Förlåt.**	furr**loat**

Questions

Where?	**Var?**	varr
Where is . . . ?	**Var är . . . ?**	varr ai
Where are . . . ?	**Var är . . . ?**	varr ai
When?	**När?**	næær
What?	**Vad?**	vard
How?	**Hur?**	hewr
How much?	**Hur mycket?**	hewr **mew**kert
How many?	**Hur många?**	hewr **mong**ah

SWEDISH

Who?	**Vem?**	vaym
Why?	**Varför?**	vahrfurr
Which?	**Vilken?**	vilkern
What do you call this?	**Vad heter det här?**	vard hayterr day hæær
What do you call that?	**Vad heter det där?**	vard hayterr day dæær
What does this mean?	**Vad betyder det här?**	vard bertewderr day hæær
What does that mean?	**Vad betyder det där?**	vard bertewderr day dæær

Do you speak ... ?

Do you speak English?	**Talar Ni engelska?**	tarlahr nee ehngerlskah
Do you speak German?	**Talar Ni tyska?**	tarlahr nee tewskah
Do you speak French?	**Talar Ni franska?**	tarlahr nee frahnskah
Do you speak Spanish?	**Talar Ni spanska?**	tarlahr nee spahnskah
Do you speak Italian?	**Talar Ni italienska?**	tarlahr nee itahliehnskah
Could you speak more slowly, please?	**Kan Ni vara snäll och tala lite långsammare?**	kahn nee varrah snehl o tarlah leeter long-sahmahrer
Please point to the phrase in the book.	**Var snäll och peka på meningen i boken.**	varr snehl o paykah poa mayningern ee bookern
Just a minute. I'll see if I can find it in this book.	**Ett ögonblick, så ska jag se om jag hittar det i den här boken.**	eht urgonblik soa skar jar(g) say om yar(g) hitahr day ee dehn hæær bookern
I understand.	**Jag förstår.**	yar(g) furrshtoar
I don't understand.	**Jag förstår inte.**	yar(g) furrshtoar inter

Can ... ?

| Can I have ... ? | **Kan jag få ... ?** | kahn yar(g) foa |
| Can we have ... ? | **Kan vi få ... ?** | kahn vee foa |

SWEDISH

Can you show me...?	**Kan Ni visa mig...?**	kahn nee **vee**sah may
Can you tell me...?	**Kan Ni säga mig...?**	kahn nee **sai**gah may
Can you help me, please?	**Kan Ni vara snäll och hjälpa mig?**	kahn nee **var**rah snehl o **yehl**pah may

Wanting

I'd like...	**Jag skulle vilja ha...**	yar(g) **skew**ller **vil**yah har
We'd like...	**Vi skulle vilja ha...**	vee **skew**ller **vil**yah har
Please give me...	**Var snäll och ge mig...**	varr snehl o yay may
Give it to me, please.	**Var snäll och ge mig den.**	varr snehl o yay may dehn
Please bring me...	**Var snäll och hämta...**	varr snehl o **hehm**tah
Bring it to me, please.	**Var snäll och hämta den.**	varr snehl o **hehm**tah dehn
I'm hungry.	**Jag är hungrig.**	yar(g) æær **hewng**ri(g)
I'm thirsty.	**Jag är törstig.**	yar(g) æær **turr**shti(g)
I'm tired.	**Jag är trött.**	yar(g) æær trurt
I'm lost.	**Jag har gått vilse.**	yar(g) harr got **vil**ser
It's important.	**Det är viktigt.**	day æær **vik**tikt
It's urgent.	**Det är brådskande.**	day æær **bros**kahnder
Hurry up!	**Skynda på!**	**shewn**dah poa

It is/There is...

It is/It's...	**Det är...**	day ai
Is it...?	**Är det...?**	ai day
It isn't...	**Det är inte...**	day ai **in**ter
There is/There are...	**Det finns...**	day finss
Is there/Are there...?	**Finns det...?**	finss day
There isn't/There aren't...	**Det finns inte...**	day finss **in**ter
There isn't any/There aren't any.	**Det finns ingen/Det finns inga.**	day finss **in**gern/day finss **in**gah

SWEDISH

A few common words

big/small	**stor/liten**	stoor/**lee**tern
quick/slow	**snabb/långsam**	snahb/**long**sahm
early/late	**tidig/sen**	**tee**di(g)/sayn
cheap/expensive	**billig/dyr**	**bil**li(g)/dewr
near/far	**nära/avlägsen**	nairah/**ahv**lehgsern
hot/cold	**varm/kall**	vahrm/kahl
full/empty	**full/tom**	fewl/toom
easy/difficult	**lätt/svår**	leht/svoar
heavy/light	**lätt/tung**	leht/tewng
open/shut	**öppen/stängd**	urpern/stehngd
right/wrong	**rätt/fel**	reht/fayl
old/new	**gammal/ny**	**gah**mahl/new
old/young	**gammal/ung**	**gah**mahl/ewng
beautiful/ugly	**vacker/ful**	**vah**kerr/fewl
good/bad	**god/dålig**	good/**doa**li(g)
better/worse	**bättre/sämre**	**beh**trer/**sehm**rer

Some prepositions and a few more useful words

at	**vid**	veed
on	**på**	poa
in	**i**	ee
to	**till**	till
from	**från**	froan
inside	**inne**	inner
outside	**ute**	ewter
up	**upp**	ewp
down	**ner**	nayr
before	**före**	furrer
after	**efter**	ehfterr
with	**med**	mayd
without	**utan**	ewtahn
through	**genom**	**yay**nom
towards	**mot**	moot
until	**till dess**	til dehss
during	**under**	**ewn**derr
and	**och**	ok
or	**eller**	**ehl**lerr
not	**inte**	inter
nothing	**ingenting**	**ing**ernting
none	**ingen**	**ing**ern
very	**mycket**	**mew**ker(t)
also	**också**	ok**soa**
soon	**snart**	snahrt

SWEDISH

perhaps	**kanske**	**kahn**sher
here	**här**	hæær
there	**där**	dæær
now	**nu**	new
then	**då**	doa

Arrival

Your passport, please.	**Passet, tack.**	**pah**sert tahk
Here it is.	**Varsågod.**	**vahr**soagood
Have you anything to declare?	**Har Ni någonting att förtulla?**	harr nee **noa**gonting aht **furr**tewlah
No, nothing at all.	**Nej, ingenting alls.**	nay **ing**ernting ahlss
Porter!	**Bärare!**	**bæær**ahrer
Can you help me with my luggage, please?	**Kan Ni vara snäll och hjälpa mig med mitt bagage?**	kahn nee **var**rah snehl o **yehl**pah may mayd mit bah**gar**sh
That's my suitcase.	**Det där är min väska.**	day dæær ai meen **vehss**kah
Where's the bus to the centre of town, please?	**Var är bussen som går till centrum?**	varr ai **bewss**ern soam goar til **sehn**troom
This way, please.	**Den här vägen.**	dehn hæær **vai**gern

Changing money

Can you change a traveller's cheque, please?	**Kan Ni växla in en resecheck?**	kahn nee **vehks**lah in ayn **rays**sershehk
Where's the nearest bank, please?	**Var ligger närmaste bank?**	varr **ligg**err **næær**mahsster bahnk

Car rental

I'd like a car.	**Jag skulle vilja hyra en bil.**	yar(g) **skewl**ler vilyah **hew**rah ayn beel
For how long?	**Hur länge?**	hewr **lehng**er
A day/Four days/ A week/Two weeks.	**En dag/Fyra dagar/ En vecka/Två veckor.**	ayn darg/**few**rah dar**gahr**/ayn **veh**kah/tvoa **veh**kor

SWEDISH

Taxi

Where can I get a taxi?	Var kan jag få tag på en taxi?	varr kahn yar(g) foa targ poa ayn **tahk**si
What's the fare to...?	Vad kostar det till...?	vard **koss**tahr day til
Take me to this address, please.	Var snäll och kör mig till den här adressen.	varr snehl o khurr may til dehn hæær ah**dress**ern
I'm in a hurry.	Jag har bråttom.	yar(g) harr **brott**om
Could you drive more slowly, please?	Skulle Ni kunna köra litet långsammare?	**skew**ller nee **kewn**nah **khurr**ah **lee**tert long**sah**mahrer

Hotel and other accommodation

My name is...	Mitt namn är...	mit nahmn ai
Have you a reservation?	Har Ni reserverat?	harr nee raysæær**vay**raht
Yes, here's the confirmation.	Ja, här är bekräftelsen.	yar hæær ai ber**krehf**terlsern
I'd like...	Jag skulle vilja ha...	yar(g) **skew**ller **vil**yah har
I'd like a single room/a double room.	Jag skulle vilja ha ett enkelrum/ett dubbelrum.	yar(g) **skew**ller **vil**yah har eht **ehng**kerlrewm/eht **dewb**berlrewm
a room with a bath/with a shower	ett rum med badrum/med dusch	eht rewm mayd **bard**rewm/med dewsh

How much?

What's the price per night/per week/per month?	Hur mycket kostar det per natt/per vecka/per månad?	hewr **mew**ker(t) **koss**tahr day pær naht/pær **veh**kah/pær **moa**nahd
May I see the room?	Kan jag få se på rummet?	kahn yar(g) foa say poa **rew**mert
I'm sorry, I don't like it.	Tyvärr, men jag tycker inte om det.	tew**væær** mayn yar(g) **tewk**kerr **in**ter om day
Yes, that's fine. I'll take it.	Ja, det här var bra. Jag tar det.	yar day hæær varr brar. yar(g) tarr day
What's my room number, please?	Vilket rumsnummer har jag?	**vil**kert **rewm**ssnewmerr har yar
Number 123.	Nummer 123.	**new**merr 123.

SWEDISH

Service, please

Who is it?	Vem är det?	vaym ai day
Just a minute.	Ett ögonblick.	eht urgonblik
Come in! The door's open.	Kom in. Dörren är öppen.	kom in durrern ai urppern
May we have breakfast in our room?	Kan vi få frukost på rummet?	kahn vee foa frewkost poa rewmert

Breakfast

I'll have...	Jag ska be att få ...	yar(g) skar bay aht foa
I'll have some fruit juice.	Jag ska be att få litet juice.	yar(g) skar bay aht foa leeter(t) yooss
a boiled egg	ett kokt ägg	eht kookt ehg
a fried egg	ett stekt ägg	eht staykt egh
some bacon/some ham	bacon/skinka	baykon/shingkah
some toast	rostat bröd	rosstaht brurd
a pot of tea	en kanna te	ayn kahnah tay
a cup of tea	en kopp te	ayn kop tay
some coffee	kaffe	kahffer
some chocolate	choklad	shooklard
more butter	mera smör	mayrah smurr
some hot water	lite hett vatten	leeter heht vahtern

Difficulties

The central heating doesn't work.	Centralvärmen fungerar inte.	sehntrarlværmern fewnggayrahr inter
the light/the socket the tap/the toilet	ljuset/kontakten vattenkranen/toaletten	yewsert/kontahktern vahternkrarnern/twahlehtern
There's no hot water.	Det finns inget varmvatten.	day finss ingert vahrmvahtern
May I see the manager, please?	Kan jag få tala med direktören, tack?	kan yar(g) foa tarlah mayd direhkturrern tahk

Telephone—Mail

There's a call for you.	Det är telefon till Er.	day ai taylayfoan til ayr
Hold the line, please.	Var god dröj, tack.	varr good drury tahk

Operator, I've been cut off.	Fröken, linjen är bruten.	frurkern linyern ai brewtern
Did anyone telephone me?	Har någon ringt mig?	harr noagon ringt may
Is there any mail for me?	Finns det post till mig?	finss day post til may
Are there any messages for me?	Finns det några meddelanden till mig.	finss day noagra mehdaylahndern til may

Checking out

May I have my bill, please?	Kan jag få räkningen, tack?	kahn yar(g) foa rehkningern tahk
We're in a great hurry.	Vi har mycket bråttom.	vee harr mewker(t) brottom
It's been a very enjoyable stay.	Det har varit mycket trevligt att bo här.	day har varrit mewker(t) trayvligt aht boo hæær

Eating out

Good evening, sir/ Good evening, madam.	God afton/God afton.	goo ahfton/goo ahfton
Good evening. I'd like a table for two, please.	God afton. Jag skulle vilja ha ett bord för två.	goo ahfton. yar(g) skewleh vilyah har eht boord furr tvoa
Do you have a fixed-price menu?	Har Ni en meny?	harr nee ayn maynew
May I see the à la carte menu?	Kan jag få se på à la carte matsedeln?	kahn yar(g) foa say poa ah lah kahrt martserderln
May we have an ashtray, please?	Kan vi få en askkopp, tack?	kahn vee foa ayn ahskkop tahk
some bread	litet bröd	leeter(t) brurd
a fork	en gaffel	ayn gahferl
a knife	en kniv	ayn kneev
a spoon	en sked	ayn shayd
a plate	en tallrik	ayn tahlrik
a glass	ett glas	eht glarss
a napkin	en servett	ayn særveht
another chair	en stol till	ayn stool til

SWEDISH

| Where's the gentlemen's toilet (men's room)? | **Var är herrtoaletten?** | varr ai **hær**twahlehtern |
| Where's the ladies' toilet (ladies' room)? | **Var är damtoaletten?** | varr ai **darm**twahlehtern |

Appetizers

I'd like some...	**Jag ska be att få...**	yar(g) skar bay aht foa
I'd like some assorted appetizers.	**Jag ska be att få några smårätter.**	yar(g) skar bay aht foa **noa**grah **smoa**rehterr
orange juice	**apelsinjuice**	ahperlseenyooss
ham	**skinka**	**shing**kah
melon	**melon**	may**loon**
pâté	**pastej**	pass**tayy**
smoked salmon	**rökt lax**	rurkt lahks
shrimps (shrimp)	**räkor**	rai**koor**

Soup

Have you any...?	**Har Ni...?**	harr nee
Have you any chicken soup?	**Har Ni kycklingsoppa?**	harr nee **khewk**lingsopah
vegetable soup	**grönsakssoppa**	**grurn**sahkssopah
onion soup	**löksoppa**	**lurk**sopah

Fish

I'd like some...	**Jag ska be att få...**	yar(g) skar bay aht foa
I'd like some fish.	**Jag ska be att få en fiskrätt.**	yar(g) skar bay aht foa ayn **fisk**reht
sole	**sjötunga**	**shur**tewngah
trout	**forell**	forehl
lobster	**hummer**	**hew**merr
crayfish	**kräftor**	**krehf**toor
prawns	**räkor**	rai**koor**
I'd like it...	**Jag skulle vilja ha den...**	yar(g) **skew**ler **vil**yah har dehn
I'd like it steamed.	**Jag skulle vilja ha den ångkokt.**	yar(g) **skew**ler **vil**yah har dehn **ong**kookt
grilled	**grillad**	**gri**lahd
boiled	**kokt**	kookt
baked	**ugnsstekt**	**ewngns**staykt
fried	**stekt**	staykt

Meat—Poultry—Game

I'd like some . . .	**Jag ska be att få . . .**	yar(g) skar bay aht foa
I'd like some beef.	**Jag ska be att få oxkött.**	yar(g) skar bay aht foa **ooks**khurt
a beef steak	**en biffstek**	ahn **bif**stayk
some roast beef	**rostbiff**	**rost**bif
a veal cutlet	**en kalvkotlett**	ahn **kahlv**kotleht
mutton	**fårkött**	**foar**khurt
lamb	**lammkött**	**lahm**khurt
a pork chop	**en fläskkotlett**	ahn **flehsk**kotleht
roast pork	**grisstek**	**greess**stayk
hare	**hare**	**harr**er
chicken	**kyckling**	**khewk**ling
roast chicken	**stekt kyckling**	staykt **khewk**ling
duck	**anka**	**ahng**kah
How do you like your meat?	**Hur vill Ni ha köttet tillagat?**	hewr vil nee har **khur**tert **til**largaht
rare	**blodig**	**bloo**dig
medium	**lagom**	**lar**gom
well done	**genomstekt**	**yay**nomstaykt

Vegetables

What vegetables have you got?	**Vad för grönsaker finns det?**	vard furr **grurn**sarkerr finss day
I'd like some . . .	**Jag ska be att få . . .**	yar(g) ska bay aht foa
I'd like some asparagus.	**Jag ska be att få sparris.**	yar(g) ska bay aht foa **spahr**riss
green beans	**haricots verts**	hahreekoavææær
mushrooms	**svamp**	svahmp
carrots	**morötter**	moo**rur**terr
onions	**lök**	lurk
red cabbage	**rödkål**	**rurd**koal
lettuce	**sallad**	**sah**lahd
spinach	**spenat**	spay**nart**
rice	**ris**	reess
peas	**ärtor**	**ær**toor
tomatoes	**tomater**	too**mar**terr
green salad	**grönsallad**	**grurn**sahlahd
potatoes	**potatis**	poo**tar**tiss

Desserts

Nothing more, thanks.	**Ingenting mer, tack.**	**ing**ernting mayr tahk
Just a small portion, please.	**Bara en liten portion, tack.**	**barr**ah ehn **lee**tern por**choon** tahk

Have you any ice-cream?	**Här Ni glass?**	har nee glahss
fruit salad	**fruktsallad**	**frewkt**sahlahd
fresh fruit	**färsk frukt**	færshk frewkt
cheese	**ost**	oost

Drink

What would you like to drink?	**Vad vill Ni ha att dricka?**	vard vil nee har aht **dri**kah
I'll have a beer, please.	**Jag tar en öl, tack.**	yar(g) tarr ehn url tahk
I'll have a whisky, please.	**Jag ska be att få en whisky, tack.**	yar(g) skar bay aht foa ehn **wiss**kew tahk

Wine

I'd like a bottle of wine.	**Jag ska be att få en flaska vin.**	yar(g) skar bay aht foa ehn **flahss**kah veen
red wine	**rödvin**	**rurd**veen
rosé wine	**rosévin**	roa**say**veen
white wine	**vitt vin**	vit veen
Cheers!	**Skål!**	skoal

The bill (check)

May I have the bill (check) please?	**Får jag be om notan, tack?**	foar yar(g) bay om **noo**tahn tahk
Is service included?	**Ingår service?**	in**goar surr**viss
Everything's included.	**Allt ingår.**	ahlt in**goar**
Thank you, that was a very good meal.	**Tack, det var en mycket god måltid.**	tahk day varr ehn **mew**ker(t) goo **moal**teed

Travelling

Where's the railway station, please?	**Var är järnvägs-stationen?**	varr ai **yærn**vehgsstah-**shoo**nern
Where's the ticket office, please?	**Var är biljettluckan?**	varr ai bil**yeht**lewkahn
I'd like a ticket to . . .	**Jag ska be att få en biljett till . . .**	yar(g) skar bay aht foa ehn bil**yeht** til
First or second class?	**Första eller andra klass?**	**furr**shtah **ehl**lerr **ahn**drah klahss

SWEDISH

First class, please.	**Första klass, tack.**	furrshtah klahss tahk
Single or return (one way or round-trip)?	**Enkel eller tur och retur?**	ehngkerl ehlerr tewr o(k) retewr
Do I have to change trains?	**Måste jag byta tåg?**	mosster yar bewtah toag
What platform does the train leave from?	**Från vilken perrong avgår tåget?**	froan vilkern pærong ahv-goar toagert
Where's the nearest underground (subway) station?	**Var ligger närmaste tunnelbanestation?**	varr ligger næærmahster tewnerlbarnerstahshoon
Where's the bus station, please?	**Var är buss-stationen?**	varr ai bewssstah-shoonern
When's the first bus to . . . ?	**När går första bus-sen till . . . ?**	næær goar furrshtah bew-ssern til
the last bus	**sista bussen/**	sisstah bewssern/
the next bus	**nästa buss**	nehsstah bewss
Please let me off at the next stop.	**Var god och låt mig gå av nästa håll-plats.**	varr goo o(k) loat may goa ahv nehsstah hol-plahts

Relaxing

What's on at the cinema (movies)?	**Vad går det på bio?**	vard goar day poa beeoo
What's on at the theatre?	**Vad ger man på teatern?**	vard yayr mahn poa tayarterrn
What time does the film begin?	**När börjar filmen?**	næær burryarr filmern
And the play?	**Och teatern?**	o tayarterrn
Are there any tickets for tonight?	**Finns det några biljetter till i kväll?**	finss day noagrah bilyehterr til ee kvehl
Where can we go dancing?	**Var kan vi gå och dansa?**	varr kahn vee goa o(k) dahnsah
Would you like to dance?	**Får jag lov?**	foar yar(g) loav

Introductions

How do you do?	**Goddag.**	goodarg
How are you?	**Hur står det till?**	hewr stoar day til
Very well, thank you. And you?	**Tack bara bra. Och Ni själv?**	tahk barrar brar. o(k) nee shehlv

SWEDISH

306

SWEDISH

English	Swedish	Pronunciation
May I introduce Miss Philips?	Får jag presentera fröken Philips?	foar yar(g) prayserntayrah frurkern Philips
My name is...	Mitt namm är...	mit nahmn æær
I'm very pleased to meet you.	Roligt att lära känna Er.	rooligt aht læærah khehnah ayr
How long have you been here?	Hur länge har Ni varit här?	hewr lehnger harr nee varrit hæær
It was nice meeting you.	Det var trevligt att träffas.	day varr trayvligt aht trehfahss

Dating

English	Swedish	Pronunciation
Would you like a cigarette?	Vill Ni ha en cigarrett?	vil nee har ehn sigahreht
May I get you a drink?	Vill Ni ha något att dricka?	vil nee har noagot aht drikar
Do you have a light, please?	Har Ni möjligen eld?	harr nee muryliggern ayld
Are you waiting for someone?	Väntar Ni på någon?	væntahr nee poa noagon
Are you free this evening?	Är Ni ledig i kväll?	ai nee laydig ee kvehl
Where shall we meet?	Var ska vi träffas?	varr skar vee trehfahss
What time shall I meet you?	När ska vi träffas?	næær skar vee trehfahss
May I take you home?	Får jag följa Er hem?	foar yar(g) furlyah ayr haym
Thank you, it's been a wonderful evening.	Tack, det har varit en underbar kväll.	tahk day har varrit ehn ewnderrbarr kvehl
What's your telephone number?	Vad har Ni för telefonnummer?	vard harr nee furr taylayfoannewmerr
Do you live alone?	Bor Ni ensam?	boor nee aynsahm
What time is your last train?	När går sista tåget?	næær goar sisstah toaget
Good-night...	God natt...	goo naht

Banks

Where's the nearest bank, please?	Var ligger närmaste bank?	varr ligger næærmahster bahnk

Where can I cash some traveller's cheques?	**Var kan jag växla in några resecheckar?**	varr kahn yar(g) **vehks**lah in **no**agrah **ray**sser-shehkahr
What time does the bank open/What time does it close?	**När öppnar banken/När stänger den?**	næær **urp**nahr **bahn**kern/næær **stehng**err dehn
I'm expecting some money from home. Has it arrived?	**Jag väntar pengar hemifrån. Har de kommit?**	yar(g) **vehn**tahr **pehng**ahr **hay**mifron. harr day **kom**mit
Can you give me some small change, please?	**Kan jag få litet växel, tack?**	kahn yar(g) foa **lee**ter(t) **vehk**serl tahk

Shops, stores and services

Where is the nearest chemist's (pharmacy)?	**Var finns närmaste apotek?**	varr finss **næær**mahster ahpoo**tayk**
the nearest hair-dresser's	**närmaste hår-frisörska**	**næær**mahster **hoar**-frisurrshkah
the photo shop	**fotoaflären**	**foo**tooahfairern
the jeweller's	**juveleraren**	yewver**lay**rahrern
the department store	**varuhuset**	**var**rewhewssert
the police station	**polisstationen**	poo**leess**stah**shoo**nern
the garage	**garaget**	gah**rar**shert
How do I get there?	**Hur kommer jag dit?**	hewr **kom**merr yar(g) deet
Is it within walking distance?	**Kan man gå dit?**	kahn mahn **goa** deet

Service

Can you help me, please?	**Kan Ni vara snäll och hjälpa mig?**	kahn nee **var**rah snehl o(k) **yehl**pah may
Can you show me this? And that, too.	**Kan Ni visa mig den här? Och den där också.**	kahn nee **vee**sah may dehn hæær? o(k) dehn dæær ok**soa**
It's too expensive/too big/too small.	**Den är för dyr/för stor/för liten.**	dehn ai furr dewr/furr stoor/furr **lee**tern
Can you show me some more?	**Kan Ni visa mig något mer?**	kahn nee **vee**sah may **noa**got mayr
something better	**någonting bättre**	**noa**gonting **beh**trer
something cheaper	**någonting billigare**	**noa**gonting **bi**ligahrer
How much is this? And that?	**Hur mycket kostar den här? Och den där?**	hewr **mew**ker(t) **kos**tar dehn hæær? o(k) dehn dæær

SWEDISH

| It's not quite what I want. | **Det är inte precis vad jag tänkt mig.** | day ai **inter praysseess** vard yar(g) tehnkt may |
| I like it. | **Jag tycker om den.** | yar(g) **tewkerr om dehn** |

Chemist's (Pharmacy)

| I'd like something for a cold/for a cough/for travel sickness. | **Jag skulle vilja ha någonting mot förkylning/mot hosta/mot ressjuka.** | yar(g) **skewler vil**yah har **noa**gonting moot turr-**khewl**ning/moot **hoo**stah/moot **rayss**shewkah |
| Can you recommend something for hay-fever/for sunburn? | **Kan Ni rekommendera någonting mot hösnuva/mot solsveda?** | kahn nee raykomehn-**dayr**ah **noa**gonting moot **hurs**newvah/moot **sool**svaydah |

Toiletry

May I have some razor blades?	**Kan jag få några rakblad?**	kahn yar(g) foa **noa**grah **rark**blahd
some shaving cream	**rakkräm**	**rark**krehm
some toothpaste	**tandkräm**	**tahnd**krehm
I'd like some soap.	**Jag ska be att få en tvål.**	yar(g) skar bay aht foa ayn tvoal
some suntan oil	**sololja**	**sool**olyah

At the barber's

I'd like a haircut, please.	**Jag skulle vilja ha håret klippt.**	yar(g) **skew**ler **vil**yah har **hoa**rert klipt
Short/Leave it long.	**Kort/Låt det vara långt.**	kort/loat day **var**rah longt
A razor cut, please.	**Klippning med rakblad, tack.**	**klip**ning mayd **rark**blahd tahk

At the hairdresser's

I'd like a shampoo and set, please.	**Jag ska be att få håret tvättat och lagt.**	yar(g) skar bay aht foa **hoa**rert **tveh**taht o(k) lahgt
I'd like a bleach.	**Jag skulle vilja ha det blekt.**	yar(g) **skew**ler **vil**yah har day blaykt
a permanent	**permanentat**	**pær**mah**nehn**taht
a colour rinse	**tonat**	**toon**aht
a manicure	**en manikyr**	ayn mahni**kewr**

Photography

I'd like a film for this camera.	**Jag ska be att få en film till den här kameran.**	yar(g) skar bay aht foa ayn film til dehn hæær **kar**mayrahn
This camera doesn't work.	**Den här kameran fungerar inte.**	dehn hæær **kar**mayrahn fewng**gay**rahr inter

At the post office

Where's the nearest post office, please?	**Var ligger närmaste postkontor?**	var **ligg**err næærmahster **posst**kontoor
I'd like to send this by express (special delivery)/by air mail.	**Jag skulle vilja skicka det här express/med flygpost.**	yar(g) **skew**ler **vil**yah **shi**kar day hæær ehks**prehss**/mayd **flewg**posst

Service stations

Where is the nearest service station, please?	**Kan Ni säga mig var närmaste bensinstation ligger?**	kahn nee **sai**gah may varr næærmahster behn**seen**stahshoon **ligg**err
Fill her up, please.	**Full tank, tack.**	fewl tahnk tahk
Check the oil, please.	**Kontrollera oljan, tack.**	kontro**lay**rah **ol**yahn tahk
Would you check the tyres?	**Skulle Ni vilja kontrollera däcken?**	**skew**ler nee **vil**yah kontro**lay**rah **deh**kern

Street directions

Can you show me on the map where I am?	**Kan Ni visa mig på kartan var jag är?**	kahn nee **vee**sah may poa **kahr**tahn varr yar(g) ai
You're on the wrong road.	**Ni är på fel väg.**	nee ai poa fayl vaig
Go back to . . .	**Kör tillbaka till . . .**	khurr til**bar**kah til
Go straight ahead.	**Kör rakt fram.**	khurr rahkt frahm
It's on the left/on the right.	**Det är till vänster/till höger.**	day ai til **vehn**sterr/til **hur**ger

Accidents

May I use your telephone?	**Kan jag få låna Er telefon?**	kahn yar(g) foa **loan**ah ayr taylay**foan**

SWEDISH

Call a doctor quickly.	**Ring genast efter en läkare.**	ring **yay**nahst **ehf**terr ayn **lai**kahrer
Call an ambulance.	**Ring på ambulansen.**	ring poa ahmbew**lahns**ern
Please call the police.	**Var snäll och ring polisen.**	varr snehl o(k) ring poo**lee**ssern

Numbers

one	**ett**	eht
two	**två**	tvoa
three	**tre**	tray
four	**fyra**	**few**rah
five	**fem**	fehm
six	**sex**	sehks
seven	**sju**	shew
eight	**åtta**	**o**tah
nine	**nio**	**nee**oo
ten	**tio**	**tee**oo
eleven	**elva**	**ehl**vah
twelve	**tolv**	tolv
thirteen	**tretton**	**treh**ton
fourteen	**fjorton**	**fyoor**ton
fifteen	**femton**	**fehm**ton
sixteen	**sexton**	**sehks**ton
seventeen	**sjutton**	**shew**ton
eighteen	**arton**	**arr**ton
nineteen	**nitton**	**nit**ton
twenty	**tjugo**	**khew**goo
twenty-one	**tjugoett**	**khew**gooeht
thirty	**trettio**	**treh**tioo
forty	**fyrtio**	**fewr**tioo
fifty	**femtio**	**fehm**tioo
sixty	**sextio**	**sehks**tioo
seventy	**sjuttio**	**shew**tioo
eighty	**åttio**	**o**tioo
ninety	**nittio**	**nit**tioo
one hundred	**hundra**	**hewn**drah
one thousand	**tusen**	**tew**sern
ten thousand	**tio tusen**	**tee**oo **tew**ssern

Days

It's Sunday.	**Det är söndag.**	day ai **surn**dar(g)
Monday	**måndag**	**moan**dar(g)
Tuesday	**tisdag**	**tiss**dar(g)
Wednesday	**onsdag**	**oonss**dar(g)

SWEDISH

Thursday	torsdag	toorshdar(g)
Friday	fredag	fraydar(g)
Saturday	lördag	lurrdar(g)
yesterday	i går	ee goar
today	i dag	ee dar(g)
tomorrow	i morgon	ee moron
morning/afternoon	förmiddag/efter-middag	furrmiddar(g)/ehfter-middar(g)
evening/night	kväll/natt	kvehl/naht

Months

January	januari	yahnewarri
February	februari	faybrewarri
March	mars	mahrsh
April	april	ahpreel
May	maj	migh
June	juni	yewni
July	juli	yewli
August	augusti	ahewgewsti
September	september	sehptehmberr
October	oktober	oktooberr
November	november	novehmberr
December	december	daysehmberr
Merry Christmas!	God Jul! Gott Nytt	goo(d) yewl! got newt oar
Happy New Year!	År!	

SWEDISH

Reference section

Weight conversion

The figure in the middle stands for both kilograms and pounds,
e.g., 1 kilogram = 2.205 lb. and 1 pound = 0.45 kilograms.

Kilograms (kg.)		Avoirdupois pounds
0.45	1	2.205
0.90	2	4.405
1.35	3	6.614
1.80	4	8.818
2.25	5	11.023
2.70	6	13.227
3.15	7	15.432
3.60	8	17.636
4.05	9	19.840
4.50	10	22.045
6.75	15	33.068
9.00	20	44.889
11.25	25	55.113
22.50	50	110.225
33.75	75	165.338
45.00	100	220.450

---

1 kilogram or kilo (kg) = 1000 grams (g)

100 g = 3.5 oz.	½ kg = 1.1 lb.
200 g = 7.0 oz.	1 kg = 2.2 lb.

1 oz. = 28.35 g
1 lb. = 453.60 g

Metres and feet

The figure in the middle stands for both metres and feet, e.g.,
1 metre = 3.281 ft. and 1 foot = 0.30 m.

Metres		Feet
0.30	1	3.281
0.61	2	6.563
0.91	3	9.843
1.22	4	13.124
1.52	5	16.403
1.83	6	19.686
2.13	7	22.967
2.44	8	26.248
2.74	9	29.529
3.05	10	32.810
3.35	11	36.091
3.66	12	39.372
3.96	13	42.635
4.27	14	45.934
4.57	15	49.215
4.88	16	52.496
5.18	17	55.777
5.49	18	59.058
5.79	19	62.339
6.10	20	65.620
7.62	25	82.023
15.24	50	164.046
22.86	75	246.069
30.48	100	328.092

Centimetres and inches

To change centimetres into inches, multiply by .39.

To change inches into centimetres, multiply by 2.54.

	in.	feet	yards
1 mm	0,039	0,003	0,001
1 cm	0,39	0,03	0,01
1 dm	3,94	0,32	0,10
1 m	39,40	3,28	1,09

	mm	cm	m
1 in.	25,4	2,54	0,025
1 ft.	304,8	30,48	0,304
1 yd.	914,4	91,44	0,914

(32 metres = 35 yards)

Temperature

To convert Centigrade into degrees Fahrenheit, multiply Centigrade by 1.8 and add 32.

To convert degrees Fahrenheit into Centigrade, subtract 32 from Fahrenheit and divide by 1.8.

The car

Miles into kilometres									
1 mile = 1.609 kilometres (km)									
miles	10	20	30	40	50	60	70	80	90	100
km	16	32	48	64	80	97	113	129	145	161

Kilometres into miles												
1 kilometre (km) = 0.62 miles												
km	10	20	30	40	50	60	70	80	90	100	110	120	130
miles	6	12	19	25	31	37	44	50	56	62	68	75	81

Tire pressure			
lb./sq. in.	kg/cm^2	lb./sq. in.	kg/cm^2
10	0.7	26	1.8
12	0.8	27	1.9
15	1.1	28	2.0
18	1.3	30	2.1
20	1.4	33	2.3
21	1.5	36	2.5
23	1.6	38	2.7
24	1.7	40	2.8

Fluid measures					
litres	imp. gal.	U.S. gal.	litres.	imp. gal.	U.S. gal.
5	1.1	1.3	30	6.6	7.8
10	2.2	2.6	35	7.7	9.1
15	3.3	3.9	40	8.8	10.4
20	4.4	5.2	45	9.9	11.7
25	5.5	6.5	50	11.0	13.0

1 litre (l) = 0.88 imp. quarts = 1.06 U.S. quarts

1 imp. quart = 1.14 l	1 U.S. quart = 0.95 l
1 imp. gallon = 4.55 l	1 U.S. gallon = 3.81 l

This is your size

Ladies

Dresses/suits						
American	10	12	14	16	18	20
British	32	34	36	38	40	42
Continental	38	40	42	44	46	48

	Stockings						Shoes			
American	8	8½	9	9½	10	10½	6	7	8	9
British										
Continental	0	1	2	3	4	5	36	38	38½	40

Gentlemen

Suits/overcoats							Shirts					
American	36	38	40	42	44	46	14	15	15½	16	16½	17
British												
Continental	46	48	50	52	54	56	36	38	39	41	42	43

Shoes							
American	5	6	7	8	9	10	11
British							
Continental	38	39	41	42	43	44	45

In Europe sizes vary somewhat from country to country, so the above must be taken as an approximate guide.

1 a.m. 2 a.m. 3 a.m. 4 a.m. 5 a.m. 6 a.m. 7 a.m. 8 a.m. 9 a.m. 10 a.m. 11 a.m. noon 11 a.m. 1 p.m. 2 p.m. 3 p.m. 4 p.m. 5 p.m. 6 p.m. 7 p.m. 8 p.m. 9 p.m. 10 p.m. 11 p.m. mid-night

Date Line

Eastern European Time

Central European Time

Western European Time (G.M.T.)

Atlantic Time

Eastern Time

Central Time

Mountain Time

Pacific Time

Alaska Time

Countries which have adopted a time differing from that in the corresponding time zone. Note that also in the USSR, official time is one hour ahead of the time in each corresponding time zone. In summer, numerous countries advance time one hour ahead of standard time.

Currency converter

In a world of fluctuating currencies, we can offer no more than this handy do-it-yourself chart. You can get information about exchange rates from banks, travel agents and tourist offices. Why not fill in this chart too, for handy reference?

REFERENCE SECTION

	£1	$1
Austria (shillings)		
Belgium (francs)		
Denmark (crowns)		
Finland (marks)		
France (francs)		
Germany (marks)		
Greece (drachmas)		
Italy (lire)		
Netherlands (guilders)		
Norway (crowns)		
Poland (zlotys)		
Portugal (escudos)		
Spain (pesetas)		
Sweden (crowns)		
Switzerland (francs)		
USSR (rubles)		
Yugoslavia (dinars)		

Emergency numbers

Ambulance . . . .

Fire . . . .

Police . . . .

Fill in these as well

Embassy . . . .

Consulate . . . .

Taxi . . . .

Airport information . . . .

Travel agent . . . .

Hotel . . . .

Restaurant . . . .

Babysitter . . . .

. . . .

. . . .

. . . .

. . . .

. . . .

. . . .

. . . .

REFERENCE SECTION

Personal data

Passport Nos. ....

....

Checking account No. ....

Credit card Nos. ....

....

Car: Licence plates ....

    Chassis No. ....

    Insurance: Company ....

    Policy No. ....

Travel Insurance: Company ....

    Policy No. ....

Blood type ....

....

....

....

....

....

....

....